C000125876

This Book Belongs To:

Andrew & Hilary Walker

A CHRISTMAS CAROL
THE UNSUNG STORY

Mr EBENEZER SCROOGE

beseeches his

long-suffering partner

Mr JACOB MARLEY

who is far from dead

(and for whom Heaven and Christmas Time be praised!)

to accept this

Christmas Present

with gratitude for the Past

and hope for the Future

A CHRISTMAS CAROL

◆

THE UNSUNG STORY

B R I A N   S I B L E Y

A LION BOOK

Text copyright © 1994 Brian Sibley
This edition copyright © 1994 Lion Publishing

The author asserts the moral right
to be identified as the author of this work

Published by
Lion Publishing plc
Sandy Lane West, Oxford, England
ISBN 0 7459 2846 3
Albatross Books Pty Ltd
PO Box 320, Sutherland, NSW 2232, Australia
ISBN 0 7324 0871 7

First edition 1994

A catalogue record for this book is available
from the British Library

Library of Congress CIP Data applied for

Printed and bound in Spain

Acknowledgments

Every effort has been made to trace the copyright holders of the
pictures in this book. Thank you to all those who have given us
permission to reproduce pictures, as indicated below (numbers
refer to page numbers):

18: The Mansell Collection;
16, 33, 37, 49, 130, 178, 187: Reproduced by courtesy of the
Dickens House Museum, London;
54: Marvel Classics Comics;
142: Copyright © Peter Brookes/Times Newspapers Ltd;
150: The Illustrated London News Picture Library;
156: Photograph by Hanson;
157: Copyright © BBC;
159, 162, 165, 172, 189: B.F.I. Stills, Posters and Designs;
170; 174: Copyright © Disney;
193: Reproduction by permission of Royal Mail;
194: Copyright © Nick Stead.

Contents

ACKNOWLEDGMENTS

There is only one edition of *A Christmas Carol*; at least, there's only one that really matters to me – and, goodness knows, I've got dozens of different editions! The cream binding has gone a nasty brown colour on the spine; the paper, which isn't very good, is turning yellow; the line and water-colour illustrations by Arthur I. Keller (first published in 1914) have seen decidedly better printings; but it is the first copy of Charles Dickens' wonderful story that I ever owned and read. That was thirty years ago: a crooked label pasted inside reveals that I received it as a school prize in 1963. And what a prize! I loved it from the first – for its humour and its humanity; for its ghosts and its generosity of spirit. I soon knew whole passages by heart, and made a vow that the story would always be a part of my Christmas celebrations.

As the years passed, I acquired – rather as one acquires various new photographs of family and friends – other copies of the book as well as recordings and, later, film versions on video. Then, in 1987, I compiled and presented 'Humbug!', a radio programme about Scrooge & Co., out of which came the idea for this book – an idea that might have come to nothing had not Pat Alexander, of Lion Publishing, decided that it was one worth putting into print, which is why I begin my acknowledgments by expressing my gratitude to her, and also to her colleague, Melanie Watson, who provided encouraging noises and editorial judgment in, fortunately, equal measures.

I am indebted to Dr David Parker, Curator of the Dickens House, for having read the manuscript of this book and offered many helpful suggestions and corrections; and his colleague Andrew Bean for assistance with finding illustrations; to Gill Henson, who also read the book in its early stages; to Denis Crutch who, many years ago, pointed me in the direction of some important books; to Richard Parlour for sharing his views on some of the many Scrooges; to Dave Goelz (and Gonzo) for talking to me about *The Muppet Christmas Carol*;

to Glyn Dearman for his recollections of being Tiny Tim, and his help in tracking down various recordings of *A Christmas Carol*; to Liz Appleby, Richard Holliss, Kevin Moore and Graham Webb, who located other much-sought after items; and to Dr Edwin A. Dawes for information on matters magical.

Special thanks is due to Nicholas Clark who contacted me following my radio programme, and has since become a valued friend. Nick not only read and commented on my text, generously sharing his considerable knowledge of *A Christmas Carol* and its sundry interpretations and transformations, but also gave me access to his own expensive collection.

Finally, I must thank David Weeks, who read and re-read every version of this manuscript – commenting on and discussing everything from ghosts to grammar – and who patiently endured long hours of watching and listening to stage, film, TV and radio versions in the cause of research!

In expressing my hopes for this book, I echo the words of the critic who, reviewing *A Christmas Carol*, shortly after publication, wrote, 'We shall have written to very little purpose if what we have said does not send every one of our readers to the pages of the Christmas Carol.' After all, as that writer observed: 'They who do not, will deprive themselves of a genuine enjoyment...'

Brian Sibley

PROLOGUE

The Story I am Going to Relate

'A merry Christmas, uncle! God save you!' cried a cheerful voice.
It was the voice of Scrooge's nephew...
'Bah!' said Scrooge, 'Humbug!'

Say 'Humbug' and people immediately think of Ebenezer Scrooge; utter the phrase: 'God bless us, every one!' and people at once recall the words of Tiny Tim. And whenever Scrooge and Tiny Tim are remembered then so, too, is Charles Dickens and what is, perhaps, his best-known and most-loved book, *A Christmas Carol*.

A host of other memories then come crowding in: poor Bob Cratchit trying to warm himself at the candle in his office; the indefatigable dancing of Old Fezziwig; the beneficent Ghost of Christmas Present with his life-enhancing torch; Mrs Cratchit's incomparable pudding; the party-games at the home of Scrooge's nephew; the prize turkey that was so big it could not have stood upon its legs; Scrooge confronting his own grave-stone and that dreadful chain-rattling apparition: the Ghost of Jacob Marley, who was undoubtedly and undeniably as dead as a door-nail!

First published in 1843, *A Christmas Carol*
holds so powerful a place in the popular imagination that, like some other universally known stories (such as *Robinson Crusoe*, *Gulliver's Travels*, *Alice in Wonderland* and *Peter Pan*), even people who have never actually read the book probably think they have!

The book's characters, though only briefly sketched, rank among the most memorable of Dickens' creations; as John Gross observed: 'Scrooge seems to have been there as a symbol and a point of reference since time began; you wonder how people ever managed without him.'

A Christmas Carol has been praised and criticized. Writing in 1907, in *The Dickensian* (the journal of the Dickens Fellowship), R.L. Stewart enthused:

In reading it, one becomes Scrooge himself: feels with him the terrible power his ghostly visitants have over him, the softening influence of the various scenes through which

Illustration by H.M. Brock

he passes, the very pangs that are caused by the ghosts' rebukes. One feels too, how very natural and how delightful it is when he is ultimately reclaimed . . .

Another reader, Samuel Rogers, was considerably less impressed; although favoured with a presentation copy of the first edition, this gentleman complained that he found the first half-hour's reading so dull that it sent him to sleep, and the next hour's worth so painful that he was 'obliged to finish it to get rid of the impression'!

An occasional critical voice is still raised against *A Christmas Carol*: politician Gerald Kaufman dismissed it as 'a cynical exercise in sentimental manipulation and emotional blackmail'. But most readers will side with G.K. Chesterton, who considered it 'the most genial and fanciful' of all the novelist's stories; or with Stephen Leacock, who answered accusations that the book was 'not true to life' by declaring, 'It is

of no consequence . . . It is better than life.'

In the 150 years since Dickens' celebrated 'Ghost Story of Christmas' was first published, the reformation of the miserly Ebenezer Scrooge by the Spirits of Christmas Past, Present and Yet To Come, appears to have lost none of its appeal; and the representing of *A Christmas Carol* – in a diversity of forms, old and new – has now become an annual obligation.

Not only has the book been reprinted many times, it has also been endlessly abridged, simplified, contracted and expanded, dramatized, sequelized, translated, pirated and parodied; it has been turned into films, plays, musicals, ballets and operas.

The book which the public read to one another around the hearth, and which Charles Dickens read upon the stage, has been subsequently retold (using every method of sound-recording from cylinder to compact disc) by a host of actors and celebrities including

America's former First Lady, Eleanor Roosevelt, and Jean-Luc Picard, of 'Star Trek: The Next Generation' – otherwise known as Patrick Stewart.

The story, originally embellished by John Leech, has since been decorated by more than a hundred artists, illustrators and cartoonists and visually interpreted in every conceivable pictorial format from the comic-strip – with its plethora of exclamation marks – to editions with hand-lettered texts and elaborate illuminations.

The characters have been turned into figurines and toby-jugs; pressed into service by politicians, theologians, moralists and propagandists and put to work by the advertisers of soups, cigars, lagers, hamburgers, electronic calculators and sundry other products.

Scrooge has also been portrayed on stage, screen, television and radio by a diversity of dramatic talent from Lionel Barrymore to Michael Caine, Basil Rathbone to Walter Matthau and Alastair Sim to Albert Finney – not to mention those cartoon characters: the myopic Mr Magoo, the gun-toting Yosemite Sam and Donald Duck's penny-pinching uncle, Scrooge McDuck.

As a result of these many variations, almost nothing that is done to the story takes us by surprise, whether it be seeing Dickens' story performed as a Muppet masquerade, or illustrated with three-dimensional grotesqueries created by the model-makers of television's 'Spitting Image'. All of these weird, wonderful, bizarre and exotic versions – from gauche pantomimes to films in which the Spirits appear in the wrong order or have two Marley's Ghosts! – have become part of our collective memories of *A Christmas Carol*.

So, how did Charles Dickens come to create, what he called, his 'little Carol'? Why did it achieve such an extraordinary worldwide fame? And why does it still move us – again and again – to laughter and to tears?

To understand the circumstances which gave birth to *A Christmas Carol*, we must begin by looking at the life of the man who has been hailed as 'the greatest popular prose writer that England has ever known' . . .

Scrooge by Kyd 'Characters from Dickens' cigarette card

Shadows of the Things
that Have Been

Charles John Huffam Dickens was born at 387 Mile End Terrace, Landport, Portsea, on 7 February 1812, the second of eight children born to John and Elizabeth Dickens. Charles' father, who worked as a clerk for the Navy Pay Office in Portsmouth, constantly lived beyond his means and was, therefore, invariably in financial difficulty.

'I know my father,' Dickens said in later years, 'to be as kindhearted and generous a man as ever lived...' However, he probably painted a more accurate – if no less affectionate – portrait of his father in the novel *David Copperfield*, where he created that eternal optimist, Wilkins Micawber, who is forever waiting for something to 'turn up'.

Dickens' early life was unsettled; during his first ten years, his father was posted from Portsmouth to London, Sheerness, Chatham, and then back to London. There were, however, compensations; notably a nursemaid with a fund of tales of the macabre and supernatural: bloodthirsty stories that may well have awakened the novelist's imagination. Certainly he never lost

his fascination with ghost stories, as the spectre of the late Jacob Marley testifies!

A delicate child, Charles spent much of his time indoors: 'The picture always arises in my mind,' he later wrote, 'of a summer evening, the boys at play in the churchyard and I sitting on my bed, reading as if for life.' That wide-ranging passion for reading began with books – such as the *Arabian Nights* and *Robinson Crusoe* – introduced to him by his father.

The relative happiness of the days in Chatham came to an end when, in 1822, the Dickens family moved back to London and overcrowded lodgings in Camden Town – an area where, later, Bob Cratchit and his family were to live. John Dickens' debts soon mounted up once more, and by 1824, the twelve-year-old Charles, who was himself not attending school, was sent to work at Warren's Blacking Factory. Housed in a dilapidated warehouse off the Strand, the factory produced boot-blacking and employed a number of poor children (including one Bob Fagin) to paste labels on the bottles of blacking.

INTERIOR OF "THE GRATE."

'I know that I worked from morning to night,' Dickens later recalled, 'with common men and boys, a shabby child . . . I know that I have lounged about the streets, insufficiently and unsatisfactorily fed. I know that, but for the mercy of God, I might have been, for any care that was taken of me, a little robber or a little vagabond . . . My whole nature was so penetrated with the grief and humiliation of such considerations, that even now, famous and caressed and happy I often forget in my dreams . . . that I am a man; and wander desolately back to that time in my life.'

Dickens' experiences at Warren's factory provided him, some twenty years later, with literary inspiration when he wrote of the early life of his semi-autobiographical hero, David Copperfield; they also fired his life-long opposition to the use of child-labour.

Charles' situation worsened when John Dickens was imprisoned for debt (with his family) in the Marshalsea debtors' prison. Charles moved into lodgings near Warren's factory and regularly visited the rest of the family in prison. Memories of the Marshalsea later found angry remembrance in many of his books – including *A Christmas Carol*, in which Ebenezer Scrooge glibly comments on the efficacy of such prisons.

On one of young Charles' visits, his father told him 'to take warning by the Marshalsea, and to observe that if a man had twenty pounds a year, and spent nineteen pounds nineteen shillings and sixpence, he would be happy; but that a shilling spent the other way would make him wretched'. Here is not just the original inspiration for the wisdom of Mr Micawber; but also, perhaps, an explanation for the obsessive anxiety about money and fear of poverty which haunted Dickens throughout his life. An obsession which informed the seasonal anger felt by Scrooge:

'What's Christmas time to you but a time for paying bills without money; a time for finding yourself a year older, and not an hour richer; a time for balancing your books and having every item in 'em through a round dozen of months presented dead against you?'

John Dickens was, as we would put it today, declared bankrupt and was released from prison. Charles was eventually sent back to school; but, just three years later, in 1827, John Dickens was once again in financial difficulties and Charles was put to work as a solicitor's clerk with the firm of Ellis and Blackmore in Gray's Inn.

Dickens heartily disliked this job – perhaps reflected in his sympathy for Scrooge's put-upon clerk, Bob Cratchit – however, he gained insights into the legal profession that were to inspire many later jibes at the law.

Teaching himself shorthand, Charles Dickens determined upon a career as a journalist and, in 1832, joined *The Mirror of Parliament*, a publication produced by his uncle, John Henry Barrow. A precursor of Hansard, *The Mirror* contained verbatim accounts of parliamentary debates. The following year, Dickens was offered a new post with the Liberal paper, the *Morning Chronicle*, and he was soon travelling around the country, reporting on political meetings and elections.

In his spare time, Dickens was experimenting with creative writing and had penned some sketches of London life. The first of these, 'A Dinner at Poplar Walk', was published in *The Monthly Magazine* in 1833, under the pen-name 'Boz', and was followed by other pieces. Three years later, a collection of these stories and essays – ranging from 'The Pawnbroker's Shop' and 'A Visit to Newgate' to 'Private Theatres' and 'The Dancing Academy' – appeared in volume form as *Sketches by 'Boz'*.

The book was a popular success, prompting the publishers, Chapman and Hall, to offer Dickens fourteen pounds a month to provide an accompanying text to a series of sporting prints by the artist Robert Seymour. Instead, Dickens persuaded the publisher to let him create a story which Seymour might illustrate. And so began a picaresque entertainment entitled *The Posthumous Papers of the Pickwick Club* – later known simply as *The Pickwick Papers*.

The serial had scarcely begun, when Robert Seymour – an emotional man – illustrated an episode showing the death of a pantomime clown (whose tragic story was recounted to Mr Pickwick), took a gun and blew his brains out.

A replacement artist was found in Hablot K. Browne; and, after a slow beginning, *Pickwick* proved a huge success: selling as many as 50,000 copies a month and doing phenomenally well when it appeared in a single volume.

At twenty-five, Dickens became a household name, and the income provided by Mr Pickwick enabled Dickens to propose marriage to Catherine (or Kate) Hogarth, the daughter of the editor of the *Evening Chronicle*. Following their wedding, in April 1836, Charles and his bride lived in chambers in Furnivall's Inn. The young couple were frequently joined by Kate's sixteen-year-old sister, Mary Hogarth, to whom Dickens became very attached.

The following year, the couple's first child, Charles, was born; the young family, together with Mary, moved into a new home, 48 Doughty Street (now the headquarters of the Dickens Fellowship). A few weeks later, in May 1837, Mary Hogarth collapsed and died, an event

Charles and Kate Dickens with Mary Hogarth, 1842

which devastated Dickens: 'I solemnly believe,' he wrote, 'that so perfect a creature never breathed... She had no fault.'

Mary haunted Dickens' memory for many years, inspiring several of his idealized heroines. And when, in 1938, Kate Dickens gave birth to a baby girl, the child was named Mary. A second daughter, Kate, followed the next year; but the marriage was, Dickens later claimed, becoming strained, and the tensions between husband and wife were not helped by Dickens' persistent adoration of the deceased Mary Hogarth.

Anthony Trollope once called Dickens 'Mr Popular Sentiment'; and he certainly had a knack for choosing subjects that enabled him to weave a strong thread of social comment through his fiction. It can be seen in *Oliver Twist*, and in the novels which followed – *Nicholas Nickleby*, *The Old Curiosity Shop* and *Barnaby Rudge*. Writing about the horrors of workhouse and prison ironically brought Dickens monetary success and stability, allowing him to lease a large, fashionable London house for himself at Number One, Devonshire Terrace.

In 1842, Dickens' fame having crossed the Atlantic, the novelist made a decision: 'After balancing, considering, and weighing the matter in every point of view, I have made up my mind (with God's leave) to go to America...'

Dickens was attracted by the idea of seeing a democratic republic at work and, on his return, to report his experiences to his readers. Charles and Kate – who now had a family of four, Walter Landor Dickens having been born two years earlier – left for America in January 1842; it

provided the novelist with a vastly contrasting series of experiences.

Lionized wherever he went, Dickens visited New York, Washington, Pittsburgh, Cincinnati and Louisville; in Boston he was greeted by the poet H.W. Longfellow and the man who was, in a spiritual sense, his American counterpart, Washington Irving – creator of Rip Van Winkle and Ichabod Crane. He sailed the Potomac River and rode a stage-coach to Columbus; he saw the Prairie, Lake Erie and Niagara Falls before visiting Canada. Dickens later wrote that he had made 'many friends in America' and felt 'a grateful interest in the country'.

Indeed, there was much that impressed him, such as the civilized conditions in which some factory workers were housed; the standard of accommodation in workhouses and institutes for the blind. But Dickens also witnessed many things that concerned him, in particular the shamefulness of slavery, the complacency of many of those who sat in the Senate and the scurrilousness of the American press.

Six months later, in June 1842, he and Kate sailed for England. Curiously, Dickens' increasingly jaundiced view of the New World seemed only to heighten his disenchantment with the Old World to which he returned.

Dickens duly published an account of his visit to the United States, as *American Notes for General Circulation*, in which he wrote of his distrust of some of 'the influences and tendencies' which he had observed. *American Notes* sold extremely well in Britain; on the other side of the Atlantic, however, Dickens' disillusionment with life in the young republic caused so much annoyance that copies of the book were burned in the streets of New York.

The year 1843 began badly for Dickens: Kate, was expecting their fifth child and a good part of his income was being eaten up by a rather too-lavish lifestyle combined with the incessant demands made by his father and other impecunious relatives: 'He and all of them,' Dickens wrote, 'look upon me as something to be plucked.'

There was nothing unusual about Dickens having financial problems, but another, more fearful spectre, was also haunting him...

The Ghost of an Idea

Could it really be that the great Dickens was losing his magic touch? It seemed unthinkable, but his new serialized novel, *Martin Chuzzlewit*, was so poorly received by the public that it seemed to raise the question of whether Dickens' remarkable career might, suddenly, be going into a decline. Whereas *The Old Curiosity Shop* had sold some 100,000 copies, the first issue of *Martin Chuzzlewit* – which was a monthly, rather than a weekly, publication – sold only 20,000 copies, a figure which hardly increased over the next few months. Publishers Chapman and Hall – who were paying the author a salary of £200 a month – reacted to this apparent lessening in his popularity by proposing a cut of £50 a month.

In the hope of boosting sales of *Martin Chuzzlewit*, Dickens decided to capitalize on the popularity of *American Notes* and to send his eponymous hero to the New World. Dickens had good reason to suppose that readers might enjoy seeing Master Chuzzlewit following in his own footsteps; and, indeed, in Britain, this proved the novel's salvation. In America, however, the strident satire in these chapters was not well received; as Dickens put it, the book made them all 'stark, raving mad across the water'.

Though desperate to earn money, Dickens did not want his public to know that he was 'writing tooth and nail for bread'. What he needed was a way of restoring his failing reputation; 'a wrong kind of fire is burning in my head,' he wrote in a moment of self-doubt, 'and I don't think I *can* write.' If only he could find a subject with which to demonstrate what he knew in his heart – that he had lost none of his old passion: 'I feel my power now more than I ever did, I have a greater confidence in myself than I ever had. That I know, if I have my health, I could sustain my place in the minds of thinking men, though fifty writers started up tomorrow. But how many readers do not think!'

So what was he to write about? One idea was to pen a response to recent parliamentary reports by the Children's Employment Commission. If Dickens had financial problems, they were as nothing compared to those of England's working poor – especially the young, who sometimes worked eighteen-hour days for very little money.

Dickens had first concerned himself with the issue of child labour in 1840, when he had a correspondence with Lord Ashley, whose impassioned speech in the House of Commons on the conditions of children working in mines and factories had prompted the setting-up of the Commission. Two years later, Dickens wrote a letter to the *Morning Chronicle*, signed 'B' (for 'Boz') defending Lord Ashley's Mines and Collieries Bill, against a decidedly Scroogish attack by Lord Londonderry.

The parliamentary reports moved several pre-eminent Victorians, including Elizabeth Barrett and Thomas Hood, to take up the pen on behalf of the poor and their children, highlighting the fact that those with nothing were often forced to live in hardship while working for the benefit of those with plenty.

Dickens had been moved to great anger when, in 1842, he read a report produced by the Parliamentary Committee for Inquiring into the Employment and Condition of Children in Mines and Manufactories. Like many of his fellow countrymen, Dickens was shocked and shamed by the scandalous facts about the hardship and suffering of children, without whose labour society would cease to function — a response that was undoubtedly intensified by bitter memories of his own childhood experiences.

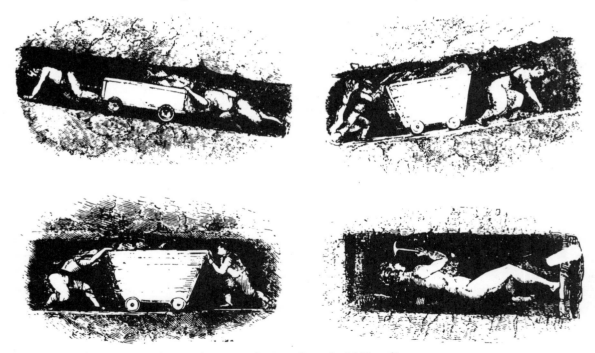

Children working in coal mines: from the 1842 parliamentary report

Illustrations in the parliamentary report showed youngsters, bare-foot and half-naked, hewing coal and pulling and pushing wagons through the low, narrow galleries in the mines. In October 1842, Dickens and three of his friends had travelled to Cornwall to see for themselves the working conditions of children in the tin-mining industry. Dickens was struck by everything about his excursion: 'If you could have followed us into the earthy old Churches we visited, and into the strange caverns on the gloomy seashore, and down into the depths of the mines...' One of those mines, which the commissioners had arranged for Dickens to visit, was the Botallack Mine at Land's End, and some years later, in his 1851 book, *A Child's History of England*, Dickens described these mines dug at the very edge of the sea:

One of them, which I have seen, is so close to it that it is hollowed out underneath the ocean; and the miners say, that, in stormy weather, when they are at work down in the deep place, they can hear the noise of the waves, thundering above their heads.

These experiences made such an impact on Dickens that he considered opening *Martin Chuzzlewit* 'in some miserable dreary iron-bound spot' on the Cornish coast. In the event, he did not do that, but when he came to write *A Christmas Carol*, he was to describe a mining community on 'a bleak and desert moor where monstrous masses of rude stone were cast about', a place where 'nothing grew but moss and furze, and coarse, rank grass'.

February 1843 saw the publication of the commission's second report, or 'blue book'. After reading it, Dickens wrote to one of the Commissioners, Dr Thomas Southwood Smith: 'I am so perfectly struck down by the blue book you have sent me, that I think (as soon as I have done my month's work) of writing, and bringing out a very cheap pamphlet, called "An appeal to the People of England, on behalf of the Poor Man's Child".'

A few days later, however, Dickens wrote again to Dr Smith saying that, for reasons he was 'not at liberty to explain' he was 'deferring the production of that pamphlet until the end of the year', although he had clearly lost none of his zeal: 'Rest assured, when you see what I do, and where, and how, you will certainly feel that a Sledge hammer has come down with twenty times the force – twenty thousand times the force – I could exert by following out my first idea.'

In September 1843, Dickens got involved in another charitable venture at the request of his wealthy, philanthropic friend Miss Burdett Coutts – to whom *Martin Chuzzlewit* was dedicated 'with the true and earnest regard of the Author'. Miss Coutts had received a request for financial assistance from one Samuel Starey, a lawyer's clerk, who was attempting to set up places of education for poor children in London. Before giving her support, Miss Coutts decided to ask Dickens' advice.

On her behalf, Dickens visited one of the so-called Ragged Schools in Field Lane, Holborn, located among the very streets he had once described in *Oliver Twist* as the setting for

Fagin's den. He found the school being held 'in three most wretched rooms on the first floor of a rotten house'. Whilst encouraging Miss Coutts to support the schools, Dickens wrote in despairing tones of what he saw there:

> To gain their attention in any way is a difficulty, quite gigantic. To impress them, even with the idea of God, when their own condition is so desolate, becomes a mon-strous task... My heart so sinks within me when I go into these scenes, that I almost lose the hope of ever seeing them changed.

Dickens offered *The Edinburgh Review* an article about the Ragged Schools and other voluntary schools that had been started in gaols. It would, Dickens told the editor, make a 'very striking paper'. Again, this article was never written, but the anger which Dickens had felt was to be voiced by the Spirit of Christmas Present on showing Scrooge two children, 'wretched, abject, frightful, hideous, miserable':

> 'Spirit! are they yours?' Scrooge could say no more.
> 'They are Man's,' said the Spirit, looking down upon them... 'This boy is Ignorance. This girl is Want. Beware them both, and all of their degree, but most of all beware this boy, for on his brow I see that written which is Doom, unless the writing be erased.'

The opportunity Dickens had been waiting for came in October: he was invited to speak at a fund-raising meeting in Manchester for the Athenaeum, a charitable institution which aimed at bringing some measure of culture and 'blameless, rational enjoyment' to the city's working class.

Dickens (like the central character in *A Christmas Carol*) had a sister named Fanny, and since she lived in Manchester, he was able to combine a visit to her with his appearance at the charity soirée. It has been suggested that Fanny's invalid son, Harry, provided the inspiration for Tiny Tim; certainly, when he died he was memorialized as Paul Dombey.

It was the evening of 5 October, and among the audience were many notable people, including the Anti-Corn Law politician, Richard Cobden, and the future prime minister, Benjamin Disraeli. Dickens began his speech by praising an institution which sought to ensure that despite 'the clanking of stupendous engines and the whirl of machinery, the immortal mechanism of God's own hand, the mind, is not forgotten in the din and uproar'.

Quoting the poet Alexander Pope, Dickens attacked the popular assertion that 'a little learning is a dangerous thing'. The same people who believed this, he pointed out, had once maintained that 'a little hanging was a dangerous thing', and, as a result, 'we had a great deal of it'; on the other hand, he added ironically, 'because a little learning was dangerous, we were to have none at all'.

But the most passionate part of Dickens' speech came when he said that he wished he could take his listeners into the gaols and nightly refuges that he himself had visited; places where, he told them, 'my own heart dies within me when I see thousands of immortal creatures condemned, without alternative or choice, to tread, not what our great poet calls "the primrose path to the everlasting bonfire", but one of jagged flints and stones, laid down by brutal ignorance'.

Dickens hated the way in which his generation dismissed the plight of the poor. He shared the anger expressed by his friend, Thomas Carlyle, who, in 1840, had described the aristocracy − 'astonishment in every feature' − responding to requests to help the poor by asking: 'Are there not treadmills, gibbets; even hospitals, poor-rates, New-Poor Law?' The same question was later asked by Ebenezer Scrooge.

Dickens remained in Manchester for three days, attending various meetings which took him, by foot, around the city. As he went about the streets, crowded with the poor and destitute, Dickens strengthened his resolve to write something that would call upon those 'truthful feelings of the people' of which he had spoken.

It was, perhaps, on one such occasion − Dickens' mind preoccupied with thoughts of finding a way of addressing the social issues concerning him, as well as touching the humanity of his readers − that an idea came to him.

It was an idea that had its origin several years before in *Sketches by 'Boz'*. One of these sketches − 'Illustrative of Every-day Life and Every-Day People' − was entitled 'A Christmas Dinner', and had begun with a proposition:

Christmas time! That man must be a misanthrope in whose breast something like a jovial feeling is not roused − in whose mind some pleasant associations are not awakened − by the recurrence of Christmas.

Supposing Dickens were to focus on the negative attitudes of one particular character − just such a misanthrope − an individual who not only ignores the plight of the poor, but is himself poor in spirit; and then supposing he were to show that character being brought to see the error of his ways? A character, as Clement Shorter has observed, who might represent 'all of us more or less'. Thus did Ebenezer Scrooge first draw breath.

Although it was expedient for Dickens, writing at the end of the year, to choose Christmas time as the setting for his new story, it proved a happy choice − not just for *A Christmas Carol*, but for Christmas itself...

3

Out Upon a Merry Christmas

Dickens' decision to write a story set at Christmas time had greater significance than the novelist could have supposed. *A Christmas Carol* is full of extreme responses to Christmas: there is Ebenezer Scrooge's enthusiastic denigration of the season:

'If I could work my will,' said Scrooge, indignantly, 'every idiot who goes about with "Merry Christmas," on his lips, should be boiled with his own pudding, and buried with a stake of holly through his heart.'

In sharp contrast, there is also the boisterous ebullience with which seemingly everyone else greets the advent of 25 December. The depiction of these responses – the one obviously bad, the other unequivocally good – has survived the 150 years since the book was written and continues to haunt our contemporary attitudes to Christmas.

However, Dickens observed in *Sketches by 'Boz'* that 'there are people who will tell you that Christmas is not what it was'; and nor was it. As G.K. Chesterton remarked: 'The popular paradox of *A Christmas Carol*, is very well symbolized in its title. Everybody has heard of Christmas carols; and certainly everybody has heard of Christmas. Yet these things are only popular because they are traditional; and the tradition has often been in need of defence, as Dickens here defended it.'

And the reason why Christmas was in need of Dickens' defence was because the spirit of the season – epitomized by the jolly giant who visits Scrooge – was less the Ghost of Christmas Present than of Christmas Past. The journalist Thomas Burke said that Dickens destroyed Christmas because he had 'found it a festival and left it a function'; but the seasonal celebrations having gone through many changes during the more than one thousand and eight hundred years since Christmas began.

Although the Gospel writers gave no indication of the date of Christ's birth, the early church celebrated the birth and the baptism of Christ on 6 January, the day on which the Western church now commemorates the visit of the wise men to the infant Christ. The move to a December celebration of Christmas took place in the fourth century, and was the result of a very different festivity. In pre-Christian Rome, the 25th of that month had been kept as *Dies Invicti Solis* ('The Day of the Invincible Sun') in celebration of the birth of the god Mithras.

It was in AD336 that this festival changed to a celebration of the incarnation of God in the birth of Christ, whom the prophet Malachi had called the 'Sun of Righteousness'. Thus the greater sun of Christianity was seen to have victoriously eclipsed the lesser, pagan sun of Mithra; and so was chosen the date, described in a lyric from one film version of *A Christmas Carol* as 'the dearest day in all the year – December the twenty-fifth!'

There was some resistance among the church fathers to the association of Christian and pagan festivals, particularly since Christmas now fell just a few days after the old Roman festival of Saturnalia. These revelries, in honour of the god Saturn and the Golden Age of Rome, were observed between 17 and 23 December, and involved a good deal of eating, drinking and merry-making.

The Saturnalian pleasures of food and drink became part of the Christmas celebration, as did aspects of the Roman New Year, during which houses were decorated with lights and greenery, and gifts were given to the young and the poor. In Europe, Christians also liberally borrowed from the Celtic Yule rites (in honour of Thor) which were similarly celebrated during the winter solstice. This festival combined the secular (the imbibing of ale brewed with malt) with the mystical (the kindling of fire and light in the darkness); and, by the year AD601, Pope Gregory I formally authorized Augustine of Canterbury to convert the Anglo Saxons into Christians and Yule into Christmas.

With the eventual sanctification of the old festivals, pagan symbols such as holly, ivy, laurel and mistletoe were similarly hallowed: any branch of evergreen was seen as hope of life in the dead depths of winter; while holly specifically came to represent Christ's passion and – in the form of a three-leafed sprig – a symbol of the Trinity. The Yule log – lit with a brand from last year's log and burned throughout the holiday – was traditionally cut from an oak, but to make it an acceptable part of Christmas, the wood used was changed to ash. The inspiration for this, was an old legend which said that the new-born Christ was bathed and dressed beside an ash-wood fire made for him by the shepherds – ash being a wood that can be burnt while still green.

Later, the ancient Northern tradition that the god Woden brought gifts to his people in the midst of winter, was de-paganized into a spirit of benevolence and provision called Old Christmas or Father Christmas. This entity was then sanctified by transferring his generosity to a fourth century bishop and saint – Nicholas by name – who, through numerous transformations, was to become Santa Claus.

During the Middle Ages, Christmas became a twelve-day festival lasting from Christmas Eve to Epiphany; it also became an increasingly elaborate celebration – especially at court where entertainments included feasts, masques and plays; while in the market square, the common people gathered to watch their own theatrical presentations, the Mystery Plays, sanctioned by the church for the teaching of the faith. And both crown and commoner enjoyed the antics of the

THE
TRYAL

OF

Old Father *Chriſtmas,*

FOR

Encouraging his MAJESTY's Subjects in Idleneſs, Gluttony, Drunkenneſs, Gaming, Swearing, Rioting, and all Manner of Extravagance and De-bauchery.

At the Aſſizes held in the

CITY of PROFUSION,

BEFORE

The Lord Chief Juſtice CHURCHMAN, Mr. Juſtice FEAST, Mr. Juſtice GAMBOL, and ſeveral other his Majeſty's Juſtices of Oyer and Terminer and Goal Delivery.

By JOSIAH KING.

LONDON:

Printed and Sold by T. BOREMAN near *Child's* Coffee-Houſe, in St. *Paul's Church-yard* ; and Sold likewiſe at his Shop at the *Cock* on *Ludgate-hill.*

M DCC XXXV.

Seventeenth-century broadsheet protesting against the celebration of Christmas

Lord of Misrule, who presided over the Christmas festivities. The embodiment of fun, frolic and disorder, the origins of this character date back to the Roman Saturnalia when people elected a mock king, wore masks, dressed-up and even cross-dressed.

So things went on, with a healthy balance of secular and religious celebrations, and a strong awareness of the simple, but positive, qualities of good-naturedness. As the sixteenth century writer, Thomas Tusser, remarked in his *Five Hundred Points of Good Husbandry*:

At Christmas play and make good cheer,
For Christmas comes but once a year.

Things changed dramatically, however, during the period of the Long Parliament which lasted from 1640 until 1653 and saw a rise in Puritanism, Civil War in England, the execution of the King and the appointment of Oliver Cromwell as Lord Protector. The Puritans denounced religious rituals associated with Roman Catholicism, performances of plays were outlawed and there was a backlash against Christmas.

The Puritans declared that men's 'stomacks must be fed with sound doctrine' rather than with 'brawne and Christmas pie, roast-beef and plum-porridge', which were condemned as profane and 'superstitious meats'. Worst of all, in Puritan eyes, was the blasphemy of linking the worship of pagan deities with Christmas, and this was now decreed 'an abomination, idolatry, superstition and Popish observance'.

In 1647, Parliament prohibited the

celebration of the nativity of Christ with other holy days. Two years later, the King went to the scaffold: and in 1652 – 'of all the good days in the year, on Christmas Eve' – Parliament declared that 'no observance shall be had of the five and twentieth day of December, commonly called Christmas Day; nor any solemnity used or exercised in churches upon that day in respect thereof'. On that day, churches were closed, shops remained open and anyone who persisted in celebrating Christmas was imprisoned. As one contemporary writer expressed it:

Gone are those golden days of yore,
When Christmas was a high day:
Whose sports we now shall see no more;
'Tis turn'd into Good Friday.

With the restoration of the monarchy in 1660, some of the traditions of those 'golden days' were revived and, as one rhyme put it, 'Loyal hearts' were once more cheered by Christmas beer, 'minc'd pies; Roast Beef and brave Plum-porridge', and by the end of the eighteenth century – thanks to a few such die-hard traditionalists, particularly in the country – a few traces of the old Christmas might still be found; but the urbanization of Britain, arriving with the Industrial Revolution, sounded a virtual death-knell for Christmas. The new factories, which had drawn thousands of people from the country into the cities, did not close for Christmas holidays and the crowded poverty and violence of the towns – with their smoggy, dirty atmosphere – were less conducive to such festivities than rural life.

Occasional attempts were made at raising the old spirits: the songs of Christmastide were collected in such anthologies as *Christmas Carols, Ancient and Modern*, edited by William Sandys who wrote: 'In the metropolis a solitary itinerant may be occasionally heard in the streets croaking out "God rest you merry gentlemen, . . ." to an ancient and simple tune.' This was the very carol which a youngster with a 'gnawed and mumbled' nose sang at Scrooge's keyhole; and which Dickens, curiously, misquoted as: 'God bless (instead of 'rest') you merry gentleman (not 'gentlemen'), May (rather than 'Let') nothing you dismay.'

Someone else who was to play an important role in the salvation of Christmas was Thomas K. Harvey, author of *The Book of Christmas*, who wrote:

The great wisdom of the world is, we presume, one of the natural consequences of its advancing age; and though we are quite conscious that some of its former pranks would be very unbecoming, now that it is getting into years . . . yet we are by no means sure that we should not have been well content to have cast our lot in the days when it was somewhat younger.

The illustrations to *The Book of Christmas* (with which Dickens was probably familiar) were by Robert Seymour, who had been the first illustrator of *The Pickwick Papers* – and indeed one of them showed a bald, broad-girthed, genial, gentleman, not unlike Mr Pickwick, sitting before a blazing fire reading the very publication in which the picture appeared: *The Book of Christmas!*

Among the many seasonal subjects depicted by Seymour are several which have a resonance with *A Christmas Carol*, among them 'The Christmas Pudding', 'Christmas Dinner' and a picture of two gentlemen greeting each other in the street with a 'Merry Christmas to you!' In another illustration, Seymour depicted 'Old Christmas': a jovial, bearded man, with ivy in his hair, riding on a goat and carrying a basket (containing a large bottle), a baby and a bowl of wassail.

This spirit — with its pagan links to Bacchus and Pan — is obviously a forebear of the second of Scrooge's Spirits. So much so, that in a critique of *A Christmas Carol* in the *Sunday Times* in December, 1993, Peter Millar wrote: 'The Ghost of Christmas Present, though hugely benign, is scarcely a Christian deity. His seat in Scrooge's sitting room is no blinding throne of angels but an all too earthly display of material plenty... Dickens without realising it, had laid the ground for a new demigod to supplant the infant Christ as a global symbol of seasonal generosity.'

Another illustration in *The Book of Christmas*, entitled 'Coming Home', shows coaches taking schoolboys home for the Christmas holidays and recalls the scene in which Scrooge sees the children of Christmas Past wishing each other 'Merry Christmas, as they parted at cross-roads and bye-ways, for their several homes'. This was a theme to which Dickens was to return, much later, in his 1850 essay, 'A Christmas Tree':

School-books shut up; Ovid and Virgil silenced; the Rule of Three, with its cool impertinent Inquiries, long disposed of; Terence and Plautus acted no more, in an arena of huddled desks and forms, all chipped, and notched, and inked... If I no more come home at Christmas-time, there will be boys and girls (thank Heaven!) while the World lasts; and they do! Yonder they dance and play... God bless them, merrily, and my heart dances and plays too!

A similar account of liberation is to be found in 'The Stage Coach', by one of Dickens' American contemporaries, Washington Irving:

I had three fine rosy-cheeked schoolboys for my fellow passengers... returning home for the holidays in high glee, and promising themselves a world of enjoyment. It was delightful to hear the gigantic plans of pleasure of the little rogues, and the impracticable feats they were to perform during the six weeks' emancipation from the abhorred thralldom of book, birch, and pedagogue.

Dickens and Irving had met during the English novelist's tour of America and Dickens would undoubtedly have read Washington Irving's *The Sketch Book of Geoffrey Crayon, Gent*. This volume, published in 1820, contained — in addition to his now-famous stories 'Rip Van Winkle' and 'The Legend of Sleepy Hollow' — a series of sketches, in which Irving recounts memories of a Christmas holiday spent at a fictional English manor-house called Bracebridge Hall.

'Of all the old festivals,' wrote Irving, 'that of Christmas awakens the strongest and most heartfelt associations. There is a tone of solemn and sacred feeling that blends with our conviviality, and lifts the spirit to a state of unalloyed and elevated enjoyment.' Washington Irving's philosophy of Christmas and, in particular, his observations of Christmas celebrations in England, pre-figures much in Dickens' seasonal writings. There are references to 'the pitchy gloom' of winter days; 'the ruddy blaze' of fires; and of people being 'brought more closely together by dependence on each other for enjoyment'.

Irving also wrote of the wassail bowl, with its concoction of 'the richest and raciest wines, highly spiced and sweetened, with roasted apples bobbing about the surface'; and described the playing of party-games in a scene that clearly pre-empts the gamesmanship exhibited at the party given by Scrooge's nephew:

I found them at the game of blind-man's buff. Master Simon, who was the leader of their revels, and seemed on all occasions to fulfill the office of that ancient potentate, the Lord of Misrule, was blinded in the midst of the hall. The little beings were ... pinching him, plucking at the skirts of his coat, and tickling him with straws. One fine blue-eyed girl of about thirteen, with her flaxen hair all in beautiful confusion, her frolic face in a glow, her frock half torn off her shoulders, a complete picture of a romp, was the chief tormentor; and from the slyness with which

Master Simon avoided the smaller game, and hemmed this wild little nymph in corners, and obliged her to jump shrieking over chairs, I suspected the rogue of being not a whit more blinded than was convenient.

Reading about the jovial celebrations at Bracebridge Hall would have delighted Dickens. Like Scrooge's nephew — a character, we are told, who 'was quite unconsciously, but most accurately, a literal description of himself' — Dickens clearly believed Christmas to be 'a good time: a kind, forgiving, charitable, pleasant time'. Recalling her father, in 1897, Mamie Dickens wrote:

Christmas was always a time which in our home was looked forward to with eagerness and delight, and to my father it was a time dearer than any other part of the year, I think. He loved Christmas for its deep significance as well as for its joy. At our holiday frolics he used sometimes to conjure for us, the equally 'noble art' of the prestidigitator being among his accomplishments.

Dickens loved parlour-games of the kind enjoyed by Scrooge's nephew and his friends. Percy Fitzgerald recalled Dickens 'going out of the room while we fixed on some subject. Then he came back and plied us with a shower of enquiries until he actually forced his way to the solution.' Sir Henry F. Dickens, the author's son, writing in 1928, recalled another entertainment known as 'The Memory Game':

One of the party started by giving a name, such as, for instance, Napoleon. The next person had to repeat this and add something of his own, such as Napoleon, Blackbeetle, and so on, until the string of names began to get long and difficult to remember. My father, after many turns, had successfully gone through the long string of words, and finished up with his own contribution, 'Warren's Blacking, 30, Strand.' He gave this with an odd twinkle in his eye and a strange inflection in his voice which at once forcibly arrested my attention and left a vivid impression on my mind for some time afterwards . . .

'Warren's Blacking, 30, Strand,' was the factory where Dickens had been forced to work as a boy; how interesting that, in the middle of so light-hearted an entertainment, Dickens should have recalled so unpleasant a time.

Again like Scrooge's nephew, Dickens venerated the 'sacred name and origin' of Christmas and saw the festival as embodying not just a commemoration of the nativity of Christ but the whole of Christ's life and ministry.

Apart from the remarks by Scrooge's nephew, there are Tiny Tim's words as reported by father: 'He told me, coming home, that he hoped the people saw him in church, because he was a cripple, and it might be pleasant to them to remember upon Christmas Day, who made lame beggars walk and blind men see.' And when, in the future, Scrooge is shown the Cratchit family mourning the death of Tiny Tim, the unfortunate child's brother, Peter, is observed reading from the family Bible: ' "And He took a child, and set him in the midst of them." ' Even Jacob Marley — shackled spectre though he is — has come to understand an aspect of the Christmas story:

Why did I walk through crowds of fellow-beings with my eyes turned down, and never raise them to that blessed Star which led the Wise Men to a poor abode? Were there no poor homes to which its light would have conducted me!

Dickens was a passionate advocate of both the holiness and the humanity of Christmas. 'He had,' said his friend, John Forster, 'identified himself with Christmas fancies. Its life and spirits, its humour in riotous abundance, of right belonged to him. Its imaginations as well as its kindly thoughts, were his; and its privilege to light up with some sort of comfort of the squalidest places, he had made his own.'

And those 'imaginations' flowed over into Dickens' writing, beginning in 1835 with the sketch 'A Christmas Dinner', which contained the exhortation: 'Reflect upon your present blessings – of which every man has many – not upon your past misfortunes, of which all men have some. Fill your glass again, with merry face and contented heart. Our life on it, but your Christmas shall be merry, and your new year a happy one!'

It was to be another book, however, in which Dickens and Christmas tied the knot of friendship beyond all doubting. 'Halfway

Illustration by Hablot K. Browne from *The Pickwick Papers* showing Mr Pickwick taking to the ice at Dingley Dell

through his first novel,' wrote Robert Cushman, 'Charles Dickens, by general consent, invented the British Christmas... If the author had been running for office as the Santa Claus of English literature, he could hardly have presented more forthright credentials.'

That book was *The Pickwick Papers*, which had begun serial publication in 1837. In 'A good-humoured Christmas Chapter', Mr Pickwick and his friends spend the festivities with Mr Wardle at Manor Farm in the fictional Kentish village of Dingley Dell. With this one episode Dickens set forth – although he may not have realized it – upon a quest to rescue the customs and traditions of Christmas. 'Dickens,' wrote G.K. Chesterton, 'saved Christmas not because it was historic, but because it was human'; and, more than anything, it was that warm, good-natured humanity of Christmas, encountered by the Pickwickians:

Christmas was close at hand, in all his bluff and hearty honesty; it was the season of hospitality, merriment, and open-heartedness; the old year was preparing, like an ancient philosopher, to call his friends around him, and amidst the sound of feasting and revelry to pass gently and calmly away... How many old recollections, and how many dormant sympathies, does Christmas time awaken!

Many of the hearts that throbbed so gaily then have ceased to beat; many of the looks that shone so brightly then have ceased to glow; the hands we grasped have grown cold; the eyes we sought have hid their lustre in the grave; and yet the old house, the room, the merry voices and smiling faces, the jest, the laugh, the most minute and trivial circumstances connected with those happy meetings, crowd upon our mind at each recurrence of the season, as if the last assemblage had been but yesterday! Happy, happy Christmas...

And the happy, happy Christmas spent at Dingley Dell caught the public imagination. Dickens raked up a fire that sent bright sparks flying and 'a rich glow that penetrated into the farthest corner of the room, and cast its cheerful tint on every face'.

Some years before Samuel Pickwick's celebrations, that other stalwart defender of Christmas, Washington Irving, had written: 'It is, indeed, the season of regenerated feeling – the season for kindling, not merely the fire of hospitality in the hall, but the genial flame of charity in the heart... He who can turn churlishly away from contemplating the felicity of his fellow-beings, and sit down darkling and repining in his loneliness when all around is joyful... wants the genial and social sympathies which constitute the charm of a merry Christmas.'

But it took Charles Dickens to create a character in which that kindling of the flame of charity was to prove so memorable that he himself became absorbed into the very mythology of Christmas. 'We must not,' said G.K. Chesterton, 'ask Dickens what Christmas is, for with all his heat and eloquence he does not know. Rather we must ask Christmas what Dickens is.'

4

Of all the Good Days in the Year, on Christmas Eve

B ack in London from Manchester, Dickens was writing furiously:

Once upon a time – of all the good days in the year, on Christmas Eve – old Scrooge sat busy in his counting-house . . .

He had no choice; apart from the burning social purpose of the story, Dickens also needed to write something that would earn him money. As his great grand-daughter, Monica Dickens, has written: 'It had to be done quickly, to get December publication. It had to be a certain seller. And so, out of the very need and greed it decried, *A Christmas Carol* was born.'

Dickens intended the book to contain an extrapolation of the views about the Christmas season which he had expressed in *Sketches by 'Boz'*. It was in one of these sketches that Dickens had asked:

Who can be insensible to the outpourings of good feeling, and the honest interchange of affectionate attachment, which abound at this season of the year? . . . There seems a magic in the very name of Christmas. Petty jealousies and discords are forgotten: social feelings are awakened in bosoms to which they had long been strangers . . . Kindly hearts that have yearned towards each other, but have been withheld by false notions of pride and self-dignity, are again united, and all is kindness and benevolence!

Here were the grains of a philosophy, but Dickens also required a story and, since there was no time to take any chances, Dickens simply lifted a plot from another book – although, to be fair, it was one of his own!

In *The Pickwick Papers*, Dickens had described the wonderful Christmas festivities enjoyed by Mr Pickwick and his friends, during their visit to Dingley Dell; and, seated around the fire, on Christmas Eve, Mr Wardle had recounted 'The Story of the Goblins who stole a Sexton', an improbable yarn about the reformation of a sour individual named Gabriel Grub – a veritable soulmate for Scrooge:

Gabriel Grub was an ill-conditioned, cross-grained, surly fellow — a morose and lonely man, who consorted with nobody but himself... who eyed each merry face, as it passed him by, with such a deep scowl of malice and ill-humour as it was difficult to meet without feeling something the worse for.

Having decided to spend his Christmas Eve digging a grave in the churchyard, Gabriel Grub encounters a goblin who demands to know: 'What man wanders among graves and churchyards on such a night?' The hapless sexton, having no satisfactory reply to this inquiry, finds himself the 'fair and lawful prize' of a whole troupe of characters, who carry him off to their underground realm, where they set about teaching him the error of his ways.

They show Grub a few pictures from a great storehouse of images: a series of scenes about a poor family who, despite their poverty, keep Christmas and know happiness and comfort. Although only lightly sketched, they are clearly forebears of the Cratchits and, indeed, have among them a sickly child:

The roses had fled from his cheek, and the light from his eye... His young brothers and sisters crowded round his little bed, and seized his tiny hand, so cold and heavy; but they shrunk back from his touch, and looked with awe on his infant face: for calm and tranquil as it was, and sleeping in rest and peace as the beautiful child seemed to be, they

saw that he was dead, and they knew that he was an angel, looking down upon and blessing them from a bright and happy heaven.

Although this angelic child undoubtedly inspired Tiny Tim, Dickens eventually decided that the child in his new story should be allowed to live: to give, perhaps, added impetus to Scrooge's conversion.

Interestingly, the sentimental way in which Dickens frequently wrote of children did not necessarily reflect his personal attitude to the young. For example, when Catherine Dickens bore their fifth child, Francis, her husband wrote: 'Kate is all right again, and so, they tell me, is the baby, but I decline (on principle) to look at the latter object.'

The outcome of Gabriel Grub being shown the goblins' visions is that he awakens on Christmas morning 'an altered man'. But Grub simply cannot 'bear the thought of returning to the place where his repentance would be scoffed at and his reformation disbelieved', so he goes wandering off through the world for the next ten years. Scrooge proved to be made of more courageous stuff.

Dickens shamelessly pillaged many other seasonal episodes from his earlier writings, especially those involving Mr Pickwick. There were echoes of the happy gathering of family and friends sitting down 'by the huge fire of blazing logs to a substantial supper, and a mighty bowl of wassail'. There was also a description of a particularly spirited Christmas dance:

Gabriel Grub confronts a goblin on Christmas Eve. An illustration by Hablot K. Browne from *The Pickwick Papers*

Away went Mr Pickwick — hands across — down the middle to the very end of the room, and half-way up the chimney, back again to the door — poussette everywhere — loud stamp on the ground — ready for the next couple — off again...

Clearly this inspired the highly energized dancing at Fezziwig's ball. Then there is Mr Pickwick's willing and good-natured participation in the party-games:

Mr Pickwick, blinded... with a silk handkerchief, falling up against the wall, and scrambling into corners, and going through all the mysteries of blindman's buff, with the utmost relish for the game, until at last he caught one of the poor relations, and then had to evade the blind-man himself, which he did with a nimbleness and agility that elicited the admiration and applause of all beholders...

An entertainment that is repeated at the Christmas Day party given by Scrooge's nephew, with an even greater disregard for the rules of the game.

As well as many such scenes of good-natured, traditional Christmas celebrations, Dickens repeated his moral that there is a duty upon those who have much to give to those who have little. Dickens intended *A Christmas Carol* as a contribution 'to the common stock of healthful cheerfulness and enjoyment'; but, more than anything, to remind his readers that Christmas was 'a time, of all others, when Want is keenly felt, and Abundance rejoices'. As Dickens so simply put it when speaking of the book: 'I meant a good thing...'

Although the story of Ebenezer Scrooge owed much to the saga of Gabriel Grub and some of his other writings, it was as if Dickens were working with an entirely new device. Writing the book had a powerful effect on him and he worked at it day and night, leading a solitary life, breaking appointments, refusing to see callers and never leaving home 'before the owls went out'.

Speaking of himself in the third person, Dickens reported having 'wept and laughed and wept again, and excited himself in a most extraordinary manner in the composition; and thinking whereof he walked about the black streets of London, fifteen and twenty miles many a night when sober folks had gone to bed'.

Much of the dynamism for the story came from the sharply defined central character. Scrooge, as first introduced, is 'a squeezing, wrenching, grasping, scraping, clutching, covetous old sinner'. His very name (a variant of the now-defunct word 'scrouge', meaning to squeeze or press and possessing more than an echo of 'scrounge') suggests something of his character, which in accord with the popular theories of physiognomy, is revealed in his appearance:

The cold within him froze his old features, nipped his pointed nose, shrivelled his cheek, stiffened his gait; made his eyes red, his thin lips blue; and spoke out shrewdly in his grating voice.

Scrooge's attitude towards his clerk, his nephew and to two gentlemen collecting for charity – and his repeated assertion that Christmas is a 'Humbug!' – show him to be a suitable case for treatment. Redemption comes in the form of three powerful spiritual beings representing Christmas Past, Present and Yet To Come, preceded by a phantom from beyond the grave, with 'death-cold eyes'. With this device Dickens inextricably linked the ghost story to Christmas with a chain 'full as heavy and as long' as that worn by Jacob Marley.

Maybe Dickens was recalling the hair-raising tales which his nursemaid had told him when he was young. Certainly there is a sense of tales recollected when Scrooge remembers hearing 'that ghosts in haunted houses were described as dragging chains'. Those chains – usually intended as a sign of some former incarceration – are ingeniously transformed by Dickens into the shackles of Mammon.

Dickens' ghosts also owe something to his love of the theatre: Marley and the Ghost of

Illustration by C.E. Brock (1905)

Christmas Future (who is surely related to the Grim Reaper) might have stepped straight out of a stage melodrama; and all the Spirits' mysterious entrances and exits – appearing in a blaze of light, emerging from mist or boldly walking through walls, windows and locked doors – show Dickens' fascination with stage magic and illusions.

The 'surprising transformation' of Scrooge's room by the Spirit of Christmas Present recalls the astonishing magical effects of such performers as Robert Houdin, who filled the stage with a profusion of objects, just as the Ghost heaps up Scrooge's chamber with a rich variety of fare.

The Spirit of Christmas Past, carrying 'a great extinguisher' – or candle-snuffer – suggests another famous illusion performed in a variety of ways by several magicians, including Henri Robin who, in his 'Soirees Magiques', placed a large extinguisher over an assistant who then disappeared – just as the first of the spirits vanishes when Scrooge seizes the extinguisher-cap and, 'by a sudden action', presses it down upon upon the head of his unearthly visitor.

Wherever he conjured them from, Dickens was clearly susceptible to the idea of such beings. 'My own mind,' he wrote the year before beginning his most famous ghost story, 'is perfectly unprejudiced and impressible on the subject of ghosts – I do not in the least pretend that such things cannot be.'

Marley's name, according to an article in the journal of the Dickens Fellowship, *The Dickensian*, in 1938, was borrowed from Dr Miles Marley of Cork Street, Piccadilly, who had met Dickens at a St Patrick's Day party in 1843. The novelist took a liking to the unusual name and allegedly told the doctor: 'Your name will be a household word before the year is out.'

As for Marley's transmogrification into a knocker, this event may well owe something to 'Our Next-Door Neighbour', a piece in *Sketches by 'Boz'*:

> Whenever we visit a man for the first time, we contemplate the features of his knocker with the greatest curiosity, for we well know, that between the man and his knocker, there will inevitably be a greater or lesser degree of resemblance and sympathy.

Dickens went on to identify different 'species' of knocker: those with 'the jolly face of a convivial lion smiling blandly as you'; or a rather different lion: 'a heavy ferocious-looking fellow, with a countenance of expressive of savage stupidity – a sort of grand master among the knockers, and a great favourite with the selfish and brutal'.

Possibly, the latter type was just the kind of knocker that Jacob Marley might have had upon the door of his chambers, later occupied by Ebenezer Scrooge. Can there be any other explanation for the fact 'that Scrooge, having his key in the lock of the door, saw in the knocker, without its undergoing any intermediate process of change: not a knocker, but Marley's face'?

Dickens used the spectral ambassadors in *A Christmas Carol* with their time-travelling powers, to teach Scrooge many lessons by which he is finally reformed. Scrooge's life, we see from these scenes, might easily have been very different, yet all is not lost, for he repeatedly shows small, but significant, indications that he may yet change his future. As Scrooge's iciness begins to thaw, he shows first a regret for the things of the past and then a concern for the future, and in particular for the fate of Tiny Tim.

The strongest indication that Scrooge has the potential to become a different man is his latent sense of humour, which is occasionally awoken; dismissing Marley's Ghost as nothing more than indigestion, Scrooge waggishly remarks: 'There's more of gravy than of grave about you, whatever you are!'

Dickens comments that 'Scrooge was not much in the habit of cracking jokes'; nevertheless, he manages the occasional facetious observation as, when being told the times at which to expect the three ghosts, he asks: 'Couldn't I take 'em all at once, and have it over, Jacob?' Here, surely, is the man who, after a modicum of haunting, is able to indulge in 'a splendid laugh, a most illustrious laugh', what Dickens describes as 'the father of a long, long, line of brilliant laughs!'

Dickens filled the book with many new and memorable scenes: among the most often-quoted being the description of Christmas dinner at the Cratchits':

There never was such a goose. Bob said he didn't believe there ever was such a goose cooked. Its tenderness and flavour, size and cheapness, were the themes of universal admiration.

Oh, a wonderful pudding!

Illustration by Emil Weiss (1944)

But some of the most affecting scenes are those depicting the young Ebenezer left alone at school in the Christmas holidays with no one to keep him company but the characters in his story-book; or, in contrast, his joyful time at the Christmas party given by his employer, Mr Fezziwig. And Dickens particularly excelled in those passages of descriptive prose evoking festive scenes which are now a part of the litany of Christmas:

There were great, round, pot-bellied baskets of chestnuts, shaped like the waistcoats of jolly old gentlemen, lolling at the doors, and tumbling out into the streets in their apoplectic opulence. There were ruddy, brown-faced, broad-girthed Spanish Onions, shining in the fatness of their growth like Spanish Friars . . . There were pears and apples, clustered high in blooming pyramids; there were bunches of grapes, made, in the shopkeepers' benevolence, to dangle from conspicuous hooks, that people's mouths might water gratis as they passed . . .

In all likelihood these glorious episodes, which have probably provided more Christmas readings than any other book apart from the Bible, present a highly romanticized view of the way life really was. Interestingly, they far outnumber those passages of social comment.

Dickens seems to have been so carried away in telling the story of Ebenezer Scrooge, and with capturing a mood of joviality – 'they were happy, grateful, pleased with one another, and contented with the time' – that he all but overlooked the terrible social conditions that had been his original motivation.

Consider the case of Martha, Bob Cratchit's eldest daughter, 'who was a poor apprentice at a milliner's'. As the family sits around the Christmas fire, Martha tells them 'what kind of work she had to do, and how many hours she worked at a stretch, and how she meant to lie a-bed to-morrow morning for a good long rest; to-morrow being a holiday she passed at home'.

Dickens might conceivably have made a more significant point if he had revealed just how many hours Martha would have been expected to work at a stretch. Contemporary reports, for example, revealed that a milliner's assistant, working in the busy pre-Christmas season, would have begun her day at seven o'clock in the morning and, apart from fifteen minute breaks for breakfast, lunch, tea and supper, might well still be working, nineteen hours later, at two o'clock the following morning.

Similarly, despite Dickens' outrage over the employment of children in mines, he raises no protesting voice in *A Christmas Carol*, beyond a description of the bleakness of the place in which they live. Indeed, if anything, Dickens' brief portrayal of life in a mining community is somewhat mawkish:

Passing through the wall of mud and stone, they found a cheerful company assembled round a glowing fire. An old, old man and woman, with their children and their children's children, and another generation beyond that, all decked out gaily in their holiday attire. The old man, in a voice that seldom rose above the howling of the wind upon the barren waste, was singing them a Christmas song . . .

It is possible that if *A Christmas Carol* had been a more didactic book it might not have achieved the same popularity, or might not have endured so well; and there is no denying that the book does contain flashes of savage satire. Scrooge, having remarked that if the poor would rather die than go to the prisons and workhouses, 'they had better do it and decrease the surplus population', later has his ruthless words thrown back at him in response to his concern about Tiny Tim:

Will you decide what men shall live what men shall die? It may be, that in the sight of Heaven, you are more worthless and less fit to live than millions like this poor man's child. Oh God! to hear the Insect on the leaf pronouncing on the too much life among his hungry brothers in the dust!

This was Dickens' scathing attack on the philosophy of Thomas Malthus, who, in 1793, had written *An Essay on the Principle of Population*. 'A man who is born into a world possessed,' wrote Malthus, 'if he cannot get subsistence from his parents, on which he has a just demand, and if society do not want his labour, has no claim of right of the smallest portion of food, and, in fact, has no business to be where he is. At Nature's mighty feast there is no vacant cover for him. She tells him to be gone...'

In a similar vein, Dickens lays about those who had recently been attempting to introduce a Sunday Observance Bill. The poor rarely had a roast meal other than on a Sundays, when they took their joints to be cooked at the bakers' shops. Legislation to close the bakeries on Sundays was being proposed by Sir Andrew Agnew and Dickens had responded with a pamphlet, written in 1836, under the name Timothy Sparks. In it he attacked Sir Andrew

and others of his class who, 'generally speaking, eat pretty comfortable dinners all the week through, and cannot be expected to understand what people feel, who have a meat dinner on one day out every seven'.

This argument reappears in *A Christmas Carol*, when Scrooge accuses the Ghost of Christmas Present of trying to deprive people of 'their means of dining every seventh day', the Spirit, denying the charge, and denounces those who claim to do such 'deeds of passion, pride, ill-will, hatred, envy, bigotry, and selfishness' in the name of Christianity.

But the impact of *A Christmas Carol* does not derive from such specifics. As G.K. Chesterton commented: 'The beauty and the real blessing of the story do not lie in the mechanical plot of it, the repentance of Scrooge, probable or improbable; they lie in the great furnace of real happiness that glows through Scrooge and everything around him; that great furnace, the heart of Dickens.'

In *Sketches by 'Boz'*, Dickens had expressed the wish that the spirit of Christmas might inform the entire behaviour of man:

Would that Christmas lasted the whole year through, and that the prejudices and passions which deform our better nature, were never called into action among those to whom, at least, they should ever be strangers.

In *A Christmas Carol*, Dickens has Scrooge make the promise: 'I will honour Christmas in my heart, and try to keep it all the year'; and, earlier in the tale, when Scrooge dismisses Christmas by saying: 'Much good may it do you! Much good has it ever done you!', Dickens gives the old man's nephew the following defence of Christmas:

I have always thought of Christmas time, when it comes round — apart from the veneration due to its sacred name and origin, if anything belonging to it can be apart from that — as a good time: a kind, forgiving, charitable, pleasant time: the only time I know of in the long calendar of the year, when men and women seem by one consent to open their shut up hearts freely, and to think of people below them as if they really were fellow passengers to the grave, and not another race of creatures bound on other journeys. And therefore, uncle, though it has never put a scrap of gold or silver in my pocket, I believe it has done me good, and will do me good; and I say God bless it!

Dickens clearly hoped that, just as Bob Cratchit had 'involuntarily applauded' this sentiment, his readers would do likewise! And, indeed, they did — and still do!

Dickens the conjuror of Christmas. A drawing by Kyd (Joseph Clayton Clarke) from 1905 edition of *The Dickensian*

5

The Greatest Little Book in the World

A famous American book-collector of the 1920s, A. Edward Newton, described Dickens' history of Scrooge as 'the greatest little book in the world'. But in 1843, no one, least of all Dickens, could have known that this small, seasonal story was destined to become something almost on a par with holy scripture.

Dickens certainly embarked on the book with high enthusiasm, but then the pressure on him was great; as he explained in a letter to his American friend, Cornelius Felton: 'To keep the "Chuzzlewit" going, and do this little book, the "Carol" in the odd times between the two parts of it, was, as you may suppose, pretty tight work.'

Tight work it may have been, but Dickens made a bold beginning. He had decided to call it *A Christmas Carol* (an interesting title, since the book is not in verse and Dickens was no poet); and pursuing the musical motif, the chapters were to be called staves. The first of these was headed 'Old Marley's Ghost' (Dickens later crossed out the word 'Old') and its opening lines are justly famous:

Marley was dead: to begin with. There is no doubt whatever about that. The register of his burial was signed by the clergyman, the clerk, the undertaker, and the chief mourner. Scrooge signed it: and Scrooge's name was good upon Change, for anything he chose to put his hand to. Old Marley was as dead as a door-nail.

Illustration by Arthur Rackham (1915)

'It's a good beginning,' Rizzo Rat tells Charles Dickens (a.k.a. Gonzo) in *The Muppet Christmas Carol*, 'it's creepy and kind of spooky!' It is also a daring beginning, if for no other reason, because the first character to be introduced – at considerable length – is not the book's central character; indeed, is not even alive!

The story has scarcely begun before Dickens is digressing with a highly idiosyncratic passage:

> Mind! I don't mean to say that I know, of my own knowledge, what there is particularly dead about a door-nail. I might have been inclined, myself, to regard a coffin-nail as the deadest piece of ironmongery in the trade. But the wisdom of our ancestors is in the simile; and my unhallowed hands shall not disturb it, or the Country's done for. You will therefore permit me to repeat, emphatically, that Marley was as dead as a door-nail.

Dickens was right to point out the antiquity of the phrase 'as dead as a door-nail'. It can be found as early as 1362, in William Langland's *The Vision of Piers Plowman*, where it appears as 'ded as a dore-nayle'. It also featured in an old ballad, 'St George for England', and in Parts Two of Shakespeare's *Henry IV* and *Henry VI*. And only two months before beginning *A Christmas Carol*, Dickens had written to his friend, Cornelius Felton:

> Apropos of dreams ... I had a good piece of absurdity in my head a night or two ago. I dreamed that somebody was dead ... It was a private gentleman and a particular friend; and I was greatly overcome when the news was broken to me (very delicately) by a gentleman in a cocked hat, top boots, and a sheet. Nothing else. 'Good God,' I said. 'Is he dead!' 'He is dead Sir,' rejoined the gentleman, 'as a door-nail. But we must all die, Mr Dickens – sooner or later my dear Sir.'

Accounts of Dickens writing *A Christmas Carol*, suggest that the book was written in a euphoric rush; he told a friend: 'I was very much affected by the little Book myself,' and was 'reluctant to lay it aside for a moment.' Nevertheless, he worked over the text many times and – whilst there are no outlines, notes or early drafts – Dickens made endless additions, deletions and revisions to the manuscript itself.

On the opening page, for example, having stressed the need for the reader to believe that Marley was dead, 'or nothing wonderful can come of the story I am going to relate', Dickens indulged in another joking aside, by drawing a comparison with the story of *Hamlet*:

> If we were not perfectly convinced that Hamlet's Father died before the play began, there would be nothing more remarkable in his taking a stroll at night, in a easterly wind, upon his own ramparts, than there would be in any other middle-aged gentleman rashly turning out after dark in a breezy spot – say Saint Paul's Churchyard for instance – literally to astonish his son's weak mind.

Illustration by Charles Green (1892)

Dickens originally continued this playful analysis:

> Perhaps you think that Hamlet's intellects were strong. I doubt it. If you could have such a son tomorrow, depend upon it, you would find him a poser. He would be a most impracticable fellow to deal with, and however creditable he might be to the family, after his decease, he would prove a special incumbrance in his lifetime, trust me.

Wisely, Dickens later deleted this paragraph; although he kept the reference to Shakespeare's play which, like *A Christmas Carol*, opens with a ghostly confrontation that haunts the rest of the story.

The full extent to which Dickens worked at the text can be seen from the manuscript, written in what John Mortimer has described as 'a sort of undulating scrawl, patterned like the waves of the sea'. On almost every line, words are crossed out or written over, and amendments are often squeezed in between the lines. Dickens changed the number of years since Marley's death from ten to the mystical seven; after a spate of deletions, he eventually named Scrooge's clerk as 'Bob Cratchit', but very nearly called his crippled child, 'Little Fred'!

On page 37, he wrote – and then crossed out – some of the most famous lines in the story. Dickens has Bob, in a tremulous voice, telling his wife that Tiny Tim is 'growing strong and hearty'; which, in the original manuscript, prompts a question from Scrooge that reflects the Victorians' obsession with infant mortality:

> 'Is that so, Spirit?' Scrooge demanded, with an interest he never felt before. 'I hope it is?'
> 'I see a vacant seat beside the chimney corner,' said the Spirit. 'The child will die.'

But having written this, Dickens deleted the exchange, finding a better place for it – a few pages later – where it added considerably to the pathos.

Dickens' style is nowhere near as effortless as it at first appears. There is a consciously created tone of intimacy in describing Scrooge coming face to face with the Ghost of Christmas Past: 'as close to it as I am now to you, and I am standing in the spirit at your elbow'. There is also his meticulousness of construction – especially in those famous descriptive passages with their opulent use of adjectives and their carefully orchestrated lists of people, things and emotions.

The book is not without its weaknesses: it is episodic and it contains major characters (Bob Cratchit and Scrooge's nephew) who have no names or proper introductions until the second half of the book. It raises awkward questions, such as why the Ghost of Christmas Past seems unsure how many children were born to Scrooge's sister; or by what power the fading Ghost of Christmas Present foretells the fate of Tiny Tim. And, occasionally, the reader is required to suspend a more than usual amount of disbelief, as when, during the visions of the future, Scrooge fails to recognize his own bed-chamber or realize that he is the man who lies there dead.

Nevertheless, there are so many strengths to the story: its undiluted energy and rich sense of good-humour; its dramatic recreation of street-life in Victorian London; its fantastical effects, as when the schoolroom ages before Scrooge's eyes in a sequence pre-echoing H.G. Wells' *The Time Machine*; and its fanciful touches – such as Dickens' speculation on the location of Scrooge's chambers:

> They were a gloomy suite of rooms, in a lowering pile of building up a yard, where it had so little business to be, that one could scarcely help fancying it must have run there when it was a young house, playing at hide-and-seek with other houses, and have forgotten the way out again.

By the second week of November 1843, Dickens had completed the manuscript and delivered it to his publishers.

Chapman and Hall were less than enthusiastic about the book, thinking it too slight to be of consequence. So Dickens undertook to pay the production costs, if the publishers would agree that – after taking a commission on copies sold – he would receive all profits.

Dickens took enormous care over the book's appearance and personally supervised all aspects of production. The book was to be bound in salmon cloth, blind-stamped with a decorative border of holly and ivy; the title (in rustic lettering) and the author's name were to be stamped in gold within a Christmas wreath, and a similar decoration was designed for the spine; the end-papers were to be green; and all three edges were to be gilded – a great luxury!

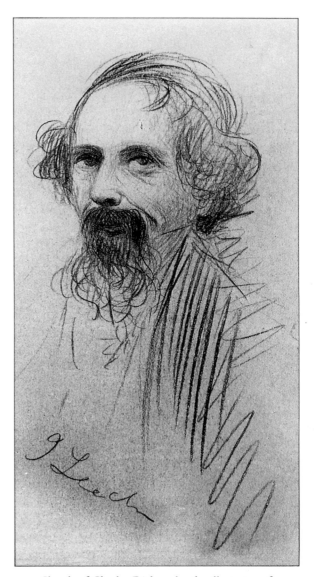

Sketch of Charles Dickens by the illustrator of *A Christmas Carol*, John Leech (1849)

Despite these expensive embellishments, Dickens insisted that the book be produced at no more than five shillings, in the hope that the greatest possible number of readers might buy the book. Although not overpriced for such a lavishly produced volume, it should be remembered that five shillings, nevertheless, represented a third of Bob Cratchit's weekly wage.

Dickens' choice of illustrator for *A Christmas Carol* was *Punch* cartoonist John Leech. The author had first encountered Leech in 1836, when the illustrator of *The Pickwick Papers*, Robert Seymour, committed suicide. Leech made a bid to take over the work and approached Dickens with a specimen illustration. This picture, drawn for an early episode in the book, illustrated the Bagman's tale of Tom Smart, who after too many glasses of punch, sees a old chair in his room undergo a curious transformation into a shrivelled old man.

Dickens told the artist that the illustration was 'well-conceived, and executed', although to Chapman and Hall he was rather more frank, remarking that 'the chair's not bad', but that Leech's notion for the bedroom looked less like a room in the rambling old house which he had described, as a room in a rather undistinguished house of the kind Dickens supposed the artist himself to inhabit!

In any event, the publishers had already selected a replacement artist for *The Pickwick Papers*, Hablot K. Browne (who drew under the pseudonym of 'Phiz'); and Dickens told Leech that he considered Phiz 'a gentleman of very great ability, with whose designs I am exceedingly well satisfied, and from whom I feel it neither my wish, not interest, to part'.

It seemed unlikely that Dickens and Leech would work together and Dickens remained critical of any examples of the artist's work which he saw. During the next few years, however, Leech's career took off and he became one of the leading contributors to *Punch*.

When in 1842, Leech once again approached Dickens, the novelist — obviously influenced by the artist's recent success — wrote Leech an ingratiating letter in which he claimed to have followed his progress 'with much interest and satisfaction'. Dickens went on: 'I congratulate you heartily on your success; and myself on having had an eye upon the means by which you have obtained it.'

Dickens and Leech eventually met, and the author thought seriously of using him as illustrator for *Martin Chuzzlewit*, but eventually Phiz — undoubtedly, at the time, a superior draughtsman — was commissioned to illustrate that book. When, however, in October 1843, Dickens began writing *A Christmas Carol*, it was clear that Phiz was too busy illustrating *Chuzzlewit* to provide decorations for the Ghost Story as well; as a result, John Leech was invited to produce four woodcuts and four steel-engravings which were to be hand-coloured.

Leech drew sketches for the woodcuts for Dickens' approval. Next, the sketches were made into finished pencil drawings for W. J. Linton, who was to cut the wood-blocks — a technique achieved by pasting the pencil drawing onto the end grain of a block of wood and then, literally, cutting through the picture into the wood. Once cut, facsimiles of the blocks were made in metal which was steel-faced so that it was possible to print thousands of copies from them without them wearing out.

As for the remaining illustrations, these were etched by Leech himself onto copper plates which were then also steel-faced for durability. Leech then produced colour-guides for the people employed to colour the printed illustrations. The method of hand-tinting involved the colourists laying out all the prints and then working with one colour at a time: painting in all blue jackets, all yellow skirts, all pink faces and so on.

This production-line approach had its drawbacks, and the artistic quality of the colourists employed by Chapman and Hall was extremely varied. The plates look decidedly more garish than subtle; what Hablot K. Browne's son described as 'certainly gay, but generally too crude to be pleasant'. Leech, a sensitive artist, was far from pleased with the way in which the plates were being coloured and complained to Dickens, who replied that he thought the artist was unconsciously exaggerating the problem, although he agreed that it was 'a point of great importance' and had, therefore, 'sent a Strong Dispatch to C and H'. To reassure Leech, he added: 'You can't think how much better they will look in a neat book, than you suppose.'

As with all illustrated books, it is interesting to speculate why the artist ignored so many potentially good illustrative subjects: the Spirit of Christmas Past; the young Scrooge in the deserted schoolroom; the confrontation with Belle; the jollifications at Scrooge's nephew's, the sordid goings-on in Old Joe's shop; and, above all, the Cratchits' Christmas Dinner with goose, pudding and all.

Leech's illustrations are sometimes disappointing, like his final picture of Scrooge and Bob discussing the Cratchit family affairs 'over a Christmas bowl of smoking bishop'; and it is curious that he chose this subject, rather than to show Scrooge and Tiny Tim, as so many of his successors have done. Nevertheless, they do have a quality of grotesque comic-horror: consider the cloud of phantoms agonized at being 'unable to assist a wretched woman with an infant upon a door step'; or the chilling visualization of Scrooge kneeling in the churchyard before the Ghost of Christmas Yet To Come.

There is also sly humour in Leech's pictures, as in the illustration of the apparition of Jacob Marley – pig-tail and coat-tails bristling – walking into Scrooge's room as an anthropomorphic candle flame, with an extremely alarmed expression, leaps up, as if crying: 'I know him! Marley's Ghost!' But, perhaps, the picture which best reflects Leech's style and the tone of Dickens' prose is the book's frontispiece, showing the ball with old Fezziwig embarking on a 'Sir Roger de Coverley' with Mrs Fezziwig: she 'one vast substantial smile'; he dancing so deftly 'that he appeared to wink with his legs, and came upon his feet again without a stagger'.

Some years later, in 1852, Leech reworked the picture for the cheap edition of the Christmas Books (a volume containing *A Christmas Carol* and its four seasonal successors), and it remains one of the most potent images associated with the story; so potent that most subsequent illustrators have produced little more than carbon-copies of that first Fezziwig.

Over the years, many other artists, illustrators and cartoonists have decorated the story with varying degrees of success. They have used pencil, pen and ink, oil paints, water colours, scraper-board and – in the case of 'Spitting Image' model makers, Fluck and Law – highly detailed, three-dimensional figures in elaborate settings.

Illustrators of *A Christmas Carol* can effectively be divided into two classes: the caricaturists, cartoonists and humorous illustrators – John Leech, Arthur Rackham, Harry Furniss, Ronald Searle and others – and those preferring a more naturalistic style, such as the American artist Greg Hildebrandt who, in a quest for realism, bases all his characterizations on family and friends – gratefully acknowledged in a list at the beginning of the book.

The realists have made a brave showing: George Alfred Williams, in 1905, giving a detailed depiction of Scrooge's office with its clutter of papers, ledgers, ink-bottles and dirty, broken windows; and, eighty-five years later, the Italian artist, Roberto Innocenti, recreating the streets around that office down to the last shutter, gutter and gas-lamp.

However, the comic illustrators have won out every time with Searle's picture of the charwoman, the laundress and the undertaker's man dancing a grotesque gavotte amongst the

Illustration by Arthur Rackham

rags and bones in Old Joe's shop; and Harry Furniss' comic vision of a portly gentleman splayed upon the ground with a huge sprig of holly through his heart.

Most illustrators have decided against showing Scrooge witnessing the various visions of Christmas past, present and future. Of the handful of artists who have chosen to include Scrooge and the Spirits in such scenes: some have depicted them as 'see-through' beings, haunting a flesh-and-blood world; while others have shown a corporeal Scrooge observing the ghostly goings-on at the Cratchits and elsewhere through a dream-like mist.

Some things, however, remain always the same: Scrooge, often balding and bespectacled, is usually drawn on the lean and hungry side; although, very occasionally, he has been shown as a man of robust physique, with a mane of silver hair and, once in a while, a moustache.

Although, for some inexplicable reason, John Leech decided not to draw a picture of Tiny Tim, later artists have shown no such restraint: the unfortunate young Cratchit — usually better fed and better dressed than might have been expected — has been depicted limping stoically along on his crutch, or riding high on his father's shoulders on the way home from church.

Michael Foreman drew a touching picture of Bob sitting at the bedside of his dead child; while, in one pseudo-religious rendering, the deceased Tim hovers in the midst of his family, suffused with an unearthly light; 'Spirit of Tiny Tim,' reads the caption, 'thy childish essence was from God.'

Other popular scenes include Mrs Cratchit's entrance with the pudding (seldom as small as Dickens says it was); Ali Baba and the other storybook characters glimpsed through the schoolroom window; the blindfolded Topper in pursuit of the plump sister at Fred's party; and, especially, the arrival of Marley's Ghost: a scene — according to Ronald Searle's illustration — that was witnessed by a tiny mouse who keeled over in terror! Searle also chose to illustrate several less familiar episodes: the young Cratchits listening to the pudding singing in the copper; Mrs Cratchit attempting to conceal her tears while sewing clothes for Tiny Tim's funeral; and the charity collectors, not arriving at Scrooge's office, but creeping dejectedly away.

Similarly, Arthur Rackham (always a good illustrator of overlooked scenes) produced a colour plate of Scrooge's lost love, Belle, surrounded by her children, 'a flushed and boisterous group'; and another, showing her husband arriving home, 'attended by a man laden with Christmas toys and presents', and being immediately pounced upon by the boisterous ones. Seeing such scenes, Scrooge might well have breathed a sigh of relief at not having married Belle!

Rackham also illustrated a snatch of conversation between two city businessmen discussing Scrooge's death: 'Well,' says one, 'Old Scratch has got his own at last, hey?' The artist shows the men shaking hands while, behind them, looms a vision of the devil (complete with cloven hoofs, horns and pitchfork), beckoning, with sinister glee, to the unfortunate Scrooge.

Marvel Comic Book's
A Christmas Carol (1981)

The same artist visualized Dickens' description of Londoners shovelling snow from their roof-tops – St Paul's rising in the distance, through the smoke and fog – while a rather less accomplished draughtsman showed the results of their labours, as the shovelled snow landed in the road below.

Despite the specificly masculine description which Dickens gave of the Ghost of Christmas Present, Honor C. Appleton rather surprisingly – and alone among illustrators – drew a female Spirit. As for the various activities instigated by Christmas Present, these have provided a fund of inspiration: apart from their night-time flights over London, the Ghost and Scrooge have been shown standing by the helmsman on board a ship; looking across a windswept waste towards a tin mine and looking across a wind-tossed sea towards a lighthouse.

On the other hand, the Ghost of Christmas Past has sorely tested illustrators, many of whom – following John Leech's example – haven't even tried their hand at the unusual visitor which Dickens described: 'It was a strange figure – like a child: yet not so like a child as like an old man, viewed through some supernatural medium, which gave him the appearance of . . . being diminished to a child's proportions.' All of which – plus 'a bright jet of clear light' springing from the top of its head – proved too complex even for Arthur Rackham.

Michael Foreman artfully showed no more

than a hand, with a sprig of holly, pulling the bed-curtains aside; others have opted to draw either a child or an old man – or a child with a beard. Maybe only Ronald Searle has succeeded in showing the Spirit simultaneously young and old, as well as capturing its rare talent for flickering in and out of sight.

Among the more ingenious illustrated editions have been versions with transforming pictures, lift-up flaps (so you can see how much Marley has got in his cash-boxes) and pop-ups. Pull this tab, and the fiddler fiddles while the Fezziwigs dance; pull that one, and the Cratchits raise their glasses; pull yet another and the Ghost of Christmas Future points to a blank headstone on which the name 'Ebenezer Scrooge' suddenly appears.

Most illustrators have revelled in the book's recurrent imagery of death: many have shown Scrooge confronting his own corpse, laid out upon the bed; and several have shown the horse-drawn hearse galloping up the stairs to Scrooge's rooms. The Marvel comic-book version – full of such visualized sounds as Marley's 'CLINK, CHINK, CLANK, CHANK' – opens with the coffin of Scrooge's partner being lowered into the grave. And illustrator John Worsley began his version with a picture of a headstone, inscribed: 'Jacob Marley 1773–1836', obviously remembering that Marley had been dead seven years when the events occurred which are described in *A Christmas Carol*.

Which takes us back to the year 1843. The story completed, Dickens made a few last-minute alterations and asked John Leech to change the colour of the robe worn by the Ghost of Christmas Present. Dickens had described it in the text as green, but Leech – inspired, perhaps, by early American images of Santa Claus – had dressed him in red.

From this sequence, Dickens also deleted a brief passage:

> The Ghost of Christmas Present rose, and as it did so Scrooge observed that [beneath] its skirts it seemed to have some object which it sought to hide. He fancied that he saw either the claw of a great bird or a foot, much smaller than the spirit's own protruding for a moment from its robe; and being curious in everything concerning these unearthly visitors, he asked the Spirit what it meant.
>
> 'They are not so many as they might be,' replied the Ghost, 'who care to know or ask. No matter what it is, just now. Are you ready to go forth with me?'

Dickens made another small, but highly significant, addition to the penultimate paragraph: '… and to Tiny Tim, who did NOT die, he was a second father'. Various commentators have criticized his decision to spare Tiny Tim, agreeing with J. Cumming Walters who said that 'Dickens was carried away by exuberance, and momentarily forgot good taste.' Good or bad taste, that sentence has become a vital part of almost every telling of the tale.

His amendments complete, Dickens penned a brief Preface. The manuscript of *A Christmas Carol* – marked in Dickens' hand: 'My own, and only, MS of the Book' – was passed to the printers, Bradbury and Evans, late in November; but, since Dickens never made fair copies of his work, the compositor had to pick his way through sixty-six closely-written pages with a myriad of textual corrections. Notwithstanding which, by 17 December, Dickens had copies of the book for inscription to friends.

Responding to a grateful acknowledgment from one of those recipients, Dickens wrote: 'I am extremely glad you feel the Carol... And when I see the effect of a little whole as that, on those for whom I care, I have a strong sense of the immense effect I could produce with an entire book.'

Dickens had completed A Christmas Carol in a frenzy of energy; as his great grand-daughter, Monica Dickens, has observed: 'What had been started as a cold-blooded money maker was finished in a white heat of emotion.' And, as Dickens himself put it: 'When it was done, I broke out like a Madman.' He held a Twelfth Night party, at which he gave a performance of magic. Mrs Thomas Carlyle, who was present, described Dickens as 'the best conjuror I ever saw'.

'A hot plum pudding,' Dickens himself recorded, 'was produced from an empty saucepan held over a blazing fire kindled in Stanfield's hat without damage to the lining' and 'a box of bran was changed into a guinea-pig, which ran between my godchild's feet.'

Mrs Carlyle's husband, the dour Scottish sage, Thomas Carlyle, was one of A Christmas Carol's most striking converts. Although, many years later, Carlyle criticized Dickens' festive philosophy for thinking that 'men ought to be buttered up, and the world made soft and accommodating for them, and all sorts of fellows have turkey for their Christmas dinner'; in 1843, his response was very different.

Carlyle refused to indulge in Christmas celebrations and was scornful of those who did: 'All mortals are tumbling about,' he wrote one year, 'in a state of drunken saturnalia... a very strange method of thanking God for sending them a Redeemer.' But then he received an advance copy of A Christmas Carol; and, according to his wife, 'the vision of Scrooge so worked upon his nervous organization that he was seized with a perfect convulsion of hospitality.'

Someone greatly amused by this information was William Makepeace Thackeray, who went into print with a reference to the 'Scotch philosopher who nationally does not keep Christmas Day,' but who, having read A Christmas Carol, 'sent out for a turkey, and asked two friends to dine – this is a fact.'

The reaction of friends, however, was one thing; Dickens knew that once A Christmas Carol went on sale, he would discover just what the critics and – more importantly – the public, thought of his 'Ghostly little book'.

At which point in this story, you can read (or, maybe, re-read) for yourself the story which began it all...

A Christmas Carol

In Prose;

Being a Short Story of Christmas.

By Charles Dickens

The Illustrations by John Leech

Chapman and Hall 186 Strand

MDCCCXLIII.

My own, and only MS of the [...]

Charles Dickens

Preface.

I have endeavoured, in this Ghostly little book, to raise the Ghost of an Idea, which shall not put my readers out of humour with themselves, with each other, with the season, or with me. May it haunt their houses pleasantly, and no one wish to lay it!

Their faithful friend and Servant

CD.

December 1843.

Contents

MARLEY'S GHOST

Marley was dead: to begin with. There is no doubt whatever about that. The register of his burial was signed by the clergyman, the clerk, the undertaker, and the chief mourner. Scrooge signed it: and Scrooge's name was good upon 'Change, for anything he chose to put his hand to. Old Marley was as dead as a door-nail.

Mind! I don't mean to say that I know, of my own knowledge, what there is particularly dead about a door-nail. I might have been inclined, myself, to regard a coffin-nail as the deadest piece of ironmongery in the trade. But the wisdom of our ancestors is in the simile; and my unhallowed hands shall not disturb it, or the Country's done for. You will therefore permit me to repeat, emphatically, that Marley was as dead as a door-nail.

Scrooge knew he was dead? Of course he did. How could it be otherwise? Scrooge and he were partners for I don't know how many years. Scrooge was his sole executor, his sole administrator, his sole assign, his sole residuary legatee, his sole friend, and sole mourner. And even Scrooge was not so dreadfully cut up by the sad event, but that he was an excellent man of business on the very day of the funeral, and solemnised it with an undoubted bargain.

The mention of Marley's funeral brings me back to the point I started from. There is no doubt that Marley was dead. This must be distinctly understood, or nothing wonderful can come of the story I am going to relate. If we were not perfectly convinced that Hamlet's Father died before the play began, there would be nothing more remarkable in his taking a stroll at night, in an easterly wind, upon his own ramparts, than there would be in any other middle-aged gentleman rashly turning out after dark in a breezy spot – say Saint Paul's Churchyard for instance – literally to astonish his son's weak mind.

Scrooge never painted out Old Marley's name. There it stood, years afterwards, above the warehouse door: Scrooge and Marley. The firm was known as Scrooge and Marley. Sometimes people new to the business called Scrooge Scrooge, and sometimes Marley, but he answered to both names. It was all the same to him.

Oh! But he was a tight-fisted hand at the grindstone, Scrooge! a squeezing, wrenching, grasping, scraping, clutching, covetous old sinner! Hard and sharp as a flint, from which no steel had ever struck out generous fire; secret, and self-contained, and solitary as an oyster. The cold within him froze his old features, nipped his pointed nose, shrivelled his cheek, stiffened his gait; made his eyes red, his thin lips blue; and spoke out shrewdly in his grating voice. A frosty rime was on his head, and on his eyebrows, and his wiry chin. He carried his own low temperature always about with him; he iced his office in the dog-days; and didn't thaw it one degree at Christmas.

External heat and cold had little influence on Scrooge. No warmth could warm, nor wintry weather chill him. No wind that blew was bitterer than he, no falling snow was more intent upon its purpose, no pelting rain less open to entreaty. Foul weather didn't know where to have him. The heaviest rain, and snow, and hail, and sleet, could boast of the advantage over him in only one respect. They often 'came down' handsomely, and Scrooge never did.

Nobody ever stopped him in the street to say, with gladsome looks, 'My dear Scrooge, how are you? when will you come to see me?' No beggars implored him to bestow a trifle, no children asked him what it was o'clock, no man or woman ever once in all his life inquired the way to such and such a place, of Scrooge. Even the blindmen's dogs appeared to know him; and when they saw him coming on, would tug their owners into doorways and up courts; and then would wag their tails as though they said, 'no eye at all is better than an evil eye, dark master!'

But what did Scrooge care! It was the very thing he liked. To edge his way along the crowded paths of life, warning all human sympathy to keep its distance, was what the knowing ones call 'nuts' to Scrooge.

Once upon a time – of all the good days in the year, on Christmas Eve – old Scrooge sat busy in his counting house. It was cold, bleak, biting weather: foggy withal: and he could hear the people in the court outside go wheezing up and down, beating their hands upon their breasts, and stamping their feet upon the pavement-stones to warm them. The city clocks had only just gone three, but it was quite dark already: it had not been light all day: and candles were flaring in the windows of the neighbouring offices, like ruddy smears upon the palpable brown air. The fog came pouring in at every chink and keyhole, and was so dense without, that although the court was of the narrowest, the houses opposite were mere phantoms. To see the dingy cloud come drooping down, obscuring everything, one might have thought that Nature lived hard by, and was brewing on a large scale.

The door of Scrooge's counting-house was open that he might keep his eye upon his clerk, who in a dismal little cell beyond, a sort of tank, was copying letters. Scrooge had a very small fire, but the clerk's fire was so very much smaller that it looked like one coal. But he couldn't replenish it, for

Scrooge kept the coal-box in his own room; and so surely as the clerk came in with the shovel, the master predicted that it would be necessary for them to part. Wherefore the clerk put on his white comforter, and tried to warm himself at the candle; in which effort, not being a man of a strong imagination, he failed.

'A merry Christmas, uncle! God save you!' cried a cheerful voice. It was the voice of Scrooge's nephew, who came upon him so quickly that this was the first intimation he had of his approach.

'Bah!' said Scrooge, 'Humbug!'

He had so heated himself with rapid walking in the fog and frost, this nephew of Scrooge's, that he was all in a glow; his face was ruddy and handsome; his eyes sparkled, and his breath smoked again.

'Christmas a humbug, uncle!' said Scrooge's nephew. 'You don't mean that, I am sure.'

'I do,' said Scrooge. 'Merry Christmas! what right have you to be merry? what reason have you to be merry? You're poor enough.'

'Come, then,' returned the nephew gaily. 'What right have you to be dismal? what reason have you to be morose? You're rich enough.'

Scrooge having no better answer ready on the spur of the moment, said, 'Bah!' again; and followed it up with 'Humbug.'

'Don't be cross, uncle,' said the nephew.

'What else can I be,' returned the uncle, 'when I live in such a world of fools as this Merry Christmas! Out upon merry Christmas. What's Christmas time to you but a time for paying bills without money; a time for finding yourself a year older, and not an hour richer; a time for balancing your books and having every item in 'em through a round dozen of months presented dead against you? If I could work my will,' said Scrooge, indignantly, 'every idiot who goes about with "Merry Christmas," on his lips, should be boiled with his own pudding, and buried with a stake of holly through his heart. He should!'

'Uncle!' pleaded the nephew.

'Nephew!' returned the uncle, sternly, 'keep Christmas in your own way, and let me keep it in mine.'

'Keep it!' repeated Scrooge's nephew. 'But you don't keep it.'

'Let me leave it alone, then,' said Scrooge. 'Much good may it do you! Much good it has ever done you!'

'There are many things from which I might have derived good, by which I have not profited, I dare say,' returned the nephew: 'Christmas among the rest. But I am sure I have always thought of Christmas time, when it has come round – apart from the veneration due to its sacred name and origin, if anything belonging to it can be apart from that – as a good time: a kind, forgiving, charitable, pleasant time: the only time I know of, in the long calendar of the year, when men and women seem by one consent to open their shut-up hearts freely, and to think of people below them as if they really were fellow-passengers to the grave, and not another race of creatures bound on other journeys. And therefore, uncle, though it has never put a scrap of gold or silver in my pocket, I believe that it *has* done me good, and *will* do me good: and I say, God bless it!'

The clerk in the tank involuntarily applauded: becoming immediately sensible of the impropriety, he poked the fire, and extinguished the last frail spark for ever.

'Let me hear another sound from *you*,' said Scrooge, 'and you'll keep your Christmas by losing your situation. You're quite a powerful speaker, sir,' he added, turning to his nephew. 'I wonder you don't go into Parliament.'

'Don't be angry, uncle. Come! Dine with us tomorrow.'

Scrooge said that he would see him – yes, indeed he did. He went the whole length of the expression, and said that he would see him in that extremity first.

'But why?' cried Scrooge's nephew. 'Why?'

'Why did you get married?' said Scrooge.

'Because I fell in love.'

'Because you fell in love!' growled Scrooge, as if that were the only thing in the world more ridiculous than a merry Christmas. 'Good afternoon!'

'Nay, uncle, but you never came to see me before that happened. Why give it as a reason for not coming now?'

'Good afternoon,' said Scrooge.

'I want nothing from you; I ask nothing of you; why cannot we be friends?'

'Good afternoon,' said Scrooge.

'I am sorry, with all my heart, to find you so resolute. We have never had any quarrel, to which I have been a party. But I have made the trial in homage to Christmas, and I'll keep my Christmas humour to the last. So A Merry Christmas, uncle!'

'Good afternoon!' said Scrooge.

'And A Happy New Year!'

'Good afternoon!' said Scrooge. His nephew left the room without an angry word, notwithstanding. He stopped at the outer door to bestow the greetings of the season on the clerk, who, cold as he was, was warmer than Scrooge; for he returned them cordially.

'There's another fellow,' muttered Scrooge; who overheard him: 'my clerk, with fifteen shillings a-week, and a wife and family, talking about a merry Christmas. I'll retire to Bedlam.'

This lunatic, in letting Scrooge's nephew out, had let two other people in. They were portly gentlemen, pleasant to behold, and now stood, with their hats off, in Scrooge's office. They had books and papers in their hands, and bowed to him.

'Scrooge and Marley's, I believe,' said one of the gentlemen, referring to his list. 'Have I the pleasure of addressing Mr Scrooge, or Mr Marley?'

'Mr Marley has been dead these seven years,' Scrooge replied. 'He died seven years ago, this very night.'

'We have no doubt his liberality is well represented by his surviving partner,' said the gentleman, presenting his credentials.

It certainly was; for they had been two kindred spirits. At the ominous word 'liberality,' Scrooge frowned, and shook his head, and handed the credentials back.

'At this festive season of the year, Mr Scrooge,' said the gentleman, taking up a pen, 'it is more than usually desirable that we should make some slight provision for the Poor and destitute, who suffer greatly at the present time. Many thousands are in want of common necessaries; hundreds of thousands are in want of common comforts, sir.'

'Are there no prisons?' asked Scrooge.

'Plenty of prisons,' said the gentleman, laying down the pen again.

'And the Union workhouses?' demanded Scrooge. 'Are they still in operation?'

'They are. Still,' returned the gentleman, 'I wish I could say they were not.'

'The Treadmill and the Poor Law are in full vigour, then?' said Scrooge.

'Both very busy, sir.'

'Oh! I was afraid, from what you said at first, that something had occurred to stop them in their useful course,' said Scrooge. 'I'm very glad to hear it.'

'Under the impression that they scarcely furnish Christian cheer of mind or body to the multitude,' returned the gentleman, 'a few of us are endeavouring to raise a fund to buy the Poor some meat and drink, and means of warmth. We choose this time, because it is a time, of all others, when Want is keenly felt, and Abundance rejoices. What shall I put you down for?'

'Nothing!' Scrooge replied.

'You wish to be anonymous?'

'I wish to be left alone,' said Scrooge. 'Since you ask me what I wish, gentlemen, that is my answer. I don't make merry myself at Christmas and I can't afford to make idle people merry. I help to support the establishments I have mentioned: they cost enough: and those who are badly off must go there.'

'Many can't go there; and many would rather die.'

'If they would rather die,' said Scrooge, 'they had better do it, and decrease the surplus population. Besides – excuse me – I don't know that.'

'But you might know it,' observed the gentleman.

'It's not my business,' Scrooge returned. 'It's enough for a man to understand his own business, and not to interfere with other people's. Mine occupies me constantly. Good afternoon, gentlemen!'

Seeing clearly that it would be useless to pursue their point, the gentlemen withdrew. Scrooge resumed his labours with an improved opinion of himself, and in a more facetious temper than was usual with him.

Meanwhile the fog and darkness thickened so that people ran about with flaring links, proffering their services to go before horses in carriages, and conduct them on their way. The ancient tower of a church, whose gruff old bell was always peeping slily down at Scrooge out of a gothic window in the wall, became invisible, and struck the hours and quarters in the clouds, with tremulous vibrations afterwards, as if its teeth were chattering in its frozen head up there. The cold became intense. In the main street at the corner of the court, some labourers were repairing the gas-pipes, and had lighted a great fire in a brazier, round which a party of ragged men and boys were gathered: warming their hands and winking their eyes before the blaze in rapture. The water-plug being left in solitude, its overflowings sullenly congealed, and turned to misanthropic ice. The brightness of the shops where holly sprigs and berries crackled in the lamp-heat of the windows, made pale faces ruddy as they passed. Poulterers' and grocers' trades became a splendid joke: a glorious pageant, with which it was next to impossible to believe that such dull principles as bargain and sale had anything to do. The Lord Mayor, in the stronghold of the mighty Mansion House, gave orders to his fifty cooks and butlers to keep Christmas as a Lord Mayor's household should; and even the little tailor, whom he had fined five shillings on the previous Monday for being drunk and blood-thirsty in the streets, stirred up tomorrow's pudding in his garret, while his lean wife and the baby sallied out to buy the beef.

Foggier yet, and colder! Piercing, searching, biting cold. If the good Saint Dunstan had but nipped the Evil Spirit's nose with a touch of such weather as that, instead of using his familiar weapons, then indeed he would have roared to lusty purpose. The owner of one scant young nose, gnawed and mumbled by the hungry cold as bones are gnawed by dogs, stooped down at Scrooge's keyhole to regale him with a Christmas carol: but at the first sound of

'God bless you merry gentleman! May nothing you dismay!'

Scrooge seized the ruler with such energy of action that the singer fled in terror, leaving the keyhole to the fog and even more congenial frost.

At length the hour of shutting up the counting-house arrived. With an ill-will Scrooge dismounted from his stool, and tacitly admitted the fact to the expectant clerk in the Tank, who instantly snuffed his candle out, and put on his hat.

'You'll want all day tomorrow, I suppose?' said Scrooge.

'If quite convenient, Sir.'

'It's not convenient,' said Scrooge, 'and it's not fair. If I was to stop half-a-crown for it, you'd think yourself ill-used, I'll be bound?'

The clerk smiled faintly.

'And yet,' said Scrooge, 'you don't think *me* ill-used, when I pay a day's wages for no work.'

The clerk observed that it was only once a year.

'A poor excuse for picking a man's pocket every twenty-fifth of December!' said Scrooge, buttoning his great-coat to the chin. 'But I suppose you must have the whole day. Be here all the earlier next morning!'

The clerk promised that he would; and Scrooge walked out with a growl. The office was closed in a twinkling, and the clerk, with the long ends of his white comforter dangling below his waist (for he boasted no great-coat), went down a slide on Cornhill, at the end of a lane of boys, twenty times, in honour of its being Christmas-eve, and then ran home to Camden Town as hard as he could pelt, to play at blindman's-buff.

Scrooge took his melancholy dinner in his usual melancholy tavern; and having read all the newspapers, and beguiled the rest of the evening with his banker's-book, went home to bed. He lived in chambers which had once belonged to his deceased partner. They were a gloomy suite of rooms, in a lowering pile of building up a yard, where it had so little business to be, that one could scarcely help fancying it must have run there when it was a young house, playing at hide-and-seek with other houses, and have forgotten the way out again. It was old enough now, and dreary enough, for nobody lived in it but Scrooge, the other rooms being all let out as offices. The yard was so dark that even Scrooge, who knew its every stone, was fain to grope with his hands. The fog and frost so hung about the black old gateway of the house, that it seemed as if the Genius of the Weather sat in mournful meditation on the threshold.

Now, it is a fact, that there was nothing at all particular about the knocker on the door, except that it was very large. It is also a fact that Scrooge had seen it night and morning during his whole residence in that place; also that Scrooge had as little of what is called fancy about him as any man in the City of London, even including – which is a bold word – the corporation, aldermen, and livery. Let it also be borne in mind that Scrooge had not bestowed one thought on Marley, since his last mention of his seven-years' dead partner that afternoon. And then let any man explain to me, if he can, how it happened that Scrooge, having his key in the lock of the door saw in the knocker, without its undergoing any intermediate process of change: not a knocker, but Marley's face.

It was not in impenetrable shadow as the other objects in the yard were, but had a dismal light about it, like a bad lobster in a dark cellar. It was not angry or ferocious, but looked at Scrooge as Marley used to look: with ghostly spectacles turned up upon its ghostly forehead. The hair was curiously stirred, as if by breath or hot-air; and though the eyes were wide open, they were perfectly motionless. That, and its livid colour, made it horrible; but its horror seemed to be, in spite of the face and beyond its control, rather than a part of its own expression.

As Scrooge looked fixedly at this phenomenon, it was a knocker again.

To say that he was not startled, or that his blood was not conscious of a terrible sensation to which it had been a stranger from infancy, would be untrue. But he put his hand upon the key he had relinquished, turned it sturdily, walked in, and lighted his candle.

He *did* pause, with a moment's irresolution, before he shut the door; and he *did* look cautiously behind it first, as if he half-expected to be terrified with the sight of Marley's pigtail sticking out into the hall. But there was nothing on the back of the door, except the screws and nuts that held the knocker on, so he said 'Pooh, pooh!' and closed it with a bang.

The sound resounded through the house like thunder. Every room above, and every cask in the wine-merchant's cellars below, appeared to have a separate peal of echoes of its own. Scrooge was not a man to be frightened by echoes. He fastened the door, and walked across the hall, and up the stairs, slowly too: trimming his candle as he went.

You may talk vaguely about driving a coach-and-six up a good old flight of stairs, or through a bad young Act of Parliament; but I mean to say you might have got a hearse up that staircase, and taken it broadwise, with the splinter-bar towards the wall and the door towards the balustrades: and done it easy. There was plenty of width for that, and room to spare; which is perhaps the reason why Scrooge thought he saw a locomotive hearse going on before him in the gloom. Half a dozen gas-lamps out of the street wouldn't have lighted the entry too well, so you may suppose that it was pretty dark with Scrooge's dip.

Up Scrooge went, not caring a button for that: darkness is cheap, and Scrooge liked it. But before he shut his heavy door, he walked through his rooms to see that all was right. He had just enough recollection of the face to desire to do that.

Sitting-room, bed-room, lumber-room. All as they should be. Nobody under the table, nobody under the sofa; a small fire in the grate; spoon and basin ready; and the little saucepan of gruel (Scrooge had a cold in his head) upon the hob. Nobody under the bed; nobody in the closet; nobody in his dressing-gown, which was hanging up in a suspicious attitude against the wall. Lumber-room as usual. Old fire-guard, old shoes, two fish-baskets, washing-stand on three legs, and a poker.

Quite satisfied, he closed his door, and locked himself in; double-locked himself in, which was not his custom. Thus secured against surprise, he took off his cravat; put on his dressing-gown and slippers, and his night-cap; and sat down before the fire to take his gruel.

It was a very low fire indeed; nothing on such a bitter night. He was obliged to sit close to it, and brood over it, before he could extract the least sensation of warmth from such a handful of fuel. The fire-place was an old one, built by some Dutch merchant long ago, and paved all round with quaint Dutch tiles, designed to illustrate the Scriptures. There were Cains and Abels; Pharaoh's daughters, Queens of Sheba, Angelic messengers descending through the air on clouds like feather-beds, Abrahams, Belshazzars, Apostles putting off to sea in butter-boats, hundreds of figures, to attract his thoughts; and yet that face of Marley, seven years dead, came like the ancient Prophet's rod, and swallowed up the whole. If each smooth tile had been a blank at first, with power to shape some picture on its surface from the disjointed fragments of his thoughts, there would have been a copy of old Marley's head on every one.

'Humbug!' said Scrooge; and walked across the room.

After several turns, he sat down again. As he threw his head back in the chair, his glance happened to rest upon a bell, a disused bell, that hung in the room, and communicated for some purpose now forgotten with a chamber in the highest story of the building. It was with great astonishment, and with a strange, inexplicable dread, that as he looked, he saw this bell begin to swing. It swung so softly in the outset that it scarcely made a sound; but soon it rang out loudly, and so did every bell in the house.

This might have lasted half a minute, or a minute, but it seemed an hour. The bells ceased as they had begun, together. They were succeeded by a clanking noise, deep down below; as if some person were dragging a heavy chain over the casks in the wine-merchant's cellar. Scrooge then remembered to have heard that ghosts in haunted houses were described as dragging chains.

The cellar-door flew open with a booming sound, and then he heard the noise much louder, on the floors below; then coming up the stairs; then coming straight towards his door.

'It's humbug still!' said Scrooge. 'I won't believe it.'

His colour changed though, when, without a pause, it came on through the heavy door, and passed into the room before his eyes. Upon its coming in, the dying flame leaped up, as though it cried 'I know him! Marley's Ghost!' and fell again.

The same face: the very same. Marley in his pig-tail, usual waistcoat, tights, and boots; the tassels on the latter bristling, like his pig-tail, and his coat-skirts, and the hair upon his head. The chain he drew was clasped about his middle. It was long, and wound about him like a tail; and it was made (for Scrooge observed it closely) of cash-boxes, keys, padlocks, legers, deeds, and heavy purses wrought in steel. His body was transparent: so that Scrooge, observing him, and looking through his waistcoat, could see the two buttons on his coat behind.

Scrooge had often heard it said that Marley had no bowels, but he had never believed it until now.

No, nor did he believe it even now. Though he looked the phantom through and through, and saw it standing before him; though he felt the chilling influence of its death-cold eyes; and marked the very texture of the folded kerchief bound about its head and chin, which wrapper he had not observed before; he was still incredulous, and fought against his senses.

'How now!' said Scrooge, caustic and cold as ever. 'What do you want with me?'

'Much!' – Marley's voice, no doubt about it.

'Who are you?'

'Ask me who I *was*.'

'Who *were* you then?' said Scrooge, raising his voice. 'You're particular – for a shade.' He was going to say 'to a shade,' but substituted this, as more appropriate.

'In life I was your partner, Jacob Marley.'

'Can you – can you sit down?' asked Scrooge, looking doubtfully at him.

'I can.'

'Do it then.'

Scrooge asked the question, because he didn't know whether a ghost so transparent might find himself in a condition to take a chair; and felt that in the event of its being impossible, it might involve the necessity of an embarrassing explanation. But the ghost sat down on the opposite side of the fire-place, as if he were quite used to it.

'You don't believe in me,' observed the Ghost.

'I don't,' said Scrooge.

'What evidence would you have of my reality beyond that of your senses?'

'I don't know,' said Scrooge.

'Why do you doubt your senses?'

'Because,' said Scrooge, 'a little thing affects them. A slight disorder of the stomach makes them cheats. You may be an undigested bit of beef, a blot of mustard, a crumb of cheese, a fragment of an underdone potato. There's more of gravy than of grave about you, whatever you are!'

Scrooge was not much in the habit of cracking jokes, nor did he feel, in his heart, by any means waggish then. The truth is, that he tried to be smart, as a means of distracting his own attention, and keeping down his terror; for the spectre's voice disturbed the very marrow in his bones.

To sit, staring at those fixed, glazed eyes, in silence for a moment, would play, Scrooge felt, the very deuce with him. There was something very awful, too, in the spectre's being provided with an infernal atmosphere of its own. Scrooge could not feel it himself, but this was clearly the case; for though the Ghost sat perfectly motionless, its hair, and skirts, and tassels, were still agitated as by the hot vapour from an oven.

'You see this toothpick?' said Scrooge, returning quickly to the charge, for the reason just asigned; and wishing, though it were only for a second, to divert the vision's stony gaze from himself.

'I do,' replied the Ghost.

'You are not looking at it,' said Scrooge.

'But I see it,' said the Ghost, 'notwithstanding.'

'Well!' returned Scrooge. 'I have but to swallow this, and be for the rest of my days persecuted by a legion of goblins, all of my own creation. Humbug, I tell you; humbug!'

At this, the spirit raised a frightful cry, and shook its chain with such a dismal and appalling noise, that Scrooge held on tight to his chair, to save himself from falling in a swoon. But how much greater was his horror, when the phantom taking off the bandage round its head, as if it were too warm to wear in-doors, its lower jaw dropped down upon its breast!

Scrooge fell upon his knees, and clasped his hands before his face.

'Mercy!' he said. 'Dreadful apparition, why do you trouble me?'

'Man of the worldly mind!' replied the Ghost, 'do you believe in me or not?'

'I do,' said Scrooge. 'I must. But why do spirits walk the earth, and why do they come to me?'

'It is required of every man,' the Ghost returned, 'that the spirit within him should walk abroad among his fellow-men, and travel far and wide – and if that spirit goes not forth in life, it is condemned to do so after death. It is doomed to wander through the world – oh, woe is me! – and witness what it cannot share, but might have shared on earth, and turned to happiness!'

Again the spectre raised a cry, and shook its chain, and wrung its shadowy hands.

'You are fettered,' said Scrooge, trembling. 'Tell me why?'

'I wear the chain I forged in life,' replied the Ghost. 'I made it link by link, and yard by yard; I girded it on of my own free will, and of my own free will I wore it. Is its pattern strange to *you*?'

Scrooge trembled more and more.

'Or would you know,' pursued the Ghost, 'the weight and length of the strong coil you bear yourself? It was full as heavy and as long as this, seven Christmas Eves ago. You have laboured on it, since. It is a ponderous chain!'

Scrooge glanced about him on the floor, in the expectation of finding himself surrounded by some fifty or sixty fathoms of iron cable: but he could see nothing.

'Jacob,' he said, imploringly. 'Old Jacob Marley, tell me more. Speak comfort to me, Jacob.'

'I have none to give,' the Ghost replied. 'It comes from other regions, Ebenezer Scrooge, and is conveyed by other ministers, to other kinds of men. Nor can I tell you what I would. A very little more, is all permitted to me. I cannot rest, I cannot stay, I cannot linger anywhere. My spirit, never walked beyond our counting-house – mark, me! – in life my spirit never roved beyond the narrow, limits of our money-changing hole; and weary journeys lie before me!'

It was a habit with Scrooge, whenever he became thoughtful, to put his hands in his breeches pockets. Pondering on what the Ghost had said, he did so now, but without lifting up his eyes, or getting off his knees.

'You must have been very slow about it, Jacob,' Scrooge observed, in a business-like manner, though with humility and deference.

'Slow!' the Ghost repeated.

'Seven years dead,' mused Scrooge. 'And travelling all the time?'

'The whole time,' said the Ghost. 'No rest, no peace. Incessant torture of remorse.'

'You travel fast?' said Scrooge.

'On the wings of the wind,' replied the Ghost.

'You might have got over a great quantity of ground in seven years,' said Scrooge.

The Ghost, on hearing this, set up another cry, and clanked its chain so hideously in the dead silence of the night, that the Ward would have been justified in indicting it for a nuisance.

'Oh! captive, bound, and double-ironed,' cried the phantom, 'not to know, that ages of incessant labour by immortal creatures, for this earth must pass into eternity before the good of which it is susceptible is all developed. Not to know that any Christian spirit working kindly in its little sphere, whatever it may be, will find its mortal life too short for its vast means of usefulness. Not to know that no space of regret can make amends for one life's opportunities misused! Yet such was I! Oh! such was I!'

'But you were always a good man of business, Jacob,' faultered Scrooge, who now began to apply this to himself.

'Business!' cried the Ghost, wringing its hands again. 'Mankind was my business. The common welfare was my business; charity, mercy, forebearance, and benevolance, were, all, my business. The dealings of my trade were but a drop of water in the comprehensive ocean of my business!'

It held up its chain at arm's length, as if that were the cause of all its unavailing grief, and flung it heavily upon the ground again.

'At this time of the rolling year,' the spectre said, 'I suffer most. Why did I walk through crowds of fellow-beings with my eyes turned down, and never raise them to that blessed Star which led the Wise Men to a poor abode? Were there no poor homes to which its light would have conducted *me*!'

Scrooge was very much dismayed to hear the spectre going on at this rate, and began to quake exceedingly.

'Hear me!' cried the Ghost. 'My time is nearly gone.'

'I will,' said Scrooge. 'But don't be hard upon me! Don't be flowery, Jacob! Pray!'

'How is it that I appear before you in a shape that you can see, I may not tell. I have sat invisible beside you many and many a day.'

It was not an agreeable idea. Scrooge shivered, and wiped the perspiration from his brow.

'That is no light part of my penance,' pursued the Ghost. 'I am here tonight to warn you, that you have yet a chance and hope of escaping my fate. A chance and hope of my procuring, Ebenezer.'

'You were always a good friend to me,' said Scrooge. 'Thank'ee!'

'You will be haunted,' resumed the Ghost, 'by Three Spirits.'

Scrooge's countenance fell almost as low as the Ghost's had done.

'Is that the chance and hope you mentioned, Jacob?' he demanded, in a faultering voice.

'It is.'

'I – I think I'd rather not,' said Scrooge.

'Without their visits,' said the Ghost, 'you cannot hope to shun the path I tread. Expect the first tomorrow, when the bell tolls One.'

'Couldn't I take 'em all at once, and have it over, Jacob?' hinted Scrooge.

'Expect the second on the next night at the same hour. The third upon the next night when the last

stroke of Twelve has ceased to vibrate. Look to see me no more; and look that, for your own sake, you remember what has passed between us!'

When it had said these words, the spectre took its wrapper from the table, and bound it round its head, as before. Scrooge knew this, by the smart sound its teeth made, when the jaws were brought together by the bandage. He ventured to raise his eyes again, and found his supernatural visitor confronting him in an erect attitude, with its chain wound over and about its arm.

The apparition walked backwards from him; and at every step it took, the window raised itself a little, so that when the spectre reached it, it was wide open. It beckoned Scrooge to approach, which he did. When they were within two paces of each other, Marley's Ghost held up its hand, warning him to come no nearer. Scrooge stopped.

Not so much in obedience, as in surprise and fear: for on the raising of the hand, he became sensible of confused noises in the air; incoherent sounds of lamentation and regret; wailings inexpressibly sorrowful and self-accusatory. The spectre, after listening for a moment, joined in the mournful dirge; and floated out upon the bleak, dark night.

Scrooge followed to the window: desperate in his curiosity. He looked out.

The air was filled with phantoms, wandering hither and thither in restless haste, and moaning as they went. Every one of them wore chains like Marley's Ghost; some few (they might be guilty governments) were linked together; none were free. Many had been personally known to Scrooge in their lives. He had been quite familiar with one old ghost in a white waistcoat, with a monstrous iron safe attached to its ankle, who cried piteously at being unable to assist a wretched woman with an infant, whom it saw below, upon a door-step. The misery with them all was, clearly, that they sought to interfere, for good, in human matters, and had lost the power for ever.

Whether these creatures faded into mist, or mist enshrouded them, he could not tell. But they and their spirit voices faded together; and the night became as it had been when he walked home. Scrooge closed the window, and examined the door by which the Ghost had entered. It was double-locked, as he had locked it with his own hands, and the bolts were undisturbed. He tried to say 'Humbug!' but stopped at the first syllable. And being, from the emotion he had undergone, or the fatigues of the day, or his glimpse of the Invisible World, or the dull conversation of the Ghost, or the lateness of the hour, much in need of repose; went straight to bed, without undressing, and fell asleep upon the instant.

THE FIRST OF THE THREE SPIRITS

When Scrooge awoke, it was so dark, that looking out of bed, he could scarcely distinguish the transparent window from the opaque walls of his chamber. He was endeavouring to pierce the darkness with his ferret eyes, when the chimes of a neighbouring church struck the four quarters. So he listened for the hour.

To his great astonishment the heavy bell went on from six to seven, and from seven to eight, and regularly up to twelve; then stopped. Twelve! It was past two when he went to bed. The clock was wrong. An icicle must have got into the works. Twelve!

He touched the spring of his repeater, to correct this most preposterous clock. Its rapid little pulse beat twelve; and stopped.

'Why, it isn't possible,' said Scrooge, 'that I can have slept through a whole day and far into another night. It isn't possible that anything has happened to the sun, and this is twelve at noon!'

The idea being an alarming one, he scrambled out of bed, and groped his way to the window. He was obliged to rub the frost off with the sleeve of his dressing-gown before he could see anything; and could see very little then. All he could make out was, that it was still very foggy and extremely cold, and that there was no noise of people running to and fro, and making a great stir, as there unquestionably would have been if night had beaten off bright day, and taken possession of the world. This was a great relief, because 'three days after sight of this First of Exchange pay to Mr Ebenezer Scrooge or his order,' and so forth, would have become a mere United States' security if there were no days to count by.

Scrooge went to bed again, and thought, and thought, and thought it over and over and over, and could make nothing of it. The more he thought, the more perplexed he was; and the more he endeavoured not to think, the more he thought Marley's Ghost bothered him exceedingly. Every time he resolved within himself, after mature inquiry, that it was all a dream, his mind flew back again, like a strong spring released, to its first position, and presented the same problem to be worked all through, 'Was it a dream or not?'

Scrooge lay in this state until the chime had gone three quarters more, when he remembered, on a sudden, that the Ghost had warned him of a visitation when the bell tolled one. He resolved to lie awake until the hour was past; and, considering that he could no more go to sleep than go to Heaven, this was perhaps the wisest resolution in his power. The quarter was so long, that he was more than once convinced he must have sunk into a doze unconsciously, and missed the clock. At length it broke upon his listening ear.

'Ding, dong!'

'A quarter past,' said Scrooge, counting.

'Ding, dong!'

'Half past!' said Scrooge.

'Ding, dong!'

'A quarter to it,' said Scrooge.

'Ding, dong!'

'The hour itself,' said Scrooge, triumphantly, 'and nothing else!'

He spoke before the hour bell sounded, which it now did with a deep, dull, hollow, melancholy ONE. Lights flashed up in the room upon the instant, and the curtains of his bed were drawn.

The curtains of his bed were drawn aside, I tell you, by a hand. Not the curtains at his feet nor the curtains at his back, but those to which his face was addressed. The curtains of his bed were drawn aside; and Scrooge, starting up into a half-recumbent attitude, found himself face to face with the unearthly visitor who drew them: as close to it as I am now to you, and I am standing in the spirit at your elbow.

It was a strange figure – like a child: yet not so like a child as like an old man, viewed through some supernatural medium, which gave him the appearance of having receded from the view, and being diminished to a child's proportions. Its hair, which hung about its neck and down its back, was white as if with age; and yet the face had not a wrinkle in it, and the tenderest bloom was on the skin. The arms were very long and muscular; the hands the same, as if its hold were of uncommon strength. Its legs and feet, most delicately formed, were, like those upper members, bare. It wore a tunic of the purest white; and round its waist was bound a lustrous belt, the sheen of which was beautiful. It held a branch of fresh green holly in its hand; and, in singular contradiction of that wintry emblem, had its dress trimmed with summer flowers. But the strangest thing about it was, that from the crown of its head there sprung a bright clear jet of light, by which all this was visible; and which was doubtless the occasion of its using, in its duller moments, a great extinguisher for a cap, which it now held under its arm.

Even this, though, when Scrooge looked at it with increasing steadiness, was *not* its strangest quality. For at its belt sparkled and glittered now in one part and now in another, and what was light one instant, at another time was dark, so the figure itself fluctuated in its distinctness: being now a thing with one arm, now with one leg, now with twenty legs, now a pair of legs without a head, now a head without a body: of which dissolving parts, no outline would be visible in the dense gloom wherein they melted away. And in the very wonder of this, it would be itself again; distinct and clear as ever.

'Are you the Spirit, sir, whose coming was foretold to me?' asked Scrooge.

'I am!'

The voice was soft and gentle. Singularly low, as if instead of being so close beside him, it were at a distance.

'Who, and what are you?' Scrooge demanded.

'I am the Ghost of Christmas Past.'

'Long past?' inquired Scrooge: observant of its dwarfish stature.

'No. Your past.'

Perhaps, Scrooge could not have told anybody why, if anybody could have asked him; but he had a special desire to see the Spirit in his cap; and begged him to be covered.

'What!' exclaimed the Ghost, 'would you so soon put out, with worldly hands, the light I give? Is it not enough that you are one of those whose passions made this cap, and force me through whole trains of years to wear it low upon my brow!'

Scrooge reverently disclaimed all intention to offend, or any knowledge of having wilfully 'bonneted' the Spirit at any period of his life. He then made bold to inquire what business brought him there.

'Your welfare!' said the Ghost.

Scrooge expressed himself much obliged but could not help thinking that a night of unbroken rest would have been more conducive to that end. The Spirit must have heard him thinking, for it said immediately:

'Your reclamation, then. Take heed!'

It put out its strong hand as it spoke, and clasped him gently by the arm.

'Rise! and walk with me!'

It would have been in vain for Scrooge to plead that the weather and the hour were not adapted to pedestrian purposes; that bed was warm, and the thermometer a long way below freezing; that he was clad but lightly in his slippers, dressing-gown, and night-cap; and that he had a cold upon him at that time. The grasp, though gentle as a woman's hand, was not to be resisted. He rose: but finding that the Spirit made towards the window, clasped its robe in supplication.

'I am a mortal,' Scrooge remonstrated, 'and liable to fall.'

'Bear but a touch of my hand *there*,' said the Spirit, laying it upon his heart, 'and you shall be upheld in more than this!'

As the words were spoken, they passed through the wall, and stood upon an open country road, with fields on either hand. The city had entirely vanished. Not a vestige of it was to be seen. The darkness and the mist had vanished with it, for it was a clear, cold, winter day, with snow upon the ground.

'Good Heaven!' said Scrooge, clasping his hands together, as he looked about him. 'I was bred in this place, I was a boy here!'

The Spirit gazed upon him mildly. Its gentle touch, though it had been light and instantaneous, appeared still present to the old man's sense of feeling. He was conscious of a thousand odours floating in the air, each one connected with a thousand thoughts, and hopes, and joys, and cares long, long, forgotten.

'Your lip is trembling,' said the Ghost. 'And what is that upon your cheek?'

Scrooge muttered, with an unusual catching in his voice, that it was a pimple, and begged the Ghost to lead him where he would.

'You recollect the way?' inquired the Spirit.

'Remember it!' cried Scrooge with fervour; 'I could walk it blindfold.'

'Strange to have forgotten it for so many years!' observed the Ghost. 'Let us go on.'

They walked along the road; Scrooge recognising every gate, and post, and tree; until a little market-town appeared in the distance, with its bridge, its church, and winding river. Some shaggy ponies now were seen trotting towards them with boys upon their backs, who called to other boys in country gigs and carts, driven by farmers. All these boys were in great spirits, and shouted to each other, until the broad fields were so full of merry music, that the crisp air laughed to hear it.

'These are but shadows of the things that have been,' said the Ghost. 'They have no consciousness of us.'

The jocund travellers came on; and as they came, Scrooge knew and named every one. Why was he rejoiced beyond all bounds to see them! Why did his cold eye glisten, and his heart leap up as they went past? Why was he filled with gladness when he heard them give each other Merry Christmas, as they parted at cross-roads and bye-ways, for their several homes! What was merry Christmas to Scrooge? Out upon merry Christmas! What good had it ever done to him?

'The school is not quite deserted,' said the Ghost. 'A solitary child, neglected by his friends, is left there still.'

Scrooge said he knew it. And he sobbed.

They left the high-road, by a well remembered lane, and soon approached a mansion of dull red brick, with a little weathercock-surmounted cupola, on the roof, and bell hanging in it. It was a large house, but one of broken fortunes; for the spacious offices were little used, their walls were damp and mossy, their windows broken, and their gates decayed. Fowls clucked and strutted in the stables; and the coach-houses and sheds were overrun with grass. Nor was it more retentive of its ancient state, within; for entering the dreary hall, and glancing through the open doors of many rooms, they found them poorly furnished, cold, and vast. There was an earthly savour in the air, a chilly bareness in the place, which associated itself somehow with too much getting up by candle-light, and not too much to eat.

They went, the Ghost and Scrooge, across the hall, to a door at the back of the house. It opened before them, and disclosed a long, bare, melancholy room, made barer still by lines of plain deal forms and desks. At one of these a lonely boy was reading near a feeble fire; and Scrooge sat down upon a form, and wept to see his poor forgotten self as he had used to be.

Not a latent echo in the house, not a squeak and scuffle from the mice behind the panneling, not a drip from the half-thawed water-spout in the dull yard behind, not a sigh among the leafless boughs of one despondent poplar, not the idle swinging of an empty store-house door, no, not a clicking in the fire, but fell upon the heart of Scrooge with softening influence, and gave a freer passage to his tears.

The Spirit touched him on the arm, and pointed to his younger self, intent upon his reading. Suddenly a man, in foreign garments: wonderfully real and distinct to look at; stood outside the window, with an axe stuck in his belt, and leading an ass laden with wood by the bridle.

'Why, it's Ali Baba!' Scrooge exclaimed in ecstacy. 'It's dear old honest Ali Baba! Yes, yes, I know! One Christmas time, when yonder solitary child was left here all alone, he *did* come, for the first time, just like that. Poor boy! And Valentine,' said Scrooge, 'and his wild brother, Orson; there they go! And what's his name, who was put down in his drawers, asleep, at the Gate of Damascus; don't you see him! And the Sultan's Groom turned upside-down by the Genii; there he is upon his head! Serve him right. I'm glad of it. What business had *he* to be married to the Princess!'

To hear Scrooge expending all the earnestness of his nature on such subjects, in a most extraordinary voice between laughing and crying; and to see his heightened and excited face; would have been a surprise to his business friends in the city, indeed.

'There's the Parrot!' cried Scrooge. 'Green body and yellow tail, with a thing like a lettuce growing out of the top of his head; there he is! Poor Robin Crusoe, he called him, when he came home again after sailing round the island. "Poor Robin Crusoe, where have you been, Robin Crusoe?" The man thought he was dreaming, but he wasn't. It was the Parrot, you know. There goes Friday, running for his life to the little creek! Halloa! Hoop! Halloo!'

Then, with a rapidity of transition very foreign to his usual character, he said, in pity for his former self, 'Poor boy!' and cried again.

'I wish,' Scrooge muttered, putting his hand in his pocket, and looking about him, after drying his eyes with his cuff: 'but it's too late now.'

'What is the matter?' asked the Spirit.

'Nothing,' said Scrooge. 'Nothing. There was a boy singing a Christmas Carol at my door last night. I should like to have given him something: that's all.'

The Ghost smiled thoughtfully, and waved its hand: saying as it did so, 'Let us see another Christmas!'

Scrooge's former self grew larger at the words, and the room became a little darker and more dirty. The pannels shrunk, the windows cracked; fragments of plaster fell out of the ceiling, and the naked laths were shown instead; but how all this was brought about, Scrooge knew no more than you do. He only knew that it was quite correct; that everything had happened so; that there he was, alone again, when all the other boys had gone home from the jolly holidays.

He was not reading now, but walking up and down despairingly. Scrooge looked at the Ghost, and with a mournful shaking of his head, glanced anxiously towards the door.

It opened; and a little girl, much younger than the boy, came darting in, and putting her arms about his neck, and often kissing him, addressed him as her 'Dear, dear brother.'

'I have come to bring you home, dear brother!' said the child, clapping her tiny hands, and bending down to laugh. 'To bring you home, home, home!'

'Home, little Fan?' returned the boy.

'Yes!' said the child, brimful of glee. 'Home, for good and all. Home, for ever and ever. Father is so much kinder than he used to be, that home's like Heaven! He spoke so gently to me one dear night when I was going to bed, that I was not afraid to ask him once more if you might come home; and he said Yes, you should; and sent me in a coach to bring you. And you're to be a man!' said the child, opening her eyes, 'and are never to come back here; but first, we're to be together all the Christmas long, and have the merriest times in the world.'

'You are quite a woman, little Fan!' exclaimed the boy.

She clapped her hands and laughed, and tried to touch his head; but being too little, laughed again, and stood on tiptoe to embrace him. Then she began to drag him, in her childish eagerness, towards the door, and he, nothing loth to go, accompanied her.

A terrible voice in the hall cried, 'Bring down Master Scrooge's box, there!' and in the hall appeared the schoolmaster himself, who glared on Master Scrooge with a ferocious condescension, and threw him into a dreadful state of mind by shaking hands with him. He then conveyed him and his sister into the veriest old well of a shivering best-parlour than ever was seen, where the maps upon the wall, and the celestial and terrestrial globes in the windows, were waxy with cold. Here he produced a decanter of curiously light wine, and a block of curiously heavy cake, and administered instalments of those dainties to the young people: at the same time, sending out a meagre servant to offer a glass of 'something' to the postboy, who answered that he thanked the gentleman, but if it was the same tap as he had tasted before, he had rather not. Master Scrooge's trunk being by this time tied on to the top of the chaise, the children bade the schoolmaster goodbye right willingly, and getting into it, drove gaily down the garden-sweep: the quick wheels dashing the hoar-frost and snow from off the dark leaves of the evergreens like spray.

'Always a delicate creature, when a breath might have withered,' said the Ghost. 'But she had a large heart!'

'So she had,' cried Scrooge. 'You're right. I will not gainsay it, Spirit. God forbid!'

'She died a woman,' said the Ghost, 'and had, as I think, children.'

'One child,' Scrooge returned.

'True,' said the Ghost. 'Your nephew!'

Scrooge seemed uneasy in his mind, and answered briefly, 'Yes.'

Although they had but that moment left the school behind them, they were now in the busy thoroughfares of a city, where shadowy passengers passed and repassed; where shadowy carts and coaches battled for the way, and all the strife and tumult of a real city were. It was made plain enough, by the dressing of the shops, that here too it was Christmas time again; but it was evening, and the streets were lighted up.

The Ghost stopped at a certain warehouse door, and asked Scrooge if he knew it.

'Know it!' said Scrooge. 'Was I apprenticed here!'

They went in. At sight of an old gentleman in a Welch wig, sitting behind such a high desk, that if he had been two inches taller he must have knocked his head against the ceiling, Scrooge cried in great excitement:

'Why, it's old Fezziwig! Bless his heart; it's Fezziwig alive again!'

Old Fezziwig laid down his pen, and looked up at the clock, which pointed to the hour of seven. He rubbed his hands; adjusted his capacious waist-coat; laughed all over himself, from his shoes to his organ of benevolence; and called out in a comfortable, oily, rich, fat, jovial voice:

'Yo ho, there! Ebenezer! Dick!'

Scrooge's former self, now grown a young man, came briskly in, accompanied by his fellow-'prentice.

'Dick Wilkins, to be sure!' said Scrooge to the Ghost. 'Bless me, yes. There he is. He was very much attached to me, was Dick. Poor Dick! Dear, dear!'

'Yo ho, my boys!' said Fezziwig. 'No more work tonight. Christmas Eve, Dick. Christmas, Ebenezer! Let's have the shutters up,' cried old Fezziwig, with a sharp clap of his hands, 'before a man can say, Jack Robinson!'

You wouldn't believe how those two fellows went at it! They charged into the street with the shutters – one, two, three – had 'em up in their places – four, five, six – barred 'em and pinned'em – seven, eight, nine – and came back before you could have got to twelve, panting like race-horses.

'Hilli-ho!' cried old Fezziwig, skipping down from the high desk, with wonderful agility. 'Clear away, my lads, and let's have lots of room here! Hilli-ho, Dick: Chirrup, Ebenezer!'

Clear away! There was nothing they wouldn't have cleared away, or couldn't have cleared away with old Fezziwig looking on. It was done in a minute. Every movable was packed off, as if it were dismissed from public life for evermore; the floor was swept and watered, the lamps were trimmed, fuel was heaped upon the fire; and the warehouse was as snug, and warm, and dry, and bright a ball-room, as you would desire to see upon a winter's night.

In came a fiddler with a music-book, and went up to the lofty desk, and made an orchestra of it, and tuned like fifty stomach-aches. In came Mrs Fezziwig, one vast substantial smile. In came the three Miss Fezziwigs, beaming and loveable. In came the six young followers whose hearts they broke. In came all the young men and women employed in the business. In came the housemaid, with her cousin, the baker. In came the cook, with her brother's particular friend, the milkman. In came the boy from over the way, who was suspected of not having board enough from his master; trying to hide himself behind the girl from next door but one, who was proved to have had her ears pulled by her Mistress. In they all came, one after another; some shyly, some boldly, some gracefully, some awkwardly, some pushing, some pulling; in they all came, anyhow and everyhow. Away they all went, twenty couples at once, hands half round and back again the other way; down the middle and up again;

round and round in various stages of affectionate grouping; old top couple always turning up in the wrong place; new top couple starting off again, as soon as they got there; all top couples at last, and not a bottom one to help them. When this result was brought about, old Fezziwig, clapping his hands to stop the dance, cried out, 'Well done!' and the fiddler plunged his hot face into a pot of porter, especially provided for that purpose. But scorning rest upon his reappearance, he instantly began again, though there were no dancers yet, as if the other fiddler had been carried home, exhausted, on a shutter; and he were a bran-new man resolved to beat him out of sight, or perish.

There were more dances, and there were forfeits, and more dances, and there was cake, and there was negus, and there was a great piece of Cold Roast, and there was a great piece of Cold Boiled, and there were mince-pies, and plenty of beer. But the great effect of the evening came after the Roast and Boiled, when the fiddler (an artful dog, mind! The sort of man who knew his business better than you or I could have told it him!) struck up 'Sir Roger de Coverley.' Then old Fezziwig stood out to dance with Mrs Fezziwig. Top couple too; with a good stiff piece of work cut out for them; three or four and twenty pair of partners; people who were not to be trifled with; people who *would* dance, and had no notion of walking.

But if they had been twice as many: ah, four times: old Fezziwig would have been a match for them, and so would Mrs Fezziwig. As to *her*, she was worthy to be his partner in every sense of the term. If that's not high praise, tell me higher, and I'll use it. A positive light appeared to issue from Fezziwig's calves. They shone in every part of the dance like moons. You couldn't have predicted, at any given time, what would become of 'em next. And when old Fezziwig and Mrs Fezziwig had gone all through the dance; advance and retire, hold hands with your partner; bow and curtsey; corkscrew; thread-the-needle, and back again to your place; Fezziwig 'cut' – cut so deftly, that he appeared to wink with his legs, and came upon his feet again without a stagger.

When the clock struck eleven, this domestic ball broke up. Mr and Mrs Fezziwig took their stations, one on either side the door, and shaking hands with every person individually as he or she went out, wished him or her a Merry Christmas. When everybody had retired but the two 'prentices, they did the same to them; and thus the cheerful voices died away, and the lads were left to their beds; which were under a counter in the back-shop.

During the whole of this time, Scrooge had acted like a man out of his wits. His heart and soul were in the scene, and with his former self. He corroborated everything, remembered everything, enjoyed everything, and underwent the strangest agitation. It was not until now, when the bright faces of his former self and Dick were turned from them, that he remembered the Ghost, and became conscious that it was looking full upon him, while the light upon its head burnt very clear.

'A small matter,' said the Ghost, 'to make these silly folks so full of gratitude.'

'Small!' echoed Scrooge.

The Spirit signed to him to listen to the two apprentices, who were pouring out their hearts in praise of Fezziwig; and when he had done so, said,

'Why! Is it not? He has spent but a few pounds of your mortal money: three or four, perhaps. Is that so much that he deserves this praise?'

'It isn't that,' said Scrooge, heated by the remark, and speaking unconsciously like his former, not his latter self. 'It isn't that, Spirit. He has the power to render us happy or unhappy; to make our service light or burdensome; a pleasure or a toil. Say that his power lies in words and looks; in things so slight and insignificant that it is impossible to add and count 'em up: what then? The happiness he gives, is quite as great as if it cost a fortune.'

He felt the Spirit's glance, and stopped.

'What is the matter?' asked the Ghost.

'Nothing particular,' said Scrooge.

'Something, I think?' the Ghost insisted.

'No,' said Scrooge, 'No. I should like to be able to say a word or two to my clerk just now! That's all.' His former self turned down the lamps as he gave utterance to the wish; and Scrooge and the Ghost again stood side by side in the open air.

'My time grows short,' observed the Spirit. 'Quick!'

This was not addressed to Scrooge, or to any one whom he could see, but it produced an immediate effect. For again Scrooge saw himself. He was older now; a man in the prime of life. His face had not the harsh and rigid lines of later years; but it had begun to wear the signs of care and avarice. There was an eager, greedy, restless motion in the eye, which showed the passion that had taken root, and where the shadow of the growing tree would fall.

He was not alone, but sat by the side of a fair young girl in a mourning-dress: in whose eyes there were tears, which sparkled in the light that shone out of the Ghost of Christmas Past.

'It matters little,' she said, softly. 'To you, very little. Another idol has displaced me; and if it can cheer and comfort you in time to come, as I would have tried to do, I have no just cause to grieve.'

'What Idol has displaced you?' he rejoined.

'A golden one.'

'This is the even-handed dealing of the world!' he said. 'There is nothing on which it is so hard as poverty; and there is nothing it professes to condemn with such severity as the pursuit of wealth!'

'You fear the world too much,' she answered, gently. 'All your other hopes have merged into the hope of being beyond the chance of its sordid reproach. I have seen your nobler aspirations fall off one by one, until the master-passion, Gain, engrosses you. Have I not?'

'What then?' he retorted. 'Even if I have grown so much wiser, what then? I am not changed towards you.'

She shook her head.

'Am I?'

'Our contract is an old one. It was made when we were both poor and content to be so, until, in good season, we could improve our worldly fortune by our patient industry. You are changed. When it was made, you were another man.'

'I was a boy,' he said impatiently.

'Your own feeling tells you that you were not what you are,' she returned. 'I am. That which promised happiness when we were one in heart, is fraught with misery now that we are two. How often and how keenly I have though of this, I will not say. It is enough that I *have* thought of it, and can release you.'

'Have I ever sought release?'

'In words. No. Never.'

'In what, then?'

'In a changed nature; in an altered spirit; in another atmosphere of life; another Hope as its great end. In everything that made my love of any worth or value in your sight. If this had never been between us,' said the girl, looking mildly, but with steadiness, upon him; 'tell me, would you seek me out and try to win me now? Ah, no!'

He seemed to yield to the justice of this supposition, in spite of himself. But he said, with a struggle, 'You think not.'

'I would gladly think otherwise if I could,' she answered, 'Heaven knows! When *I* have learned a Truth like this, I know how strong and irresistible it must be. But if you were free today, tomorrow, yesterday, can even I believe that you would choose a dowerless girl — you who, in your very confidence with her, weigh everything by Gain: or, choosing her, if for a moment you were false enough to your one guiding principle to do so, do I not know that your repentance and regret would surely follow? I do; and I release you. With a full heart, for the love of him you once were.'

He was about to speak; but with her head turned from him, she resumed.

'You may – the memory of what is past half makes me hope you will – have pain in this. A very, very brief time, and you will dismiss the recollection of it, gladly, as an unprofitable dream, from which it happened well that you awoke. May you be happy in the life you have chosen!'

She left him; and they parted.

'Spirit!' said Scrooge, 'show me no more! Conduct me home. Why do you delight to torture me?'

'One shadow more!' exclaimed the Ghost.

'No more!' cried Scrooge. 'No more. I don't wish to see it. Show me no more!'

But the relentless Ghost pinioned him in both his arms, and forced him to observe what happened next.

They were in another scene and place: a room, not very large or handsome, but full of comfort. Near to the winter fire sat a beautiful young girl, so like the last that Scrooge believed it was the same, until he saw *her*, now a comely matron, sitting opposite her daughter. The noise in this room was perfectly tumultuous, for there were more children there, than Scrooge in his agitated state of mind could count; and, unlike the celebrated herd in the poem, they were not forty children conducting themselves like one, but every child was conducting itself like forty. The consequences were uproarious beyond belief; but no one seemed to care; on the contrary, the mother and daughter laughed heartily, and enjoyed it very much; and the latter, soon beginning to mingle in the sports, got pillaged by the young brigands most ruthlessly. What would I not have given to be one of them! Though I never could have been so rude, no, no! I wouldn't for the wealth of all the world have crushed that braided hair, and torn it down; and for the precious little shoe, I wouldn't have plucked it off, God bless my soul! to save my life. As to measuring her waist in sport, as they did, bold young brood, I couldn't have done it; I should have expected my arm to have grown round it for a punishment, and never come straight again. And yet I should have dearly liked, I own, to have touched her lips; to have questioned her, that she might have opened them; to have looked upon the lashes of her downcast eyes, and never raised a blush; to have let loose waves of hair, an inch of which would be a keepsake beyond price: in short, I should have liked, I do confess, to have had the lightest licence of a child, and yet been man enough to know its value.

But now a knocking at the door was heard, and such a rush immediately ensued that she with laughing face and plundered dress was borne towards it the centre of a flushed and boisterous group, just in time to greet the father, who came home attended by a man laden with Christmas toys and presents. Then the shouting and the struggling, and the onslaught that was made on the defencelss porter! The scaling him, with chairs for ladders, to dive into his pockets, despoil him of brown-paper parcels, hold on tight by his cravat, hug him round the neck, pommel his pack, and kick his legs in irrepressible affection! The shouts of wonder and delight with which the development of every package was received! The terrible announcement that the baby had been taken in the act of putting a doll's frying-pan into his mouth, and was more than suspected of having swallowed a fictitious turkey, glued on a wooden platter! The immense relief of finding this a false alarm! The joy, and gratitude, and ecstacy! They are all indescribable alike. It is enough that by degrees the children and their emotions got out of the parlour and by one stair at a time, up to the top of the house; where they went to bed, and so subsided.

And now Scrooge looked on more attentively than ever, when the master of the house, having his daughter leaning fondly on him, sat down with her and her mother at his own fireside; and when he thought that such another creature, quite as graceful and as full of promise, might have called him father, and been a spring-time in the haggard winter of his life, his sight grew very dim indeed.

'Belle,' said the husband, turning to his wife with a smile, 'I saw an old friend of yours this afternoon.'

'Who was it?'

'Guess!'

'How can I? Tut, don't I know,' she added in the same breath, laughing as he laughed. 'Mr Scrooge.'

'Mr Scrooge it was. I passed his office window; and as it was not shut up, and he had a candle inside, I could scarcely help seeing him. His partner lies upon the point of death, I hear; and there he sat alone. Quite alone in the world, I do believe.'

'Spirit!' said Scrooge in a broken voice, 'remove me from this place.'

'I told you these were shadows of the things that have been,' said the Ghost. 'That they are what they are, do not blame me!'

'Remove me!' Scrooge exclaimed. 'I cannot bear it!'

He turned upon the Ghost, and seeing that it looked upon him with a face, in which in some strange way there were fragments of all the faces it had shown him, wrestled with it.

'Leave me! Take me back. Haunt me no longer!'

In the struggle, if that can be called a struggle in which the Ghost with no visible resistance on its own part was undisturbed by any effort of its adversary, Scrooge observed that its light was burning high and bright; and dimly connecting that with its influence over him, he seized the extinguisher-cap, and by a sudden action pressed it down upon its head.

The Spirit dropped beneath it, so that the extinguisher covered its whole form; but though Scrooge pressed it down with all his force, he could not hide the light: which streamed from under it, in an unbroken flood upon the ground.

He was conscious of being exhausted, and overcome by an irresistible drowsiness; and, further, of being in his own bedroom. He gave the cap a parting squeeze, in which his hand relaxed; and had barely time to reel to bed, before he sank into a heavy sleep.

THE SECOND OF THE THREE SPIRITS

Awaking in the middle of a prodigiously tough snore, and sitting up in bed to get his thoughts together, Scrooge had no occasion to be told that the bell was again upon the stroke of One. He felt that he was restored to consciousness in the right nick of time, for the especial purpose of holding a conference with the second messenger despatched to him through Jacob Marley's intervention. But finding that he turned uncomfortably cold when he began to wonder which of his curtains this new spectre would draw back, he put them every one aside with his own hands; and lying down again, established a sharp look-out all round the bed. For he wished to challenge the Spirit on the moment of its appearance, and did not wish to be taken by surprise and made nervous.

Gentlemen of the free-and-easy sort, who plume themselves on being acquainted with a move or two, and being usually equal to the time-of-day, express the wide range of their capacity for adventure by observing that they are good for anything from pitch-and-toss to manslaughter; between which opposite extremes, no doubt, there lies a tolerably wide and comprehensive range of subjects. Without venturing for Scrooge quite as hardily as this I don't mind calling on you to believe that he was ready for a good broad field of strange appearances, and that nothing between a baby and a rhinoceros would have astonished him very much.

Now, being prepared for almost anything, he was not by any means prepared for nothing; and, consequently, when the Bell struck One, and no shape appeared, he was taken with a violent fit of trembling. Five minutes, ten minutes, a quarter of an hour went by, yet nothing came. All this time, he lay upon his bed, the very core and centre of a blaze of ruddy light, which streamed upon it when the clock proclaimed the hour; and which being only light, was more alarming than a dozen ghosts, as he was powerless to make out what it meant, or would be at; and was sometimes apprehensive that he might be at that very moment an interesting case of spontaneous combustion, without having the consolation of knowing it. At last, however, he began to think – as you or I would have thought at first; for it is always the person not in the predicament who knows what ought to have been done in it, and would unquestionably have done it too – at last, I say, he began to think that the source and secret of this ghostly light might be in the adjoining room: from whence, on further tracing it, it seemed to shine. This idea taking full possession of his mind, he got up softly and shuffled in his slippers to the door.

The moment Scrooge's hand was on the lock, a strange voice called him by his name, and bade him enter. He obeyed.

It was his own room. There was no doubt about that. But it had undergone a surprising transformation. The walls and ceiling were so hung with living green, that it looked a perfect grove, from every part of which, bright gleaming berries glistened. The crisp leaves of holly, mistletoe, and ivy reflected back the light, as if so many little mirrors had been scattered there; and such a mighty blaze went roaring up the chimney, as that dull petrifaction of a hearth had never known in Scrooge's time, or Marley's, or for many and many a winter season gone. Heaped up upon the floor, to form a kind of throne, were turkeys, geese, game, poultry, brawn, great joints of meat, sucking-pigs, long wreaths of sausages, mince-pies, plum-puddings, barrels of oysters, red-hot chestnuts, cherry-cheeked apples, juicy oranges, luscious pears, immense twelfth-cakes, and seething bowls of punch, that made the chamber dim with their delicious steam. In easy state upon this couch, there sat a jolly Giant, glorious to see; who bore a glowing torch, in shape not unlike Plenty's horn, and held it up, high up, to shed its light on Scrooge, as he came peeping round the door.

'Come in!' exclaimed the Ghost. 'Come in! and know me better, man!'

Scrooge entered timidly, and hung his head before this Spirit. He was not the dogged Scrooge he had been; and though its eyes were clear and kind, he did not like to meet them.

'I am the Ghost of Christmas Present,' said the Spirit. 'Look upon me!'

Scrooge reverently did so. It was clothed in one simple deep green robe, or mantle, bordered with white fur. This garment hung so loosely on the figure, that its capacious breast was bare, as if disdaining to be warded or concealed by any artifice. Its feet, observable beneath the ample folds of the garment, were also bare; and on its head it wore no other covering than a holly wreath set here and there with shining icicles. Its dark brown curls were long and free: free as its genial face, its sparkling eye, its open hand, its cheery voice, its unconstrained demeanour, and its joyful air. Girded round its middle was an antique scabbard; but no sword was in it, and the ancient sheath was eaten up with rust.

'You have never seen the like of me before!' exclaimed the Spirit.

'Never,' Scrooge made answer to it.

'Have never walked forth with the younger members of my family; meaning (for I am very young) my elder brothers born in these later years?' pursued the Phantom.

'I don't think I have,' said Scrooge. 'I am afraid I have not. Have you had many brothers, Spirit?'

'More than eighteen hundred,' said the Ghost. 'A tremendous family to provide for!' muttered Scrooge.

The Ghost of Christmas Present rose.

'Spirit,' said Scrooge submissively, 'conduct me where you will. I went forth last night on compulsion, and I learnt a lesson which is working now. Tonight, if you have ought to teach me, let me profit by it.'

'Touch my robe!'

Scrooge did as he was told, and held it fast.

Holly, mistletoe, red berries, ivy, turkeys, geese, game, poultry, brawn, meat, pigs, sausages, oysters, pies, puddings, fruit and punch, all vanished instantly. So did the room, the fire, the ruddy glow, the hour of night, and they stood in the city streets on Christmas morning, where (for the weather was severe) the people made a rough, but brisk and not unpleasant kind of music, in scraping the snow from the pavement in front of their dwellings, and from the tops of their houses; whence it was mad delight to the boys to see it come plumping down into the road below, and splitting into artificial little snowstorms.

The house fronts looked black enough, and the windows blacker, contrasting with the smooth white sheet of snow upon the roofs, and with the dirtier snow upon the ground; which last deposit had been ploughed up in deep furrows by the heavy wheels of carts and waggons; furrows that crossed and recrossed each other hundreds of times where the great streets branched off; and made intricate channels, hard to trace, in the thick yellow mud and icy water. The sky was gloomy, and the shortest streets were choked up with a dingy mist, half thawed half frozen, whose heavier particles descended in a shower of sooty atoms, as if all the chimneys in Great Britain had, by one consent, caught fire, and were blazing away to their dear hearts' content. There was nothing very cheerful in the climate of the town, and yet there was an air of cheerfulness abroad that the clearest summer air and brightest summer sun might have endeavoured to diffuse in vain.

For the people who were shovelling away on the house-tops were jovial and full of glee; calling out to one another from the parapets, and now and then exchanging a facetious snowball – better-natured missile far than many a wordy jest – laughing heartily if it went right, and not less heartily if it went wrong. The poulterers' shops were still half open, and the fruiterers' were radiant in their glory. There were great, round, pot-bellied baskets of chestnuts, shaped like the waistcoats of jolly old gentlemen, lolling at the doors, and tumbling out into the street in their apoplectic opulence. There were ruddy, brown-faced, broad-girthed Spanish Onions, shining in the fatness of their growth like Spanish Friars; and winking from the shelves in wanton slyness at the girls as they went by, and glanced demurely at the hung-up mistletoe. There were pears and apples, clustered high in blooming pyramids; there were bunches of grapes, made, in the shopkeepers benevolence, to dangle from conspicuous hooks, that people's mouths might water gratis as they passed; there were piles of filberts, mossy and brown, recalling, in their fragrance, ancient walks among the woods, and pleasant shufflings ankle deep through withered leaves; there were Norfolk Biffins, squab and swarthy, setting off the yellow of the oranges and lemons, and, in the great compactness of their juicy persons, urgently entreating and beseeching to be carried home in paper bags and eaten after dinner. The very gold and silver fish, set forth among these choice fruits in a bowl, though members of a dull and stagnant-blooded race, appeared to know that there was something going on; and, to a fish, went gasping round and round their little world in slow and passionless excitement.

The Grocers'! oh the Grocers'! nearly closed, with perhaps two shutters down, or one; but through those gaps such glimpses! It was not alone that the scales descending on the counter made a merry sound, or that the twine and roller parted company so briskly, or that the canisters were rattled up and down like juggling tricks, or even that the blended scents of tea and coffee were so grateful to the nose, or even that the raisins were so plentiful and rare, the almonds so extremely white, the sticks of cinnamon so long and straight, the other spices so delicious, the candied fruits so caked and spotted with molten sugar as to make the coldest lookers-on feel faint and subsequently bilious. Nor was it that the figs were moist and pulpy, or that the French plums blushed in modest tartness from their highly-decorated boxes, or that everything was good to eat and in its Christmas dress: but the customers were all so hurried and so eager in the hopeful promise of the day, that they tumbled up against each other at the door, crashing their wicker baskets wildly, and left their purchases upon the counter, and came running back to fetch them, and committed hundreds of the like mistakes, in the best humour possible; while the Grocer and his people were so frank and fresh that the polished hearts with which they fastened their aprons behind might have been their own, worn outside for general inspection, and for Christmas daws to peck at if they chose.

But soon the steeples called good people all, to church and chapel, and away they came, flocking through the streets in their best clothes, and with their gayest faces. And at the same time there emerged from scores of bye streets, lanes, and nameless turnings, innumerable people, carrying their dinners to the bakers' shops. The sight of these poor revellers appeared to interest the Spirit very much, for he stood with Scrooge beside him in a baker's doorway, and taking off the covers as their bearers passed, sprinkled incense on their dinners from his torch. And it was a very uncommon kind of torch, for once or twice when there were angry words between some dinner-carriers who had jostled with each other, he shed a few drops of water on them from it, and their good humour was restored directly. For they said, it was a shame to quarrel upon Christmas Day. And so it was! God love it, so it was!

In time the bells ceased, and the bakers' were shut up; and yet there was a genial shadowing forth of all these dinners and the progress of their cooking, in the thawed blotch of wet above each baker's oven; where the pavement smoked as if its stones were cooking too.

'Is there a peculiar flavour in what you sprinkle from your torch?' asked Scrooge.

'There is. My own.'

'Would it apply to any kind of dinner on this day?' asked Scrooge.

'To any kindly given. To a poor one most.'

'Why to a poor one most?' asked Scrooge.

'Because it needs it most.'

'Spirit,' said Scrooge, after a moment's thought, 'I wonder you, of all the beings in the many worlds about us, should desire to cramp these people's opportunities of innocent enjoyment.'

'I!' cried the Spirit.

'You would deprive them of their means of dining every seventh day, often the only day on which they can be said to dine at all,' said Scrooge. 'Wouldn't you?'

'I!' cried the Spirit.

'You seek to close these places on the Seventh Day?' said Scrooge. 'And it comes to the same thing.'

'*I* seek!' exclaimed the Spirit.

'Forgive me if I am wrong. It has been done in your name, or at least in that of your family,' said Scrooge.

'There are some upon this earth of yours,' returned the Spirit, 'who lay claim to know us, and who do their deeds of passion, pride, ill-will, hatred, envy, bigotry, and selfishness in our name; who are as strange to us and all our kith and kin, as if they had never lived. Remember that, and charge their doings on themselves, not us.'

Scrooge promised that he would; and they went on, invisible, as they had been before, into the suburbs of the town. It was a remarkable quality of the Ghost (which Scrooge had observed at the baker's) that notwithstanding his gigantic size, he could accomodate himself to any place with ease; and that he stood beneath a low roof quite as gracefully and like a supernatural creature, as it was possible he could have done in any lofty hall.

And perhaps it was the pleasure the good Spirit had in showing off this power of his, or else it was his own kind, generous, hearty nature, and his sympathy with all poor men, that led him straight to Scrooge's clerk's; for there he went, and took Scrooge with him, holding to his robe; and on the threshold of the door the Spirit smiled, and stopped to bless Bob Cratchit's dwelling with the sprinklings of his torch. Think of that! Bob had but fifteen 'Bob' a-week himself; he pocketed on Saturdays but fifteen copies of his Christian name; and yet the Ghost of Christmas Present blessed his four-roomed house!

Then up rose Mrs Cratchit, Cratchit's wife, dressed out but poorly in a twice-turned gown, but brave in ribbons, which are cheap and make a goodly show for sixpence; and she laid the cloth, assisted by Belinda Cratchit, second of her daughters, also brave in ribbons; while Master Peter Cratchit plunged a fork into the saucepan of potatoes, and getting the corners of his monstrous shirt-collar (Bob's private property, conferred upon his son and heir in honour of the day) into his mouth, rejoiced to find himself so gallantly attired, and yearned to show his linen in the fashionable Parks. And now two smaller Cratchits, boy and girl, came tearing in, screaming that outside the baker's they had smelt the goose, and known it for their own; and basking in luxurious thoughts of sage-and-onion, these young Cratchits danced about the table, and exalted Master Peter Cratchit to the skies, while he (not proud, although his collars nearly choked him) blew the fire, until the slow potatoes bubbling up, knocked loudly at the saucepan-lid to be let out and peeled.

'What has ever got your precious father then,' said Mrs Cratchit. 'And your brother, Tiny Tim! And Martha warn't as late last Christmas Day by half-an-hour!'

'Here's Martha, mother!' said a girl, appearing as she spoke.

'Here's Martha, mother!' cried the two young Cratchits. 'Hurrah! There's such a goose, Martha!'

'Why, bless your heart alive, my dear, how late you are!' said Mrs Cratchit, kissing her a dozen times, and taking off her shawl and bonnet for her with officious zeal.

'We'd a deal of work to finish up last night,' replied the girl, 'and had to clear away this morning, mother!'

'Well! Never mind so long as you are come,' said Mrs Cratchit. 'Sit ye down before the fire, my dear, and have a warm, Lord bless ye!'

'No no! There's father coming,' cried the two young Cratchits, who were everywhere at once. 'Hide Martha, hide!' So Martha hid herself, and in came little Bob, the father, with at least three feet of comforter exclusive of the fringe, hanging down before him; and his thread-bare clothes darned up and brushed, to look seasonable; and Tiny Tim upon his shoulder. Alas for Tiny Tim, he bore a little crutch, and had his limbs supported by an iron frame!

'Why, where's our Martha?' cried Bob Cratchit looking round.

'Not coming,' said Mrs Cratchit.

'Not coming!' said Bob, with a sudden declension in his high spirits; for he had been Tim's blood horse all the way from church, and had come home rampant. 'Not coming upon Christmas Day!'

Martha didn't like to see him disappointed, if it were only in joke; so she came out prematurely from behind the closet door, and ran into his arms, while the two young Cratchits hustled Tiny Tim, and bore him off into the wash-house, that he might hear the pudding singing in the copper.

'And how did little Tim behave?' asked Mrs Cratchit, when she had rallied Bob on his credulity and Bob had hugged his daughter to his heart's content.

'As good as gold,' said Bob, 'and better. Somehow he gets thoughtful, sitting by himself so much, and thinks the strangest things you ever heard. He told me, coming home, that he hoped the people saw him in the church, because he was a cripple, and it might be pleasant to them to remember upon Christmas Day, who made lame beggars walk and blind men see.'

Bob's voice was tremulous when he told them this, and trembled more when he said that Tiny Tim was growing strong and hearty.

His active little crutch was heard upon the floor, and back came Tiny Tim before another word was spoken, escorted by his brother and sister to his stool beside the fire; and while Bob, turning up his cuffs – as if, poor fellow, they were capable of being made more shabby – compounded some hot mixture in a jug with gin and lemons, and stirred it round and round and put it on the hob to simmer; Master Peter and the two ubiquitous young Cratchits went to fetch the goose, with which they soon returned in high procession.

Such a bustle ensued that you might have thought a goose the rarest of all birds; a feathered phenomenon, to which a black swan was a matter of course; and in truth it was something very like it in that house. Mrs Cratchit made the gravy (ready beforehand in a little saucepan) hissing hot; Master Peter mashed the potatoes with incredible vigour; Miss Belinda sweetened up the apple-sauce; Martha dusted the hot plates; Bob took Tiny Tim beside him in a tiny corner at the table; the two young Cratchits set chairs for everybody, not forgetting themselves, and mounting guard upon their posts, crammed spoons into their mouths, lest they should shriek for goose before their turn came to be helped. At last the dishes were set on, and grace was said. It was succeeded by a breathless pause, as Mrs Cratchit, looking slowly all along the carving-knife, prepared to plunge it in the breast; but when she did, and when the long expected gush of stuffing issued forth, one murmur of delight arose all round the board, and even Tiny Tim, excited by the two young Cratchits, beat on the table with the handle of his knife, and feebly cried Hurrah!

There never was such a goose. Bob said he didn't believe there ever was such a goose cooked. Its tenderness and flavour, size and cheapness, were the themes of universal admiration. Eked out by the apple-sauce and mashed potatoes, it was a sufficient dinner for the whole family; indeed, as Mrs Cratchit said with great delight (surveying one small atom of a bone upon the dish), they hadn't ate it all at last! Yet every one had had enough, and the youngest Cratchits in particular, were steeped in sage and onion to the eyebrows! But now, the plates being changed by Miss Belinda, Mrs Cratchit left the room alone – too nervous to bear witnesses – to take the pudding up, and bring it in.

Suppose it should not be done enough! Suppose it should break in turning out! Suppose somebody should have got over the wall of the back-yard, and stolen it, while they were merry with the goose; a supposition at which the two young Cratchits became livid! All sorts of horrors were supposed.

Hallo! A great deal of steam! The pudding was out of the copper. A smell like a washing-day! That was the cloth. A smell like an eating-house, and a pastry cook's next door to each other, with a laundress's next door to that! That was the pudding. In half a minute Mrs Cratchit entered: flushed, but smiling proudly; with the pudding, like a speckled cannon-ball, so hard and firm, blazing in half of half-a-quartern of ignited brandy, and bedight with Christmas holly stuck into the top.

Oh, a wonderful pudding! Bob Cratchit said, and calmly too, that he regarded it as the greatest success achieved by Mrs Cratchit since their marriage. Mrs Cratchit said that now the weight was off her mind, she would confess she had had her doubts about the quantity of flour. Everybody had something to say about it, but nobody said or thought it was at all a small pudding for a large family. It would have been flat heresy to do so. Any Cratchit would have blushed to hint at such a thing.

At last the dinner was all done, the cloth was cleared, the hearth swept, and the fire made up. The compound in the jug being tasted and considered perfect, apples and oranges were put upon the table, and a shovel-full of chestnuts on the fire. Then all the Cratchit family drew round the hearth, in what Bob Cratchit called a circle, meaning half a one; and at Bob Cratchit's elbow stood the family display of glass; two tumblers, and a custard-cup without a handle. These held the hot stuff from the jug, however, as well as golden goblets would have done; and Bob served it out with beaming looks, while the chestnuts on the fire sputtered and crackled noisily. Then Bob proposed:

'A Merry Christmas to us all, my dears. God bless us!'

Which all the family re-echoed.

Mr. Fezziwig's Ball.

John Leech

Marley's Ghost.

'God bless us every one!' said Tiny Tim, the last of all.

He sat very close to his father's side, upon his little stool. Bob held his withered little hand in his, as if he loved the child, and wished to keep him by his side, and dreaded that he might be taken from him.

'Spirit,' said Scrooge, with an interest he had never felt before, 'tell me if Tiny Tim will live.'

'I see a vacant seat,' replied the Ghost, 'in the poor chimney corner, and a crutch without an owner, carefully preserved. If these shadows remain unaltered by the Future, the child will die.'

'No, no,' said Scrooge. 'Oh no, kind Spirit! say he will be spared.'

'If these shadows remain unaltered by the Future, none other of my race,' returned the Ghost, 'will find him here. What then? If he be like to die, he had better do it, and decrease the surplus population.'

Scrooge hung his head to hear his own words quoted by the Spirit, and was overcome with penitence and grief.

'Man,' said the Ghost, 'if man you be in heart, not adamant, forbear that wicked cant until you have discovered What the surplus is, and Where it is. Will you decide what men shall live, what men shall die? It may be, that in the sight of Heaven, you are more worthless and less fit to live than millions like this poor man's child. Oh God! to hear the Insect on the leaf pronouncing on the too much life among his hungry brothers in the dust!'

Scrooge bent before the Ghost's rebuke, and trembling cast his eyes upon the ground. But he raised them speedily, on hearing his own name.

'Mr Scrooge!' said Bob; 'I'll give you Mr Scrooge, the Founder of the Feast!'

'The Founder of the Feast indeed!' cried Mrs Cratchit, reddening. 'I wish I had him here. I'd give him a piece of my mind to feast upon, and I hope he'd have a good appetite for it.'

'My dear,' said Bob, 'the children; Christmas Day.'

'It should be Christmas Day, I am sure,' said she, 'on which one drinks the health of such an odious, stingy, hard, unfeeling man as Mr Scrooge. You know he is, Robert! Nobody knows it better than you do, poor fellow!'

'My dear,' was Bob's mild answer, 'Christmas Day.'

'I'll drink his health for your sake and the Day's,' said Mrs Cratchit, 'not for his. Long life to him! A merry Christmas and a happy new year! He'll be very merry and very happy, I have no doubt!'

The children drank the toast after her. It was the first of their proceedings which had no heartiness in it. Tiny Tim drank it last of all, but he didn't care twopence for it. Scrooge was the Ogre of the family. The mention of his name cast a dark shadow on the party, which was not dispelled for full five minutes.

After it had passed away, they were ten times merrier than before, from the mere relief of Scrooge the Baleful being done with. Bob Cratchit told them how he had a situation in his eye for Master Peter, which would bring in, if obtained, full five-and-sixpence weekly. The two young Cratchits laughed tremendously at the idea of Peter's being a man of business; and Peter himself looked thoughtfully at the fire from between his collars, as if he were deliberating what particular investments he should favour when he came into the receipt of that bewildering income. Martha, who was a poor apprentice at a milliner's, then told them what kind of work she had to do, and how many hours she worked at a stretch, and how she meant to lie a-bed tomorrow morning for a good long rest; tomorrow being a holiday she passed at home. Also how she had seen a countess and a lord some days before, and how the lord 'was much about as tall as Peter;' at which Peter pulled up his collars so high that you couldn't have seen his head if you had been there. All this time the chesnuts and the jug went round and round; and bye and bye they had a song, about a lost child travelling in the snow, from Tiny Tim; who had a plaintive little voice, and sang it very well indeed.

There was nothing of high mark in this. They were not a handsome family; they were not well dressed; their shoes were far from being waterproof; their clothes were scanty; and Peter might have known, and very likely did, the inside of a pawnbroker's. But they were happy, grateful, pleased with one another, and contented with the time; and when they faded, and looked happier yet in the bright sprinklings of the Spirit's torch at parting, Scrooge had his eye upon them, and especially on Tiny Tim, until the last.

By this time it was getting dark, and snowing pretty heavily; and as Scrooge and the Spirit went along the streets, the brightness of the roaring fires in kitchens, parlours, and all sorts of rooms, was wonderful. Here, the flickering of the blaze showed preparations for a cosy dinner, with hot plates baking through and through before the fire, and deep red curtains, ready to be drawn, to shut out cold and darkness. There, all the children of the house were running out into the snow to meet their married sisters, brothers, cousins, uncles, aunts, and be the first to greet them. Here, again, were shadows on the window-blind of guests assembling; and there a group of handsome girls, all hooded and fur-booted, and all chattering at once, tripped lightly off to some near neighbour's house; where, woe upon the single man who saw them enter – artful witches: well they knew it – in a glow!

But if you had judged from the numbers of people on their way to friendly gatherings, you might have thought that no one was at home to give them welcome when they got there, instead of every house expecting company, and piling up its fires half-chimney high. Blessings on it, how the Ghost exulted! How it bated its breadth of breast, and opened its capacious palm, and floated on, outpouring, with a generous hand, its bright and harmless mirth on everything within its reach! The very lamplighter, who ran on before, dotting the dusky street with specks of light, and who was dressed to spend the evening somewhere, laughed out loudly as the Spirit passed: though little kenned the lamplighter that he had any company but Christmas!

And now, without a word of warning from the Ghost, they stood upon a bleak and desert moor, where monstrous masses of rude stones were cast about, as though it were the burial-place of giants; and water spread itself wheresoever it listed; or would have done so, but for the frost that held it prisoner; and nothing grew but moss and furze, and coarse, rank grass. Down in the west the setting sun had left a streak of fiery red, which glared upon the desolation for an instant, like a sullen eye, and frowning lower, lower, lower yet, was lost in the thick gloom of darkest night.

'What place is this?' asked Scrooge.

'A place where Miners live, who labour in the bowels of the earth,' returned the Spirit. 'But they know me. See!'

A light shone from the window of a hut, and swiftly they advanced towards it. Passing through the wall of mud and stone, they found a cheerful company assembled round a glowing fire. An old, old man and woman, with their children and their children's children, and another generation beyond that, all decked out gaily in their holiday attire. The old man, in a voice that seldom rose above the howling of the wind upon the barren waste, was singing them a Christmas song; it had been a very old song when he was a boy; and from time to time they all joined in the chorus. So surely as they raised their voices, the old man got quite blithe and loud; and so surely as they stopped, his vigour sank again. The Spirit did not tarry here, but bade Scrooge hold his robe, and passing on above the moor, sped whither? Not to sea? To sea. To Scrooge's horror, looking back, he saw the last of the land, a frightful range of rocks, behind them; and his ears were deafened by the thundering of water, as it rolled, and roared, and raged among the dreadful caverns it had worn, and fiercely tried to undermine the earth.

Built upon a dismal reef of sunken rocks, some league or so from shore, on which the waters chafed and dashed, the wild year through, there stood a solitary lighthouse. Great heaps of sea-weed clung to its base, and storm-birds – born of the wind one might suppose, as sea-weed of the water – rose and fell about it, like the waves they skimmed.

But even here, two men who watched the light had made a fire, that through the loophole in the thick stone wall shed out a ray of brightness on the awful sea. Joining their horny hands over the rough table at which they sat, they wished each other Merry Christmas in their can of grog; and one of them: the elder, too, with his face all damaged and scarred with hard weather, as the figure-head of an old ship might be: struck up a sturdy song that was like a Gale in itself.

Again the Ghost sped on, above the black and heaving sea – on, on – until, being far away, as he told Scrooge, from any shore, they lighted on a ship. They stood beside the helmsman at the wheel, the look-out on the bow, the officers who had the watch; dark, ghostly figures in their several stations; but every man among them hummed a Christmas tune, or had a Christmas thought, or spoke below his breath to his companion of some bygone Christmas Day, with homeward hopes belonging to it. And every man on board, waking or sleeping, good or bad, had had a kinder word for another on that day than on any day in the year; and had shared to some extent in its festivities; and had remembered those he cared for at a distance, and had known that they delighted to remember him.

It was a great surprise to Scrooge, while listening to the moaning of the wind, and thinking what a solemn thing it was to move on through the lonely darkness over an unknown abyss, whose depths were secret as profound as Death: it was a great surprise to Scrooge, while thus engaged, to hear a hearty laugh. It was a much greater surprise to Scrooge to recognise it as his own nephew's, and to find himself in a bright, dry, gleaming room, with the Spirit standing smiling by his side, and looking at the same nephew with approving affability!

'Ha, ha!' laughed Scrooge's nephew. 'Ha, ha, ha!'

If you should happen, by any unlikely chance, to know a man more blest in a laugh than Scrooge's nephew, all I can say is, I should like to know him too. Introduce him to me, and I'll cultivate his acquaintance. It is a fair, even-handed, noble adjustment of things, that while there is infection in disease and sorrow, there is nothing in the world so irresistibly contagious as laughter and good-humour. When Scrooge's nephew laughed in this way: holding his sides, rolling his head, and twisting his face into the most extravagant contortions: Scrooge's niece, by marriage, laughed as heartily as he. And their assembled friends being not a bit behindhand, roared out, lustily.

'Ha, ha! Ha, ha, ha, ha!'

'He said that Christmas was a humbug, as I live!' cried Scrooge's nephew. 'He believed it too!'

'More shame for him, Fred!' said Scrooge's niece, indignantly. Bless those women; they never do anything by halves. They are always in earnest.

She was very pretty: exceedingly pretty. With a dimpled, surprised-looking, capital face; a ripe little mouth, that seemed made to be kissed – as no doubt it was; all kinds of good little dots about her chin, that melted into one another when she laughed: and the sunniest pair of eyes you ever saw in any little creature's head. Altogether she was what you have called provoking, you know; but satisfactory, too. Oh, perfectly satisfactory!

'He's a comical old fellow,' said Scrooge's nephew, 'that's the truth; and not so pleasant as he might be. However, his offences carry their own punishment, and I have nothing to say against him.'

'I'm sure he is very rich, Fred,' hinted Scrooge's niece. 'At least you always tell *me* so.'

'What of that, my dear!' said Scrooge's nephew. 'His wealth is of no use to him. He don't do any good with it. He don't make himself comfortable with it. He hasn't the satisfaction of thinking — ha, ha, ha! — that he is ever going to benefit Us with it.'

'I have no patience with him,' observed Scrooge's niece. Scrooge's niece's sisters, and all the other ladies, expressed the same opinion.

'Oh, I have!' said Scrooge's nephew. 'I am sorry for him; I couldn't be angry with him if I tried. Who suffers by his ill whims? Himself, always. Here, he takes it into his head to dislike us, and he won't come and dine with us. What's the consequence? He don't lose much of a dinner.'

'Indeed, I think he loses a very good dinner,' interrupted Scrooge's niece. Everybody else said the same, and they must be allowed to have been competent judges, because they had just had dinner; and, with the dessert upon the table, were clustered round the fire, by lamplight.

'Well! I am very glad to hear it,' said Scrooge's nephew, 'because I haven't any great faith in these young housekeepers. What do *you* say, Topper?'

Topper had clearly got his eye upon one of Scrooge's niece's sisters, for he answered that a bachelor was a wretched outcast, who had no right to express an opinion on the subject. Whereat Scrooge's niece's sister — the plump one with the lace tucker: not the one with the roses — blushed.

'Do go on, Fred,' said Scrooge's niece, clapping her hands. 'He never finishes what he begins to say! He is such a ridiculous fellow!'

Scrooge's nephew revelled in another laugh, and as it was impossible to keep the infection off; though the plump sister tried hard to do it with aromatic vinegar; his example was unanimously followed.

'I was only going to say,' said Scrooge's nephew 'that the consequence of his taking a dislike to us, and not making merry with us, is, as I think, that he loses some pleasant moments, which could do him no harm. I am sure he loses pleasanter companions than he can find in his own thoughts, either in his mouldy old office, or his dusty chambers. I mean to give him the same chance every year, whether he likes it or not, for I pity him. He may rail at Christmas till he dies, but he can't help thinking better of it — I defy him — if he finds me going there, in good temper, year after year, and saying Uncle Scrooge, how are you? If it only puts him in the vein to leave his poor clerk fifty pounds, *that's* something; and I think I shook him, yesterday.'

It was their turn to laugh now, at the notion of his shaking Scrooge. But being thoroughly good-natured, and not much caring what they laughed at, so that they laughed at any rate, he encouraged them in their merriment, and passed the bottle, joyously.

After tea, they had some music. For they were a musical family, and knew what they were about, when they sung a Glee or Catch, I can assure you: especially Topper, who could growl away in the bass like a good one, and never swell the large veins in his forehead, or get red in the face over it. Scrooge's niece played well upon the harp; and played among other tunes a simple little air (a mere nothing: you might learn to whistle it in two minutes), which had been familiar to the child who fetched Scrooge from the boarding-school, as he had been reminded by the Ghost of Christmas Past. When this strain of music sounded, all the things that Ghost had shown him, came upon his mind; he softened more and more; and though that if he could have listened to it often, years ago, he might have cultivated the kindnesses of life for his own happiness with his own hands, without resorting to the sexton's spade that buried Jacob Marley.

But they didn't devote the whole evening to music. After a while they played at forfeits; for it is good to be children sometimes, and never better than at Christmas, when its mighty Founder was a child himself. Stop! There was first a game at blind-man's buff. Of course there was. And I no more believe Topper was really blind than I believe he had eyes in his boots. My opinion is, that it was a done thing between him and Scrooge's nephew; and that the Ghost of Christmas Present knew it. The way he went after that plump sister in the lace tucker, was an outrage on the credulity of human nature. Knocking down the fire-irons, tumbling over the chairs, bumping up against the piano, smothering himself among the curtains, wherever she went, there went he. He always knew where the plump sister was. He wouldn't catch anybody else. If you had fallen up against him, as some of them did, and stood there; he would have made a feint of endeavouring to seize you, which would have been an affront to your understanding; and would instantly have sidled off in the direction of the plump sister. She often cried out that it wasn't fair; and it really was not. But when at last, he caught her; when, in spite of all her silken rustlings, and her rapid flutterings past him, he got her into a corner whence there was no escape; then his conduct was the most execrable. For his pretending not to know her; his pretending that it was necessary to touch her head-dress, and, further to assure himself of her identity by pressing a certain ring upon her finger, and a certain chain about her neck; was vile, monstrous! No doubt she told him her opinion of it, when, another blind-man being in office, they were so very confidential together, behind the curtains.

Scrooge's niece was not one of the blind-man's buff party, but was made comfortable with a large chair and a footstool, in a snug corner, where the Ghost and Scrooge were close behind her. But she joined in the forfeits, and loved her love to admiration with all the letters of the alphabet. Likewise at the game of How, When, and Where, she was very great, and to the secret joy of Scrooge's nephew, beat her sisters hollow: though they were sharp girls too, as Topper could have told you. There might have been twenty people there, young and old, but they all played, and so did Scrooge; for, wholly forgetting in the interest he had in what was going on, that his voice made no sound in their ears, he sometimes came out with his guess quite loud, and very often guessed right, too; for the sharpest needle, best Whitechapel, warranted not to cut in the eye, was not sharper than Scrooge: blunt as he took it in his head to be.

The Ghost was greatly pleased to find him in this mood, and looked upon him with such favour that he begged like a boy to be allowed to stay until the guests departed. But this the Spirit said could not be done.

'Here is a new game,' said Scrooge. 'One half hour, Spirit, only one!' It was a Game called Yes and No, where Scrooge's nephew had to think of something, and the rest must find out what; he only answering to their questions yes or no as the case was. The brisk fire of questioning to which he was exposed, elicited from him that he was thinking of an animal, a live animal, rather a disagreeable animal, a savage animal, an animal that growled and grunted sometimes, and talked sometimes, and lived in London, and walked about the streets, and wasn't made a show of, and wasn't led by anybody, and didn't live in a menagerie, and was never killed in a market, and was not a horse, or an ass, or a cow, or a bull, or a tiger, or a dog, or a pig, or a cat, or a bear. At every fresh question that was put to him, this nephew burst into a fresh roar of laughter; and was so inexpressibly tickled, that he was obliged to get up off the sofa and stamp. At last the plump sister, falling into a similar state, cried out:

'I have found it out! I know what it is, Fred! I know what it is!'

'What is it?' cried Fred.

'It's your Uncle Scro-o-o-o-ge!'

Which it certainly was. Admiration was the universal sentiment, though some objected that the reply to 'Is it a bear?' ought to have been 'Yes;' inasmuch as an answer in the negative was sufficient to have diverted their thoughts from Mr Scrooge, supposing they had ever had any tendency that way.

'He has given us plenty of merriment, I am sure,' said Fred, 'and it would be ungrateful not to drink his health. Here is a glass of mulled wine ready to our hand at the moment; and I say "Uncle Scrooge!"'

'Well! Uncle Scrooge!' they cried.

'A Merry Christmas and a happy New Year to the old man, whatever he is!' said Scrooge's nephew.

'He wouldn't take it from me, but may he have it, nevertheless. Uncle Scrooge!'

Uncle Scrooge had imperceptibly become so gay and light of heart, that he would have pledged the unconscious company in return, and thanked them in an inaudible speech, if the Ghost had given him time. But the whole scene passed off in the breath of the last word spoken by his nephew; and he and the Spirit were again upon their travels.

Much they saw, and far they went, and many homes they visited, but always with a happy end. The Spirit stood beside sick beds, and they were cheerful; on foreign lands, and they were close at home; by struggling men, and they were patient in their greater hope; by poverty, and it was rich. In almshouse, hospital, and jail, in misery's every refuge, where vain man in his little brief authority had not made fast the door, and barred the Spirit out, he left his blessing, and taught Scrooge his precepts. It was a long night, if it were only a night; but Scrooge had his doubts of this, because the Christmas Holidays appeared to be condensed into the space of time they passed together. It was strange, too, that while Scrooge remained unaltered in his outward form, the Ghost grew older, clearly older. Scrooge had observed this change, but never spoke of it, until they left a children's Twelfth Night party, when, looking at the Spirit as they stood together in an open place, he noticed that its hair was gray.

'Are spirits' lives so short?' asked Scrooge.

'My life upon this globe, is very brief,' replied the Ghost. 'It ends tonight.'

'Tonight!' cried Scrooge.

'Tonight at midnight. Hark! The time is drawing near.'

The chimes were ringing the three quarters past eleven at that moment.

'Forgive me if I am not justified in what I ask,' said Scrooge, looking intently at the Spirit's robe, 'but I see something strange, and not belonging to yourself, protruding from your skirts. Is it a foot or a claw!'

'It might be a claw, for the flesh there is upon it,' was the Spirit's sorrowful reply. 'Look here.'

From the foldings of its robe, it brought two children; wretched, abject, frightful, hideous, miserable. They knelt down at its feet, and clung upon the outside of its garment.

'Oh, Man! look here. Look, look, down here!' exclaimed the Ghost.

They were a boy and a girl. Yellow, meagre, ragged, scowling, wolfish; but prostrate, too, in their humility. Where graceful youth should have filled their features out, and touched them with its freshest tints, a stale and shrivelled hand, like that of age, had pinched, and twisted them, and pulled them into shreds. Where angels might have sat enthroned, devils lurked, and glared out menacing. No change, no degradation, no perversion of humanity, in any grade, through all the mysteries of wonderful creation, has monsters half so horrible and dread.

Scrooge started back, appalled. Having them shown to him in this way, he tried to say they were fine children, but the words choked themselves, rather than be parties to a lie of such enormous magnitude.

'Spirit! are they yours?' Scrooge could say no more.

'They are Man's,' said the Spirit, looking down upon them. 'And they cling to me, appealing from their fathers. This boy is Ignorance. This girl is Want. Beware them both, and all of their degree, but most of all beware this boy, for on his brow I see that written which is Doom, unless the writing be erased. Deny it!' cried the Spirit, stretching out its hand towards the city. 'Slander those who tell it ye! Admit it for your factious purposes, and make it worse! And bide the end!'

'Have they no refuge or resource?' cried Scrooge.

'Are there no prisons?' said the Spirit, turning on him for the last time with his own words. 'Are there no workhouses?'

The bell struck twelve.

Scrooge looked about him for the Ghost, and saw it not. As the last stroke ceased to vibrate, he remembered the prediction of old Jacob Marley, and lifting up his eyes, beheld a solemn Phantom, draped and hooded, coming, like a mist along the ground, towards him.

THE LAST OF THE SPIRITS

The Phantom slowly, gravely, silently, approached. When it came near him, Scrooge bent down upon his knee; for in the very air through which this Spirit moved it seemed to scatter gloom and mystery.

It was shrouded in a deep black garment, which concealed its head, its face, its form, and left nothing of it visible save one outstretched hand. But for this it would have been difficult to detach its figure from the night, and separate it from the darkness by which it was surrounded.

He felt that it was tall and stately when it came beside him, and that its mysterious presence filled him with a solemn dread. He knew no more, for the Spirit neither spoke nor moved.

'I am in the presence of the Ghost of Christmas Yet To Come?' said Scrooge.

The Spirit answered not, but pointed onward with its hand.

'You are about to show me shadows of the things that have not happened, but will happen in the time before us,' Scrooge pursued. 'Is that so, Spirit?'

The upper portion of the garment was contracted for an instant in its folds, as if the Spirit had inclined its head. That was the only answer he received.

Although well used to ghostly company by this time, Scrooge feared the silent shape so much that his legs trembled beneath him, and he found that he could hardly stand when he prepared to follow it. The Spirit paused a moment, as observing his condition, and giving him time to recover.

But Scrooge was all the worse for this. It thrilled him with a vague uncertain horror, to know that behind the dusky shroud, there were ghostly eyes intently fixed upon him, while he, though he stretched his own to the utmost, could see nothing but a spectral hand and one great heap of black.

'Ghost of the Future!' he exclaimed, 'I fear you more than any Spectre I have seen. But, as I know your purpopse is to do me good, and as I hope to live to be another man from what I was, I am prepared to bear your company, and do it with a thankful heart. Will you not speak to me?'

It gave him no reply. The hand was pointed straight before them.

'Lead on!' said Scrooge. 'Lead on! The night is waning fast, and it is precious time to me, I know.

Lead on, Spirit!' The Phantom moved away as it had come towards him. Scrooge followed in the shadow of its dress, which bore him up, he thought, and carried him along.

They scarcely seemed to enter the city; for the city rather seemed to spring up about them, and encompass them of its own act. But there they were, in the heart of it; on Change, amongst the merchants; who hurried up and down, and chinked the money in their pockets, and conversed in groups, and looked at their watches, and trifled thoughtfully with their great gold seals; and so forth, as Scrooge had seen them often.

The Spirit stopped beside one little knot of business men. Observing that the hand was pointed to them, Scrooge advanced to listen to their talk.

'No,' said a great fat man with a monstrous chin, 'I don't know much about it, either way. I only know he's dead.'

'When did he die?' inquired another.

'Last night, I believe.'

'Why, what was the matter with him?' asked a third, taking a vast quantity of snuff out of a very large snuff-box. 'I thought he'd never die.'

'God knows,' said the first, with a yawn.

'What has he done with his money?' asked a red-faced gentleman with a pendulous excrescence on the end of his nose, that shook like the gills of a turkey-cock.

'I haven't heard,' said the man with the large chin, yawning again. 'Left it to his Company, perhaps. He hasn't left it to *me*. That's all I know.'

This pleasantry was received with a general laugh.

'It's likely to be a very cheap funeral,' said the same speaker; 'for upon my life I don't know of anybody to go to it. Suppose we make up a party and volunteer?'

'I don't mind going if a lunch is provided,' observed the gentleman with the excrescence on his nose. 'But I must be fed, if I make one.'

Another laugh.

'Well, I am the most disinterested among you after all,' said the first speaker, 'for I never wear black gloves, and I never eat lunch. But I'll offer to go, if anybody else will. When I come to think of it, I'm not at all sure that I wasn't his most particular friend; for we used to stop and speak whenever we met. Bye, bye!'

Speakers and listeners strolled away, and mixed with other groups. Scrooge knew the men and looked towards the Spirit for an explanation.

The Phantom glided on into a street. Its finger pointed to two persons meeting. Scrooge listened again, thinking that the explanation might lie here.

He knew these men, also, perfectly. They were men of business: very wealthy, and of great importance. He had made a point always of standing well in their esteem: in a business point of view, that is; strictly in a business point of view.

'How are you?' said one.

'How are you?' returned the other.

'Well!' said the first. 'Old Scratch has got his own at last, hey?'

'So I am told,' returned the second. 'Cold, isn't it?'

'Seasonable for Christmas time. You're not a skater, I suppose?'

'No. No. Something else to think of. Good morning!'

Not another word. That was their meeting, their conversation, and their parting.

Scrooge was at first inclined to be surprised that the Spirit should attach importance to conversations apparently so trivial; but feeling assured that they must have some hidden purpose, he set himself to consider what it was likely to be. They could scarcely be supposed to have any bearing on the death of Jacob, his old partner, for that was Past, and this Ghost's province was the Future. Nor could he think of any one immediately connected with himself, to whom he could apply them. But nothing doubting that to whomsoever they applied they had some latent moral for his own improvement, he resolved to treasure up every word he heard, and everything he saw; and especially to observe the shadow of himself when it appeared. For he had an expectation that the conduct of his future self would give him the clue he missed, and would render the solution of these riddles easy.

He looked about in that very place for his own image; but another man stood in his accustomed corner, and though the clock pointed to his usual time of day for being there, he saw no likeness of himself among the multitudes that poured in through the Porch. It gave him little surprise, however; for he had been revolving in his mind a change of life, and thought and hoped he saw his new-born resolutions carried out in this. Quiet and dark, beside him stood the Phantom, with its outstretched hand. When he roused himself from his thoughtful quest, he fancied from the turn of the hand, and its situation in reference to himself, that the Unseen Eyes were looking at him keenly. It made him shudder, and feel very cold.

They left the busy scene, and went into an obscure part of the town, where Scrooge had never penetrated before, although he recognised its situation, and its bad repute. The ways were foul and narrow; the shops and houses wretched; the people half-naked, drunken, slipshod, ugly. Alleys and archways, like so many cesspools, disgorged their offences of smell; and dirt, and life, upon the straggling streets; and the whole quarter reeked with crime, with filth, and misery.

Far in this den of infamous resort, there was a low-browed, beetling shop, below a pent-house roof, where iron, old rags, bottles, bones, and greasy offal, were bought. Upon the floor within, were piled up heaps of rusty keys, nails, chains, hinges, files, scales, weights, and refuse iron of all kinds. Secrets that few would like to scrutinise were bred and hidden in mountains of unseemly rags, masses of corrupted fat, and sepulchres of bones. Sitting in among the wares he dealt in, by a charcoal-stove, made of old bricks, was a gray-haired rascal, nearly seventy years of age; who had screened himself from the cold air without, by a frousy curtaining of miscellaneous tatters, hung upon a line; and smoked his pipe in all the luxury of calm retirement.

Scrooge and the Phantom came into the presence of this man, just as a woman with a heavy bundle slunk into the shop. But she had scarcely entered, when another woman, similarly laden, came in too; and she was closely followed by a man in faded black, who was no less startled by the sight of them, than they had been upon the recognition of each other. After a short period of blank astonishment, in which the old man with the pipe had joined them, they all three burst into a laugh.

'Let the charwoman alone to be the first!' cried she who had entered first. 'Let the laundress alone to be the second, and let the undertaker's man alone to be the third. Look here, old Joe, here's a chance! If we haven't all three met here without meaning it!'

'You couldn't have met in a better place,' said old Joe, removing his pipe from his mouth. 'Come into the parlour. You were made free of it long ago, you know; and the other two an't strangers. Stop till I shut the door of the shop. Ah! How it skreeks! There an't such a rusty bit of metal in the place as its own hinges, I believe; and I'm sure there's no such old bones here, as mine. Ha, ha! We're all suitable to our calling, we're well matched. Come into the parlour. Come into the parlour.'

The parlour was the space behind the screen of rags. The old man raked the fire together with an old stair-rod, and having trimmed his smoky lamp (for it was night), with the stem of his pipe, put it in his mouth again.

While he did this, the woman who had already spoken threw her bundle on the floor and sat down in a flaunting manner on a stool; crossing her elbows on her knees, and looking with a bold defiance at the other two.

'What odds then! What odds, Mrs Dilber?' said the woman. 'Every person has a right to take care of themselves. *He* always did!'

'That's true, indeed!' said the laundress. 'No man more so.'

'Why then, don't stand staring as if you was afraid, woman; who's the wiser? We're not going to pick holes in each other's coats, I suppose?'

'No, indeed!' said Mrs Dilber and the man together. 'We should hope not.'

'Very well, then!' cried the woman. 'That's enough. Who's the worse for the loss of a few things like these? Not a dead man, I suppose.'

'No, indeed,' said Mrs Dilber, laughing.

'If he wanted to keep 'em after he was dead, a wicked old screw,' pursued the woman, 'why wasn't he natural in his lifetime! If he had been, he'd have had somebody to look after him when he was struck with Death, instead of lying gasping out his last there, alone by himself.'

'It's the truest word that ever was spoke,' said Mrs Dilber. 'It's a judgment on him.'

'I wish it was a little heavier judgment,' replied the woman; 'and it should have been, you may depend upon it, if I could have laid my hands on anything else. Open that bundle, old Joe, and let me know the value of it. Speak out plain. I'm not afraid to be the first, nor afraid for them to see it. We knew pretty well that we were helping ourselves, before we met here, I believe. It's no sin. Open the bundle, Joe.'

But the gallantry of her friends would not allow of this; and the man in faded black, mounting the breach first, produced *his* plunder. It was not extensive. A seal or two, a pencil-case, a pair of sleeve-buttons, and a brooch of no great value were all. They were severally examined and appraised by old Joe, who chalked the sums he was disposed to give for each, upon the wall, and added them up into a total when he found that there was nothing more to come.

'That's your account,' said Joe, 'and I wouldn't give another sixpence, if I was to be boiled for not doing it. Who's next?' Mrs Dilber was next. Sheets and towels, a little wearing apparel, two old-fashioned silver teaspoons, a pair of sugar-tongs, and a few boots. Her account was stated on the wall in the same manner.

'I always give too much to ladies. It's a weakness of mine, and that's the way I ruin myself,' said old Joe. 'That's your account. If you asked me for another penny, and made it an open question, I'd repent of being so liberal, and knock off half-a-crown.'

'And now undo *my* bundle, Joe,' said the first woman.

Joe went down on his knees for the greater convenience of opening it, and having unfastened a great many knots, dragged out a large and heavy roll of some dark stuff.

'What do you call this?' said Joe. 'Bed-curtains!'

'You don't mean to say you took 'em down, rings and all, with him lying there?' said Joe.

'Yes I do,' replied the woman. 'Why not?'

'You were born to make your fortune,' said Joe, 'and you'll certainly do it.'

'I certainly shan't hold my hand, when I can get anything in it by reaching it out, for the sake of such a man as He was, I promise you, Joe,' returned the woman coolly. 'Don't drop that oil upon the blankets, now.'

'His blankets?' asked Joe.

'Whose else's do you think?' replied the woman. 'He isn't likely to take cold without 'em, I dare say.'

'I hope he didn't die of anything catching? Eh?' said old Joe, stopping in his work, and looking up.

'Don't you be afraid of that,' returned the woman. 'I an't so fond of his company that I'd loiter about him for such things, if he did. Ah! You may look through that shirt till your eyes ache; but you won't find a hole in it, nor a threadbare place. It's the best he had, and a fine one too. They'd have wasted it, if it hadn't been for me.'

'What do you call wasting of it?' asked old Joe.

'Putting it on him to be buried in, to be sure,' replied the woman with a laugh. 'Somebody was fool enough to do it, but I took it off again. If calico an't good enough for such a purpose, it isn't good enough for anything. It's quite as becoming to the body. He can't look uglier than he did in that one.'

Scrooge listened to this dialogue in horror. As they sat grouped about their spoil, in the scanty light afforded by the old man's lamp, he viewed them with a detestation and disgust, which could hardly have been greater, though they had been obscene demons, marketing the corpse itself.

'Ha, ha!' laughed the same woman, when old Joe, producing a flannel bag with money in it, told out their several gains upon the ground. 'This is the end of it, you see! He frightened every one away from him when he was alive, to profit us when he was dead! Ha, ha, ha!'

'Spirit!' said Scrooge, shuddering from head to foot. 'I see, I see. The case of this unhappy man might be my own. My life tends that way, now. Merciful Heaven, what is this!'

He recoiled in terror, for the scene had changed, and now he almost touched a bed: a bare, uncurtained bed: on which, beneath a ragged sheet, there lay a something covered up, which, though it was dumb, announced itself in awful language.

The room was very dark, too dark to be observed with any accuracy, though Scrooge glanced round it in obedience to a secret impulse, anxious to know what kind of room it was. A pale light, rising in the outer air, fell straight upon the bed; and on it, plundered and bereft, unwatched, unwept, uncared for, was the body of this man.

Scrooge glanced towards the Phantom. Its steady hand was pointed to the head. The cover was so

Scrooge's third Visitor.

The Last of the Spirits.

carelessly adjusted that the slightest raising of it, the motion of a finger upon Scrooge's part, would have disclosed the face. He thought of it, felt how easy it would be to do, and longed to do it; but had no more power to withdraw the veil than to dismiss the spectre at his side.

Oh cold, cold, rigid, dreadful Death, set up thine altar here, and dress it with such terrors as thou hast at they command: for this is thy dominion! But of the loved, revered, and honoured head, thou canst not turn one hair to thy dread purposes, or make one feature odious. It is not that the hand is heavy and will fall down when released; it is not that the heart and pulse are still; but that the hand WAS open, generous, and true; the heart brave, warm, and tender; and the pulse a man's. Strike, Shadow, strike! And see his good deeds springing from the wound, to sow the world with life immortal.

No voice pronounced these words in Scrooge's ears, and yet he heard them when he looked upon the bed. He thought, if this man could be raised up now, what would be his foremost thoughts? Avarice, hard dealing, griping cares? They have brought him to a rich end, truly!

He lay, in the dark empty house, with not a man, a woman, or a child, to say he was kind to me in this or that, and for the memory of one kind word I will be kind to him. A cat was tearing at the door, and there was a sound of gnawing rats beneath the hearth-stone. What *they* wanted in the room of death, and why they were so restless and disturbed, Scrooge did not dare to think.

'Spirit!' he said, 'this is a fearful place. In leaving it, I shall not leave its lesson, trust me. Let us go!'

Still the Ghost pointed with an unmoved finger to the head.

'I understand you,' Scrooge returned, 'and I would do it, if I could. But I have not the power, Spirit. I have not the power.'

Again it seemed to look upon him.

'If there is any person in the town, who feels emotion caused by this man's death,' said Scrooge quite agonized, 'show that person to me, Spirit, I beseech you!'

The phantom spread its dark robe before him for a moment, like a wing; and withdrawing it, revealed a room of daylight, where a mother and her children were.

She was expecting some one, and with anxious eagerness; for she walked up and down the room; started at every sound; looked out from the window; glanced at the clock; tried, but in vain, to work with her needle; and could hardly bear the voices of the children in their play.

At length the long-expected knock was heard. She hurried to the door, and met her husband; a man whose face was care-worn and depressed, though he was young. There was a remarkable expression in it now; a kind of serious delight of which he felt ashamed, and which he struggled to repress.

He sat down to the dinner that had been hoarding for him by the fire; and when she asked him faintly what news (which was not until after a long silence), he appeared embarrassed how to answer.

'Is it good,' she said, 'or bad?' – to help him.

'Bad,' he answered.

'We are quite ruined?'

'No. There is hope yet, Caroline.'

'If *he* relents,' she said, amazed, 'there is! Nothing is past hope, if such a miracle has happened.'

'He is past relenting,' said her husband. 'He is dead.'

She was a mild and patient creature if her face spoke truth; but she was thankful in her soul to hear it, and she said so, with clasped hands. She prayed forgiveness the next moment, and was sorry; but the first was the emotion of her heart.

'What the half-drunken woman whom I told you of last night, said to me, when I tried to see him and obtain a week's delay; and what I thought was a mere excuse to avoid me; turns out to have been quite true. He was not only very ill, but dying, then.'

'To whom will our debt be transferred?'

'I don't know. But before that time we shall be ready with the money; and even though we were not, it would be bad fortune indeed to find so merciless a creditor in his successor. We may sleep tonight with light hearts, Caroline!'

Yes. Soften it as they would, their hearts were lighter. The children's faces, hushed and clustered round to hear what they so little understood, were brighter; and it was a happier house for this man's death! The only emotion that the Ghost could show him, caused by the event, was one of pleasure.

'Let me see some tenderness connected with a death,' said Scrooge; 'or that dark chamber, Spirit, which we left just now, will be for ever present to me.'

The Ghost conducted him through several streets familiar to his feet; and as they went along, Scrooge looked here and there to find himself, but nowhere was he to be seen. They entered poor Bob Cratchit's house; the dwelling he had visited before; and found the mother and the children seated round the fire.

Quiet. Very quiet. The noisy little Cratchits were as still as statues in one corner, and sat looking up at Peter, who had a book before him. The mother and her daughters were engaged in sewing. But surely they were very quiet!

' "And he took a child, and set him in the midst of them." '

Where had Scrooge heard those words? He had not dreamed them. The boy must have read them out, as he and the Spirit crossed the threshold. Why did he not go on?

The mother laid her work upon the table, and put her hand up to her face.

'The colour hurts my eyes,' she said.

The colour? Ah, poor Tiny Tim!

'They're better now again,' said Cratchit's wife. 'It makes them weak by candle-light; and I wouldn't show weak eyes to your father when he comes home, for the world. It must be near his time.'

'Past it rather,' Peter answered, shutting up his book. 'But I think he has walked a little slower than he used, these few last evenings, mother.'

They were very quiet again. At last she said, and in a steady cheerful voice, that only faultered once:

'I have known him walk with – I have known him walk with Tiny Tim upon his shoulder, very fast indeed.'

'And so have I,' cried Peter. 'Often.'

'And so have I!' exclaimed another. So had all.

'But he was very light to carry,' she resumed, intent upon her work, 'and his father loved him so, that it was no trouble: no trouble. And there is your father at the door!'

She hurried out to meet him; and little Bob in his comforter – he had need of it, poor fellow – came in. His tea was ready for him on the hob, and they all tried who should help him to it most. Then the two young Cratchits got upon his knees and laid, each child a little cheek, against his face, as if they said, 'Don't mind it, father. Don't be grieved!'

Bob was very cheerful with them, and spoke pleasantly to all the family. He looked at the work upon the table, and praised the industry and speed of Mrs Cratchit and the girls. They would be done long before Sunday he said.

'Sunday! You went today then, Robert?' said his wife.

'Yes, my dear,' returned Bob. 'I wish you could have gone. It would have done you good to see how green a place it is. But you'll see it often. I promised him that I would walk there on a Sunday. My little, little child!' cried Bob. 'My little child!'

He broke down all at once. He couldn't help it. If he could have helped it, he and his child would have been farther apart perhaps than they were.

He left the room, and went up stairs into the room above, which was lighted cheerfully, and hung with Christmas. There was a chair set close beside the child, and there were signs of some one having been there, lately. Poor Bob sat down in it, and when he had thought a little and composed himself, he kissed the little face. He was reconciled to what had happened, and went down again quite happy.

They drew about the fire, and talked; the girls and mother working still. Bob told them of the extraordinary kindness of Mr Scrooge's nephew, whom he had scarcely seen but once, and who, meeting him in the street that day, and seeing that he looked a little – 'just a little down you know,' said Bob, enquired what had happened to distress him. 'On which,' said Bob, 'for he is the pleasantest-spoken gentleman you ever heard, I told him. "I am heartily sorry for it, Mr Cratchit," he said, "and heartily sorry for your good wife." By the bye, how he ever knew *that*, I don't know.'

'Knew what, my dear?'

'Why, that you were a good wife,' replied Bob.

'Everybody knows that!' said Peter.

'Very well observed, my boy!' cried Bob. 'I hope they do. "Heartily sorry," he said, "for your good wife. If I can be of service to you in any way," he said, giving me his card, "that's where I live. Pray come to me." Now, it wasn't,' cried Bob, 'for the sake of anything he might be able to do for us, so much as for his kind way, that this was quite delightful. It really seemed as if he had known our Tiny Tim, and felt with us.'

'I'm sure he's a good soul!' said Mrs Cratchit.

'You would be surer of it, my dear,' returned Bob, 'if you saw and spoke to him. I shouldn't be at all surprised, mark what I say, if he got Peter a better situation.'

'Only hear that, Peter,' said Mrs Cratchit.

'And then,' cried one of the girls, 'Peter will be keeping company with some one, and setting up for himself.'

'Get along with you!' retorted Peter, grinning.

'It's just as likely as not,' said Bob, 'one of these days; though there's plenty of time for that my dear. But however and whenever we part from one another, I am sure we shall none of us forget poor Tiny Tim – shall we – or this first parting that there was among us?'

'Never, father!' cried they all.

'And I know,' said Bob, 'I know, my dears, that when we recollect how patient and how mild he was; although he was a little, little child; we shall not quarrel easily among ourselves, and forget poor Tiny Tim in doing it.'

'No, never, father!' they all cried again.

'I am very happy,' said little Bob, 'I am very happy!'

Mrs Cratchit kissed him, his daughters kissed him, the two young Cratchits kissed him, and Peter and himself shook hands. Spirit of Tiny Tim, thy childish essence was from God!

'Spectre,' said Scrooge, 'something informs me that our parting moment is at hand. I know it, but I know not how. Tell me what man that was whom we saw lying dead?'

The Ghost of Christmas Yet To Come conveyed him, as before – though at a different time, he thought: indeed, there seemed no order in these latter visions, save that they were in the Future – into the resorts of business men, but showed him not himself. Indeed, the Spirit did not stay for anything, but went straight on, as to the end just now desired, until besought by Scrooge to tarry for a moment.

'This court,' said Scrooge, 'through which we hurry now, is where my place of occupation is, and has been for a length of time. I see the house. Let me behold what I shall be, in days to come.'

The Spirit stopped; the hand was pointed elsewhere.

'The house is yonder,' Scrooge exclaimed. 'Why do you point away?'

The inexorable finger underwent no change.

Scrooge hastened to the window of his office, and looked in. It was an office still, but not his. The furniture was not the same, and the figure in the chair was not himself. The Phantom pointed as before.

He joined it once again, and wondering why and whither he had gone, accompanied it until they reached an iron gate. He paused to look round before entering.

A churchyard. Here, then, the wretched man whose game he had now to learn, lay underneath the ground. It was a worthy place. Walled in by houses; overrun by grass and weeds, the growth of vegetation's death, not life; choked up with too much burying; fat with repleted appetite. A worthy place!

The Spirit stood among the graves, and pointed down to One. He advanced towards it trembling. The Phantom was exactly as it had been, but he dreaded that he saw new meaning in its solemn shape.

'Before I draw nearer to that stone to which you point,' said Scrooge, 'answer me one question. Are these the shadows of the things that Will be, or are they shadows of the things that May be, only?'

Still the Ghost pointed downward to the grave by which it stood.

'Men's courses will foreshadow certain ends, to which, if persevered in, they must lead,' said Scrooge. 'But if the courses be departed from, the ends will change. Say it is thus with what you show me!'

The Spirit was immovable as ever. Scrooge crept towards it, trembling as he went; and following the finger, read upon the stone of the neglected grave his own name, EBENEZER SCROOGE.

'Am *I* that man who lay upon the bed?' he cried, upon his knees.

The finger pointed from the grave to him, and back again.

'No, Spirit! Oh no, no!'

The finger still was there.

'Spirit!' he cried, tight clutching at its robe, 'hear me! I am not the man I was. I will not be the man I must have been but for this intercourse. Why show me this, if I am past all hope?'

For the first time the hand appeared to shake.

'Good Spirit!' he pursued, as down upon the ground he fell before it: 'Your nature intercedes for me, and pities me. Assure me that I yet may change these shadows you have shown me, by an altered life!'

The kind hand trembled.

'I will honour Christmas in my heart, and try to keep it all the year. I will live in the Past, the Present, and the Future. The Spirits of all Three shall strive within me. I will not shut out the lessons that they teach. Oh, tell me I may sponge away the writing on this stone!'

In his agony, he caught the spectral hand. It sought to free itself, but he was strong in his entreaty, and detained it. The Spirit, stronger yet, repulsed him.

Holding up his hands in one last prayer to have his fate reversed, he saw an alteration in the Phantom's hood and dress. It shrunk, collapsed, and dwindled down into a bedpost.

THE END OF IT

Yes! and the bedpost was his own. The bed was his own, the room was his own. Best and happiest of all, the time before him was his own, to make amends in!

'I will live in the Past, the Present, and the Future!' Scrooge repeated, as he scrambled out of bed. The Spirits of all Three shall strive within me. Oh Jacob Marley! Heaven, and the Christmas Time be praised for this. I say it on my knees, old Jacob; on my knees!'

He was so fluttered and so glowing with his good intentions, that his broken voice would scarcely answer to his call. He had been sobbing violently in his conflict with the Spirit, and his face was wet with tears.

'They are not torn down,' cried Scrooge, folding one of his bed-curtains in his arms, 'they are not torn down, rings and all. They are here: I am here: the shadows of the things that would have been, may be dispelled. They will be. I know they will!'

His hands were busy with his garments all this time: turning them inside out, putting them on upside down, tearing them, mislaying them, making them parties to every kind of extravagance.

'I don't know what to do!' cried Scrooge, laughing and crying in the same breath: and making a perfect Laocoön of himself with his stockings. 'I am as light as a feather, I am as happy as an angel, I am as merry as a school-boy. I am as giddy as a drunken man. A merry Christmas to everybody! A happy New Year to all the world. Hallo here! Whoop! Hallo!'

He had frisked into the sitting-room and was now standing there: perfectly winded.

'There's the saucepan that the gruel was in!' cried Scrooge, starting off again, and going round the fire-place. 'There's the door, by which the Ghost of Jacob Marley entered! There's the corner where the Ghost of Christmas Present, sat! There's the window where I saw the wandering Spirits! It's all right, it's all true, it all happened. Ha ha ha!'

Really, for a man who had been out of practice for so many years, it was a splendid laugh, a most illustrious laugh. The father of a long, long, line of brilliant laughs!

'I don't know what day of the month it is!' said Scrooge. 'I don't know how long I've been among the

Spirits. I don't know anything. I'm quite a baby. Never mind. I don't care. I'd rather be a baby. Hallo! Whoop! Hallo here!'

He was checked in his transports by the churches ringing out the lustiest peals he had ever heard. Clash, clang, hammer, ding, dong, bell. Bell, dong, ding, hammer, clang, clash! Oh, glorious, glorious!

Running to the window, he opened it, and put out his head. No fog, no mist: clear, bright, jovial, stirring, cold, cold, piping for the blood to dance to; Golden sunlight; Heavenly sky; sweet fresh air; merry bells. Oh, glorious. Glorious!

'What's today?' cried Scrooge, calling downward to a boy in Sunday clothes, who perhaps had loitered in to look about him.

'Eh?' returned the boy, with all his might of wonder.

'What's today, my fine fellow?' said Scrooge.

'Today!' replied the boy. 'Why, CHRISTMAS DAY.'

'It's Christmas Day!' said Scrooge to himself. 'I haven't missed it. The Spirits have done it all in one night. They can do anything they like. Of course they can. Of course they can. Hallo, my fine fellow!'

'Hallo!' returned the boy.

'Do you know the Poulterer's, in the next street but one, at the corner?' Scrooge inquired.

'I should hope I did,' replied the lad.

'An intelligent boy!' said Scrooge. 'A remarkable boy! Do you know whether they've sold the prize Turkey that was hanging up there? Not the little prize Turkey; the big one?'

'What, the one as big as me?' returned the boy.

'What a delightful boy!' said Scrooge. 'It's a pleasure to talk to him. Yes, my buck!'

'It's hanging there now,' replied the boy.

'Is it?' said Scrooge. 'Go and buy it.'

'Walk-ER!' exclaimed the boy.

'No, no,' said Scrooge, 'I am in earnest. Go and buy it, and tell 'em to bring it here, that I may give them the direction where to take it. Come back with the man, and I'll give you a shilling. Come back with him in less than five minutes, and I'll give you half-a-crown!'

The boy was off like a shot. He must have had a steady hand at a trigger who could have got a shot off half so fast.

'I'll send it to Bob Cratchit's!' whispered Scrooge, rubbing his hands, and splitting with a laugh. 'He shan't know who sends it. It's twice the size of Tiny Tim. Joe Miller never made such a joke as sending it to Bob's will be!'

The hand in which he wrote the address was not a steady one, but write it he did, somehow, and went down stairs to open the street door, ready for the coming of the poulterer's man. As he stood there, waiting his arrival, the knocker caught his eye.

'I shall love it, as long as I live!' cried Scrooge, patting it with his hand. 'I scarcely ever looked at it before. What an honest expression it has in its face! It's a wonderful knocker! – Here's the Turkey. Hallo! Whoop! How are you! Merry Christmas!'

It *was* a Turkey! He never could have stood upon his legs, that bird. He would have snapped 'em short off in a minute, like sticks of sealing-wax.

'Why, it's impossible to carry that to Camden Town,' said Scrooge. 'You must have a cab.'

The chuckle with which he said this, and the chuckle with which he paid for the Turkey, and the chuckle with which he paid for the cab, and the chuckle with which he recompensed the boy, were only to be exceeded by the chuckle with which he sat down breathless in his chair again, and chuckled till he cried.

Shaving was not an easy task, for his hand continued to shake very much; and shaving requires attention, even when you don't dance while you are at it. But if he had cut the end of his nose off, he would have put a piece of sticking-plaster over it, and been quite satisfied.

He dressed himself 'all in his best,' and at last got out into the streets. The people were by this time pouring forth, as he had seen them with the Ghost of Christmas Present; and walking with his hands behind him, Scrooge regarded every one with a delighted smile. He looked so irresistibly pleasant, in a word, that three or four good-humoured fellows said, 'Good morning, sir! A merry Christmas to you!' And Scrooge said often afterwards, that of all the blithe sounds he had ever heard, those were the blithest in his ears.

He had not gone far, when coming on towards him he beheld the portly gentleman, who had walked into his counting-house the day before and said, 'Scrooge and Marley's, I believe?' It sent a pang across his heart to think how this old gentleman would look upon him when they met; but he knew what path lay straight before him, and he took it.

'My dear sir,' said Scrooge, quickening his pace, and taking the old gentleman by both his hands. 'How do you do? I hope you succeeded yesterday. It was very kind of you. A merry Christmas to you, sir!'

'Mr Scrooge?'

'Yes,' said Scrooge. 'That is my name, and I fear it may not be pleasant to you. Allow me to ask your pardon. And will you have the goodness – ' here Scrooge whispered in his ear.

'Lord bless me!' cried the gentleman, as if his breath were gone. 'My dear Mr Scrooge, are you serious?'

'If you please,' said Scrooge. 'Not a farthing less. A great many back-payments are included in it, I assure you. Will you do me that favour?'

'My dear sir,' said the other, shaking hands with him. 'I don't know what to say to such munifi – '

'Don't say anything, please,' retorted Scrooge. 'Come and see me. Will you come and see me?'

'I will!' cried the old gentleman. And it was clear he meant to do it.

'Thank'ee,' said Scrooge. 'I am much obliged to you. I thank you fifty times. Bless you!'

He went to church, and walked about the streets, and watched the people hurrying to and fro, and patted children on the head, and questioned beggars, and looked down into the kitchens of houses, and up to the windows: and found that everything could yield him pleasure. He had never dreamed that any walk – that anything – could give him so much happiness. In the afternoon, he turned his steps towards his nephew's house.

He passed the door a dozen times, before he had the courage to go up and knock. But he made a dash and did it:

'Is your master at home, my dear!' said Scrooge to the girl. Nice girl! Very.

'Yes sir.'

'Where is he, my love?' said Scrooge.

'He's in the dining-room, sir, along with mistress. I'll show you up stairs, if you please.'

'Thank'ee. He knows me,' said Scrooge, with his hand already on the dining-room lock. 'I'll go in here, my dear.'

He turned it gently, and sidled his face in, round, the door. They were looking at the table (which was spread out in great array); for these young housekeepers are always nervous on such points, and like to see that everything is right.

'Fred!' said Scrooge.

Dear heart alive, how his niece by marriage started! Scrooge had forgotten, for the moment, about her sitting in the corner with the footstool, or he wouldn't have done it, on any account.

'Why bless my soul!' cried Fred, 'who's that?'

'It's I. Your uncle Scrooge. I have come to dinner. Will you let me in, Fred?'

Let him in! It is a mercy he didn't shake his arm off. He was at home in five minutes. Nothing could be heartier. His niece looked just the same. So did Topper when *he* came. So did the plump sister, when *she* came. So did every one when *they* came. Wonderful party, wonderful games, wonderful unanimity, won-der-ful happiness!

But he was early at the office next morning. Oh he was early there. If he could only be there first, and catch Bob Cratchit coming late! That was the thing he had set his heart upon.

And he did it; yes he did! The clock struck nine. No Bob. A quarter past. No Bob. He was full eighteen minutes and a half, behind his time. Scrooge sat with his door wide open, that he might see him come into the Tank.

His hat was off, before he opened the door; his comforter too. He was on his stool in a jiffy; driving

away with his pen, as if he were trying to overtake nine o'clock.

'Hallo!' growled Scrooge, in his accustomed voice as near as he could feign it. 'What do you mean by coming here at this time of day?'

'I am very sorry, sir,' said Bob. 'I *am* behind my time.'

'You are?' repeated Scrooge. 'Yes. I think you are. Step this way, if you please.'

'It's only once a year, sir,' pleaded Bob, appearing from the Tank. 'It shall not be repeated. I was making rather merry yesterday, sir.'

'Now, I'll tell you what, my friend,' said Scrooge, 'I am not going to stand this sort of thing any longer. And therefore,' he continued, leaping from his stool, and giving Bob such a dig in the waistcoat that he staggered back into the Tank again: 'and therefore I am about to raise your salary!'

Bob trembled, and got a little nearer to the ruler. He had a momentary idea of knocking Scrooge down with it; holding him; and calling to the people in the court for help and a strait-waistcoat.

'A merry Christmas, Bob!' said Scrooge, with an earnestness that could not be mistaken, as he clapped him on the back. 'A merrier Christmas, Bob, my good fellow, than I have given you, for many a year! I'll raise your salary, and endeavour to assist your struggling family, and we will discuss your affairs this very afternoon, over a Christmas bowl of smoking bishop, Bob! Make up the fires, and buy another coal-scuttle before you dot another i, Bob Cratchit!'

Scrooge was better than his word. He did it all, and infinitely more; and to Tiny Tim, who did NOT die, he was a second father. He became as good a friend, as good a master, and as good a man, as the good old city knew, or any other good old city, town, or borough, in the good old world. Some people laughed to see the alteration in him, but he let them laugh, and little heeded them; for he was wise enough to know that nothing ever happened on this globe, for good, at which some people did not have their fill of laughter in the outset: and knowing that such as these would be blind anyway, he thought it quite as well that they should wrinkle up their eyes in grins, as have the malady in less attractice forms. His own heart laughed: and that was quite enough for him.

He had no further intercourse with Spirits, but lived upon the Total Abstinence Principle, ever afterwards; and it was always said of him, that he knew how to keep Christmas well, if any man alive possessed the knowledge. May that be truly said of us, and all of us! And so, as Tiny Tim observed, God Bless Us, Every One!

THE END

6

A National Benefit

'... And so, as Tiny Tim observed,
God bless Us, Every One!'

The last words read, the critics dipped their pens in their inkwells and passed judgment:

Who can listen to objections regarding such a book as this? It seems to me a national benefit, and to every man or woman who reads it a personal kindness.

This review, in *Fraser's Magazine*, was by William Makepeace Thackeray, who also recorded having overheard two very different people speaking of Dickens' book: 'neither knew the other, or the author, and both said, by way of criticism, "God bless him!" ... What a feeling is this for a writer to be able to inspire and what a reward to reap.'

There were those who did not warm to *A Christmas Carol*: one critic thought the book did little more than promote 'the immense spiritual power of the Christmas turkey'; and Dickens told John Forster that 'the Westminster Review

considered Scrooge's presentation of the turkey to Bob Cratchit as grossly incompatible with political economy'. What the writer actually said was:

A great part of the enjoyments of life are summed up in eating and drinking at the cost of munificent patrons of the poor... The processes whereby poor men are to be enabled to earn good wages, wherewith to buy turkeys for themselves, does not enter into the account... Who went without turkey and punch in order that Bob Cratchit might get them – for, unless there were turkey and punch in surplus, some one must go without – is a disagreeable reflection wholly out of sight.

Another attack on what some saw as the secular indulgence preached in *A Christmas Carol* appeared – this time in verse – in a Scottish publication:

What's Christmas, indeed,
But a season to feed:
Why should it be more in the Christian's eye!
'Twas made but for this;
But to revel and kiss
And spoil one's digestion with brandied
    mince-pie.
With pleasure unfeign'd,
This lesson I've gained
From the new 'Christmas Carol,' invented by
    Boz,
And I mean never more
To be sober, before
I have emptied the cellar, entirely that's poz.

But such criticisms mattered little, for the book had more than enough champions. *The Athenaeum* described it at as a 'jovial, genial piece of Christmas fare'; the *Gentleman's Magazine* expressed the view that 'Tiny Tim is quite perfection'; while the Tory weekly, *Britannia*, praised Dickens' 'sympathy for human suffering... not for imaginary and fictitious distresses but for the real grinding sorrows of life'. The *Sunday Times* said it was 'perfectly delightful, and its moral purpose deserving of the highest praise', adding: 'generally the tone of the story is sweet and subdued, but occasionally it soars and becomes altogether sublime'.

The poet Thomas Hood described *A Christmas Carol* – 'with its opulence of good cheer, and all the Gargantuan festivity of hospitable tide' – as being 'a happy inspiration of the heart that warms every page. It is impossible to read, without a glowing bosom and burning cheeks, between love and shame for our kind.'

Dickens was deeply moved by the critical response to the book: he told Thackeray that his review had 'touched him to the quick, encouraged him and done him good'; while to another reviewer, Laman Blanchard (who had written that the book would be 'heard and remembered a hundred Christmases to come') he wrote: 'You have filled my heart up to the brim, and it is running over... your elegant and fervent praise has touched me in the tenderest place.'

Lord Jeffrey, the editor of the *Edinburgh Review*, had written to the author: 'Blessings on your kind heart, my dear Dickens... We are all charmed with your "Carol"; chiefly I think for the genuine goodness which breathes all through it, and is the true inspiring angel by which its genius had been awakened...' Jeffrey was particularly generous in his praise, saying that Dickens had 'done more good, and not only fostered more kindly feelings, but prompted more positive acts of beneficence, by this little publication, than can be traced to all the pulpits and confessionals in Christendom since Christmas 1842'.

Dickens soon discovered that the enthusiasm of critics and friends was endorsed by the public, and the first printing of 6,000 copies sold well. Initially, these sales must have been rather surprising to Dickens, who was convinced that Chapman and Hall weren't publicizing the book sufficiently: 'Can you believe,' he had complained on publication, 'that with the exception of Blackwood's, the Carol is not advertised in One of the Magazines!'

Dickens' printers, Bradbury and Evans,

advised him that 'nothing but a tremendous push can possibly atone for such fatal negligence'; so the author had written to his publishers and said: 'Do this – Do that – Do the other – keep away from me – and be damned.' This and that was duly done and, on 27 December, Dickens was writing to his solicitor, Thomas Mitton, to say that 'as the orders were coming in fast from town and country', it would be necessary to reprint. A week later, on 3 January, 1844, Dickens had learned that 'two thousand of the three printed for second and third editions are already taken by the trade'; and by the end of the year, no less than 14,930 copies had been sold.

When the printers returned the manuscript, Dickens had it bound in red morocco, had the name 'Thomas Mitton Esqre.' stamped on the front cover and presented the volume to his solicitor. It was a handsome gesture of friendship, for the manuscript was precious to Dickens; but it was also, no doubt, intended as partial mitigation of his indebtedness to Mitton, who had loaned him £270 during the previous year and had received little in the way of fees.

Mitton kept the manuscript until 1875, five years after Dickens' death, when he sold it – for, possibly as little as £50 – to a London bookseller, Francis Harvey. An autograph collector, Henry George Churchill, saw an advertisement for its sale, immediately hailed a cab to take him to the book shop where he, there and then, wrote a cheque and 'bore off the prize in triumph'. In 1882, Churchill put the manuscript up for sale at a book shop in Birmingham, where crowds of people flocked to

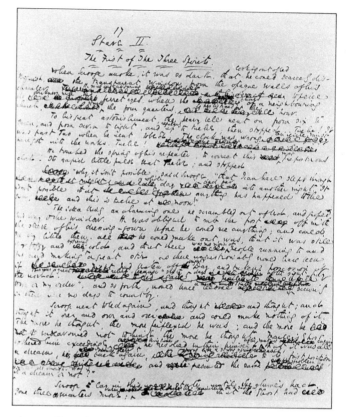

A page from the original manuscript of *A Christmas Carol*

see it. The London booksellers, Robson and Kerslake, paid £200 for the manuscript and at once offered it for sale at £300, which sum was paid by a Dickens collector, Stuart M. Samuel. A facsimile was published in 1890, and, some years later, the original passed to the American collector, J. Pierpont Morgan; and it is in the New York library, named after Pierpont Morgan, that Dickens' 'own and only' manuscript of *A Christmas Carol* now resides.

In 1843, whilst the future value of the manuscript was of little consequence, the book itself had an extraordinary effect on a wide range of people. By every post, Dickens reported, 'all manner of strangers write all manner of letters'. These letters, Dickens' friend John Forster recalled, were 'not literary at all, but of the simplest, domestic kind; of which the general burden was to tell him, amid many confidences about their homes, how the Carol had come to be read aloud there and was to be kept upon a little shelf by itself, and was to do them no end of good'. Indeed, the success of *A Christmas Carol* was, as the author himself put it, 'the greatest, as I am told, that this ruffian and rascal has ever achieved'.

Such a success, Dickens hoped, would bring him an appropriate financial reward; he confessed to having set his 'heart and soul upon a Thousand clear', enough, in fact, to clear his considerable debts. Imagine then his horror, when his first royalty statement, in February 1844, showed a mere £230. 'Such a night as I have passed! I really believed I should never get up again, until I had passed through all the horrors of a fever.'

To Thomas Mitton he wrote: 'Prepare yourself for a shock! I was never so knocked over in my life, as when I opened this Carol account on Saturday night; and though I had got over it by yesterday and could look the thing good humouredly in the face, I have slept badly as Macbeth ever since...'

Or as badly, perhaps, as Ebenezer Scrooge! Dickens was quick to blame Chapman and Hall:

'I have not the least doubt that they have run the expenses up anyhow purposely to bring me back and disgust me with the charges.' However, the real cause of the book not showing a greater profit was the high costs of production. Although the actual printing of the text and plates accounted for only 16 per cent of the total expenses, the elaborate binding and the hand-tinted plates were responsible for no less than 60 per cent. 'If you add up the different charges for the plates,' Dickens complained, 'you will find that they cost me even more than I get.'

A year after publication, his total royalties were still only £726, and the extent of Dickens' disappointment can be judged from a letter written to his friend John Forster: 'What a wonderful thing it is, that such a great success should occasion me such intolerable anxiety and disappointment!'

The solution to his problems came in the form of an offer from the printers, Bradbury and Evans: if he left Chapman and Hall and joined them, they would settle Dickens' debts with his former publishers and pay him the sum of £2,800. This arrangement, however, was not without its drawbacks, for Dickens had to agree to give the printers a one-fourth share of everything he would write over the next eight years. 'Ironically,' the literary commentator, Michael Patrick Hearn has remarked, 'the sentiments of good-fellowship and mercy, the tone of *A Christmas Carol*, did not touch its purveyor in his dealings with his publishers.'

The popular success of *A Christmas Carol* resulted in its being translated into French as

Les Apparitions de Noel, published in the French magazine, *Revue Britannique*; it was to be the first of many translations into almost every language including Gaelic, Russian, Chinese, Japanese, Eskimo and Modern Hebrew. In Italian it is called *Cantico di Natale*; in Spanish it is *Los Fantasmas de Nochebuena*; in Dutch, *Een Kerssprookje*; and in Turkish *Dznunti yerk*. The book has also been transliterated into shorthand and, as B.W. Matz observed, 'if it ever happens that Esperanto becomes the universal language, an edition in that language is already made for the terrible contingency'.

Almost immediately, following publication, a German edition of the English text was issued by Tauchnitz of Leipzig, for which Dickens was reputedly well paid. Not so, an unauthorized American edition of *A Christmas Carol*, published in 1844 by Carey & Hart of Philadelphia. Dickens, whose earlier books had already been pirated in America, may not have even been aware of this volume, but, even if he had, he would have been powerless to do anything about it, since there was no so such thing as international copyright protection. He did, however, know of another unauthorized edition that was published rather closer to home.

It was Twelfth Night, 6 January, 1844, and a magazine called *Parley's Illuminated Library*, published 'A Christmas Ghost Story', which was saucily described as being 'Re-originated from the Original by Charles Dickens, Esq., and Anylitically [sic] Condensed Expressly for this Work.' On the front cover was a ludicrous illustration of the Ghost of Christmas Present

towering over the Cratchit's dinner-table and putting his torch to the celebrated pudding, here shown considerably larger than 'a speckled cannon-ball'; so large, in fact, that Mrs Crachit could not possibly have lifted it!

Following a number of literary quotations, including one from Hamlet – 'There are more things in heaven and earth [Horatio] than are dreamt of in [your] philosophy' – the reader was offered a text that sounded only vaguely familiar:

> Everybody, as the phrase goes, knew the firm of 'Scrooge and Marley;' for, though Marley had 'long been dead' at the period we have chosen for the commencement of our story, the name of the deceased partner still maintained its place above the warehouse door; somewhat faded, to be sure, but there it was...

There were occasional changes to the original, that were probably mistakes, such as the printing of Fezziwig as Fuzziwig; but, as Dickens woefully observed: 'The story is practically the same... the incidents are the same, and follow in the same order.' Very frequently, Dickens noted, even the language was the same, and 'where it is not, it is weakened, degraded; made tame, vile, ignorant, and mawkish'. Dickens' anger was in full flood when he instructed his solicitor, Thomas Mitton to act against this 'gang of Robbers':

> I have not the least doubt that if these Vagabonds can be stopped, they must be. So let us go to work in such terrible earnest that everything tumble down before it.

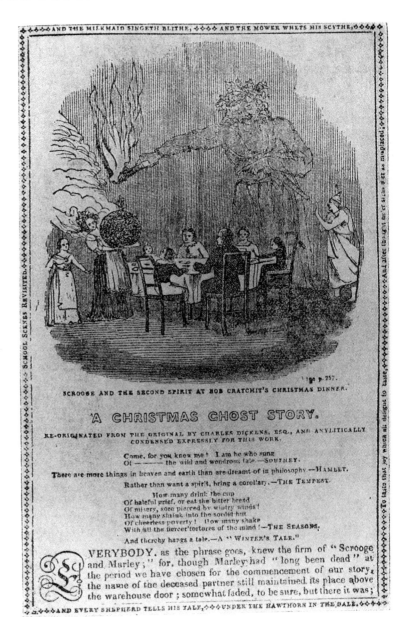

The infamous pirated version of *A Christmas Carol*, published in *Parley's Illuminated Library*, January 1844

He realized that if he did not respond like a 'sledge-hammer' over a small volume like *A Christmas Carol*, 'I shall be beset by hundreds of the same crew, when I come out with a long story'. The defendants, Messrs Lee and Haddock, moved to dissolve the injunction on the grounds that Dickens had taken no action when, three years earlier, *Parley's Illuminated Library* had 'analysed, abridged, re-originated and published the plaintiff's well known and then recently published works *The Old Curiosity Shop* and *Barnaby Rudge*'.

It was also claimed that the writer, Henry Hewitt, had 'made very considerable improvements, and in some instances large original additions', such as inventing a carol of sixty lines for Tiny Tim's song 'about a lost child travelling in the snow'. The defendants also claimed that their writer had 'tastefully remedied' what were described as 'numerous incongruities' and 'defects or wants of harmony'. Mr Hewitt himself attested to the fact that he had found Dickens' book so filled with flaws that he had been induced 'in numerous instances to abandon the plot of the plaintiff's tale and to substitute a more artistical style of expression and of incident'.

Coming to the court of Chancery, the case was heard before the Vice-Chancellor, Sir J. Knight Bruce, who refused to accept the defendants' propositions, demanding that they 'produce a passage which was not an expanded or contracted idea from Dickens' original book'. Whenever they offered such a passage, the judgment was given: 'That is Mr Dickens' case. Find another!'

Dickens triumphantly reported that the Vice-Chancellor considered that 'there was not a shadow of doubt upon the matter ... the piracy going beyond all previous instances'. With the judgment given in Dickens' favour, he wrote to John Forster, in a state of considerable excitement: 'The Pirates are beaten flat. They are bruised, bloody, battered, smashed, squelched, and utterly undone.'

But, unfortunately, there were yet more twists in the tale to come. Being given judgment did not ensure that Dickens would necessarily receive compensation. He demanded £1,000 in damages (a sum which might have gone some way towards making up for his disappointing royalties), but Lee and Haddock declared themselves bankrupt and Dickens had to pursue his claim against their assignees whose situation turned out to be 'quite desperate'.

By the end of January 1844, Dickens was forced to admit that due to 'the villainy of the law, which after declaring me robbed, obliges me to bring action against men for whom it demands no security for the expenses to which I shall be put'. Despite facing legal fees of £300, Dickens remained resolute: 'I declare war against the Black Flag; and down it shall come, if strong and constant hauling will do it.'

Four months later, Dickens still hadn't achieved a settlement and since the defendants had no assets, he finally abandoned his suits against 'the bankrupt Pirates'. He remained liable, however, for the court costs, a sum which eventually amounted to around £700. 'I shall not easily forget,' he bitterly wrote two years later, when he was again troubled by plagiarists, 'the expense, and anxiety, and horrible injustice of the Carol case, wherein, in asserting the plainest right on earth, I was really treated as if I were the robber instead of the robbed.'

Now that the author is no longer around to protest (and his book is no longer in copyright), re-originations of *A Christmas Carol* proliferate. Dickens himself, it should be said, provided what is, perhaps, the most succinct synopsis of his story when, in 1868, he added a series of descriptive headlines for each of the chapters. Although not strictly an abridgement, it certainly attempts to capture the essential elements of the story:

STAVE ONE:
Out upon Merry Christmas! – God bless you, merry gentleman! – Scrooge's Fireside – The Ghost – The Ghost's departure

STAVE TWO:
Another unearthly Visitor – Scrooge's School-Days – The Fezziwig Ball – Scrooge's old Love – Expecting a Third Visitor

STAVE THREE:
Christmas Shops – At Bob Cratchit's – Tiny Tim And Mr Scrooge – Over Land and Sea – Games at Forfeits – Ignorance and Want

STAVE FOUR:
A Death has occurred – Ghoules – Poor Tiny Tim! – The name of the dead man

STAVE FIVE:
A delightful Boy – Scrooge reclaimed by Christmas

For the many contemporary writers and editors who have embarked on an abridgement

Illustration by Arthur Rackham (1915)

of *A Christmas Carol*, the first stumbling-block is invariably Dickens' opening sentence: 'Marley was dead: to begin with.'

Apart from such oddities as the version which opens by establishing the period – 'This story begins just after Queen Victoria came to the throne' – most start straight in with Marley's surviving partner:

It was Christmas Eve. Ebenezer Scrooge was working at his desk ...
    or
Once upon a time on Christmas Eve, Ebenezer Scrooge sat busy in his counting-house ...

There is also the occasional volume that begins with enumerating the failings of this character: 'Ebenezer Scrooge, merchant in the City of London, cared for one thing only: money. Not for what it could buy, but for itself alone ...'

Dickens' own description of Scrooge – 'Oh! But he was a tight-fisted hand at the grindstone, Scrooge! a squeezing, wrenching, grasping, scraping, clutching, covetous old sinner!' – has particularly suffered by abridgment. In one book it is reduced to: 'Oh! he was a hard, tight-fisted old man!'; in another: 'He was a mean, close-fisted old miser'; elsewhere, 'he was a hard, sour-tempered man of business, intent only on saving and making money ...' But perhaps the most unlikely rendition is one that reads: 'Oh! but he was a tight-fisted old geezer, that Scrooge!'

Brevity may well be the soul of wit, but the briefer versions of *A Christmas Carol* are not necessarily among the wittiest. In one of the shortest (and, at only 8 x 7 centimetres, one of the smallest), Dickens' text is scarcely recognizable; it opens:

It will surprise you all very much to hear that there was once a man who did not like Christmas. In fact, he had been heard on several occasions to use the word humbug with regard to it. His name was Scrooge ...

And, fourteen pages later, it ends:

Tiny Tim did not die, not a bit of it ... Mr Scrooge loved him, and well he might, for was it not Tiny Tim, who had unconsciously, through the Christmas dream-spirit, touched his hard heart, and caused him to become a good and happy man.

Nicholas Clark recalls having seen what is probably the perfect minimalist version, comprising three thick cardboard pages. The first, depicting a nasty fellow in a night-cap, began the story with words to this effect: 'Once there was a horrible man called Scrooge.' The next page – 'He was visited by three ghosts,' – showed three traditional white-sheeted spectres, all appearing simultaneously. Lastly, came a picture of a smiling man: 'And he became nice.'

Other abridgers have taken out with one hand and put back in with another, as with the writer who cut Marley's explanation of his fetters – 'I wear the chain I forged in life ... I made it link by link, and yard by yard' – and substituted: 'Do you see these heavy chains? Each link represents a thoughtless word or action during my life; the heavy chests – the wealth I accumulated but failed to put to good use.'

Many of these changes have been decidedly odd: such as Scrooge's former fiancée (no longer named Belle) who, rather than confront her lover, writes him a letter:

> . . . You see, there is something you love more than me – money. So, my dear Ebenezer, I hope you will remember me when you are rich. Goodbye.
> Your own sweetheart, Clara.

The sharpness of Dickens' original prose is frequently dulled – as when lines such as Scrooge's verdict: 'If they would rather die, they had better do it, and decrease the surplus population,' are rendered as 'Well, let the poor die then! There are far too many destitutes as it is.'

Elsewhere, Dickens' dramatic intentions are severely frustrated as when the pending death-sentence on Tiny Tim – 'If these shadows remain unaltered by the Future, the child will die,' – is inexplicably commuted by the Ghost of Christmas Present with the words: 'Tiny Tim is such a happy child, but he may never walk again.'

In a similar vein, is a heavily truncated version in which Tiny Tim's famous benediction appears to have been motivated by nothing more than a greedy appetite:

And so, as Tiny Tim observed when he saw the turkey arrive by Hackney cab that Christmas morning, 'God bless us, every one!'

Like that early version in *Parley's Illuminated Library*, most of these retellings (often described as being in 'simple language') suffer from the loss of Dickens' imaginative descriptions; so the account of Marley's face in the knocker having 'a dismal light about it, like a bad lobster in a dark cellar', becomes changed to 'a dismal shade of green, rather like bad fish glowing in the dark'.

Poor Marley has, repeatedly, been a candidate for the chop: in one edition he was obliged to do all his haunting in knocker-form; while, in several other versions, the knocker is dispensed with altogether. One is tempted to wish that those responsible for such uglifications might find themselves haunted by the Ghost of Charles Dickens himself!

Today's abridgers and simplifiers may be aiming their travesties at the very young or those with reading difficulties (indeed some of them contain questions and lists of 'New Words', such as 'bedpost', 'undertaker' and, surprisingly, 'tiny'). However, the piracy against which Dickens' was fighting was motivated solely by the enormous popularity of the book; a popularity which also clearly indicated a need for there to be a sequel . . .

As Like the Carol as May Be

It had caused Dickens more anxiety and heartache than anything else he had ever written; but it also turned out to be one of his most popular books. Dickens now referred to himself in print as being 'the author of *A Christmas Carol* in prose and other works', and was well aware that he needed to follow up its success with another story. In the short term, however, he still had money problems.

With no quick or easy remedy to the financial débâcle over *A Christmas Carol*, and with the birth of their fifth child, Francis Jeffrey, Dickens decided to let the house in Devonshire Terrace and take the family abroad where they might live more cheaply. Leaving England, they travelled to Genoa in Italy, living first in the gaudy but dilapidated Villa di Bella Vista at Albano (described by Dickens as a 'pink gaol'), then in the beautiful Palazzo Peschiere, where the novelist was soon busy writing a successor to *A Christmas Carol*.

In a whimsical article entitled 'Sketches by Zizz', published in *Punch*, in 1986, Keith Waterhouse speculates on how Dickens might have approached the task of creating that sequel. Sitting before the fire, he fantasized, Dickens

must have mused on how close he had been to getting things wrong with his last book: after all, he had almost called the central character 'Ebenezer Golightly', and had very nearly made him an alcoholic instead of a miser – the book, Waterhouse confides, was to have been called *The Reformed Drunkard*!

Now Dickens had to come up with a new idea. Various titles suggest themselves – such as *A Christmas Cracker* – before he finally decided on a story, set in France, about the reformation of a profligate character who might possibly be called 'Sydney Carlton'. It would open with the words: 'It was the best of times, it was the worst of times... (etcetera, etcetera)... it was Christmas Eve'; and would end with the line: 'It is a far, far better thing that I do than I have ever done, ho ho ho.' According to Waterhouse, Dickens would call this new book – *A Tale of Two Christmases*!

In reality, inspiration for a sequel to *A Christmas Carol* came from endlessly hearing the bells of Genoa, which Dickens, at first, had found 'maddening'. Then, suddenly they gave him an idea. Writing to his friend, John Forster, Dickens quoted Falstaff from Act 3 of Shakespeare's

Henry IV, Part Two: 'We have heard The chimes at midnight, Master Shallow!' And *The Chimes* became the title for his new Christmas Book.

Although Dickens missed the crowded streets of London 'to plunge into at night', he was as energized over this story as he had been over *A Christmas Carol*: 'I am in a regular, ferocious excitement with *The Chimes*... I am fierce to finish in a spirit bearing some affinity to those of truth and mercy, and to shame the cruel and canting'. Subtitled: 'A Goblin Story of Some Bells That Rang an Old Year Out and a New Year In', the book was completed on 3 November 1844, whereupon Dickens had 'what women call "a real good cry"'.

Dickens believed *The Chimes* would prove 'a great blow for the poor' but he also wanted the story 'to be tender too and cheerful; as like the Carol in that respect as may be, and as unlike it as much as a thing can be. The duration of the action will resemble it a little, but I trust to the novelty of the machinery to carry that off; and if my design be anything at all, it has a grip upon the very throat of the public.'

This new Christmas volume would provide Dickens with another opportunity to attack those who supported Malthus' theories on the 'surplus population':

'Ah!' cried Mr Filer with a groan... 'A man may live to be as old as Methuselah... and may labour all his life for the benefit of such people as those; and may heap up facts on figures, facts on figures, facts on figures, mountains high and dry; and he can no more hope to persuade 'em that they have no right or business to be married, than he can hope to persuade 'em that they have no earthly right or business to be born.'

The Spirits of the Bells by Daniel Maclise, from *The Chimes* (1844)

However, whereas *A Christmas Carol* had been a story of Christmas Eve, *The Chimes* was a tale of New Year's Eve; the Christmas ghosts replaced by a group of goblin spirits who lived among the bells:

He saw them ugly, handsome, crippled, exquisitely formed. He saw them young, he saw them old, he saw them kind, he saw them cruel, he saw them merry, he saw them grim; he saw them dance, and heard them sing; he saw them tear their hair, and heard them howl. He saw the air thick with them.

The most apparent difference was that the sombre mood in parts of *The Chimes* was unrelieved by the kind of purely celebratory episodes that are one of the joys of *A Christmas Carol*. It was also an altogether more satirical tract, with controversial talk of 'a Sea of Time' that would one day rise and sweep away, 'like leaves', those who wrong and oppress the poor.

In order to gauge the power of his new book, Dickens returned to London in December to read *The Chimes* aloud to a circle of friends including John Forster, Thomas Carlyle, William Macready and the artist Daniel Maclise who, afterwards told Kate Dickens that he did not think 'there was ever such a triumphant hour for Charles'; the audience, he reported, had given way to 'shrieks of laughter... and floods of tears as a relief to them'.

Dickens returned to Genoa for Christmas, confident that he had 'written a tremendous book' that would create 'a great uproar'. Published on 16 December 1844, *The Chimes* sold almost 20,000 copies over the next few months.

But the critics were divided; and hostile notices appeared of a kind that had never been generated by *A Christmas Carol*. Whilst some considered it 'the finest thing Dickens has ever written', others complained that 'the fierce tone of menace to the rich is unreasonable and ignorant'.

Dickens was back in London in June 1845, involving himself in all kinds of projects. As well as being actor-manager of an amateur theatrical group, he was also toying with the idea of starting-up, and editing, a cheap weekly magazine that would feature what he called the Carol philosophy: 'cheerful views, sharp anatomization of humbug, jolly good temper' and 'a vein of glowing, hearty, generous, mirthful, beaming references in everything to Home and Fireside.' This periodical would be called *The Cricket*, and would carry a quotation from a volume of Natural History: 'A Cheerful creature that chirrups on the Hearth'.

Dickens told Forster that he thought of producing 'a prospectus on the subject of the Cricket that should put everybody in a good temper, and make such a dash at people's fenders and arm-chairs as hasn't been made for many a long day... and I would chirp, chirp, chirp away in every number until I chirped it up to – well, you shall say how many hundred thousand!'

The Cricket, however, was put aside when Dickens became involved with plans for establishing a new Liberal newspaper, the *Daily News*, which he was also to edit. Meanwhile Dickens had not totally abandoned his little Cricket: 'It would be a delicate and beautiful fancy for a Christmas book,' he noted, 'making the Cricket a little household god – silent in the wrong and sorrow of the tale, and loud again when all went well and happy'.

It was in August that Dickens got 'a good notion' for *The Cricket* – what he called 'a decided chirp!' – but November found him, as he put it, grinding his teeth, and the new story was not finished until the beginning of December. *The Cricket on the Hearth* – subtitled 'A Fairy Tale of Home' – introduced another remarkable cavalcade of Dickens characters, including the toy-maker, Caleb Plummer, and his poor blind daughter.

'To have a Cricket on the Hearth,' says one of the characters, 'is the luckiest thing in all the world.' And it was certainly a lucky omen for Dickens. Dedicated to Lord Jeffrey, who had been so full of praise for *A Christmas Carol, The Cricket* proved hugely popular with the public and the critics, one of whom described the appearance of a new Christmas book as being 'as regularly expected as a pantomime'.

Within a month of publication, no fewer than seventeen dramatizations of the story were being presented on the London stage, though they must have been hard pressed to capture the book's more elusive magic:

> Good Heaven, how it chirped! Its shrill sharp, piercing voice resounded through the house and seemed to twinkle in the outer darkness like a Star. There was an indescribable little trill and tremble in it, at its loudest which suggested its being carried off its legs, and made to leap again, by its own intense enthusiasm...

Illustration by John Leech for
The Cricket on the Hearth (1845)

In 1846, having resigned from the editorship of the *Daily News*, Dickens and his family were abroad once more, this time in Switzerland, first in Geneva and then in Lausanne. Another novel was begun – *Dombey and Son* – and, between whiles, Dickens began struggling with another seasonal volume: 'An odd shadowy undefined idea is at work within me, that I could connect a great battle-field somehow with my little Christmas story'.

The pressures of producing the monthly installments of *Dombey and Son* left Dickens with little time or inspiration, and he seriously thought of giving up his plan to produce a new Christmas book; Dickens was no longer the man who had once crammed the writing of *A Christmas Carol* between writing issues of *Martin Chuzzlewit*.

However, he kept at it and *The Battle of Life*, 'A Love Story', eventually appeared in December 1846. The book is decidedly the odd man out: containing no goblins, no fairies and no spirits. In the opinion of one commentator it is 'the feeblest piece of writing of Dickens' entire career'.

On the reputation of the earlier books, *The Battle of Life* sold 23,000 copies, but the critics dismissed it as nothing more than 'exaggerated, absurd, impossible sentimentality'. This response probably persuaded Dickens – who, the following year, was still writing *Dombey and Son* – to give up any idea of writing a story for the next Christmas, although he was 'very loath to lose the money. And still more so to leave any gap at Christmas firesides which I ought to fill.'

Not that he was without an idea; although the one that was occupying him was, he confessed, 'very ghostly and wild'. The following autumn, he was staying in Broadstairs, Kent, and attempting to do something with that 'wild idea'. By November, Dickens reported that he was once more 'grinding' away at a Christmas book – a curiously significant phrase when one recalls how little 'grinding' had been required to write *A Christmas Carol*.

Entitled *The Haunted Man and the Ghost's Bargain*, the new book appeared in December 1848, and told the strange history of Mr Redlaw, a chemist who is haunted by the ghost of his dead

self, who offers to cancel all remembrance of the 'sorrow, wrong and trouble' that he has known. 'Of course,' Dickens wrote, 'my point is that bad and good are inextricably linked in remembrance, and that you could not choose the enjoyment of recollecting only the good.'

That aim certainly impressed itself on the novelist, Robert Louis Stevenson, who – after reading *A Christmas Carol* and *The Haunted Man* – wrote to a friend:

I wonder if you have ever read Dickens' Christmas Books? ... I have only read two yet, but I have cried my eyes out, and had a terrible fight not to sob. But oh, dear God, they are good – and I feel so good after them – I shall do good and lose no time – I want to go out and comfort someone – I shall give money. Oh, what a jolly thing it is for a man to have written books like these and just filled people's hearts with pity.

Stevenson's reaction appears to endorse Dickens' conviction that *The Haunted Man* would appeal to 'thoughtful readers'; thoughtful critics, however, were unmoved. If ghosts 'talk such nonsense as Mr Dickens' ghost talks,' commented one, then it was scarcely surprising that people were afraid of them!

Nevertheless, there were a number of successful theatrical versions of *The Haunted Man*. It was first staged, during the month in which the book was published, at London's Adelphi Theatre. Dramatized by Mark Lemon, one of the founders of *Punch* (working at break-neck speed from proofs of the book), the play used remarkable visual illusions that were among the latest creations of the popular stage magicians. The phantom made a spectacular entrance gliding from the roof and Dickens later recalled: 'I well remember the strangely weird effect of the cleverly-managed first appearance of the ghost.'

Another production of *The Haunted Man* opened on Christmas Eve, 1862, and on this occasion, the ghost found it possible to pass through walls and furniture. This startling effect was achieved by means of a device known as 'Pepper's Ghost'. Invented by John Henry Pepper and Henry Dircks, the illusion used a large sheet of glass (unseen by the audience) that was angled out from the stage over the orchestra pit. In the pit, an actor playing the ghost was illuminated so that his image was reflected up onto the glass. The ghost would then appear, translucently, on stage where an actor could respond to its presence – even (in some plays) attempt to engage it in a fight. It is appropriate that a story by Dickens, a distinguished amateur conjuror, should have provided the first public demonstration of a classic magic illusion.

When Dickens had completed his second Christmas book, *The Chimes*, he wrote that he believed he had 'knocked the Carol out of the field', but it was not to be. Not even the tremendous theatrical success of *The Haunted Man* could eclipse the popularity of *A Christmas Carol*; which is probably why so many others have tried so desperately to recreate the formula...

Illustration by John Leech for *The Haunted Man* (1848)

8

You Have Never Seen the Like of Me Before!

Charles Dickens described himself as 'the inventor of this sort of story', but other hands have subsequently tinkered with the invention. Whether viewed as outrageous plagiarism or as the sincerest form of flattery, it is a fact that, for 150 years, people have been rewriting *A Christmas Carol* and telling new stories about Scrooge and company with such titles as 'A Modern Scrooge', 'The New Christmas Carol' or 'Scrooge Up to Date'.

One of the earliest of these, written anonymously in 1869, had the rather protracted title *Christmas Eve with the Spirits; or, the Canon's Wanderings through Ways Unknown; with some further tidings of the lives of Scrooge and Tiny Tim.* Those further tidings revealed that Scrooge had given up his counting-house in order to pursue philanthropic works. The firm was now managed by his nephew and Bob Cratchit had been promoted to foreman. When, according to the author, Scrooge passes from the world, he is touchingly mourned by the child whose life he has saved:

Tiny Tim laid a wreath of roses upon the coffin, and would have flung himself upon it in his passionate grief, had not they withheld him. – Most truly could it be said of him, 'In sure and certain hope of the resurrection to eternal life,' for nobly had he redeemed his time.

Many other writers have since speculated on what became of Scrooge and friends. Keith Waterhouse dreamed up a comic fantasy in which Dickens thought of writing a sequel in which Cratchit inherited the counting-house. The Great Author (via Waterhouse) turns Bob into a character that out-Scrooges Scrooge. Confusing some details from his original, Dickens imagines a scene in which Cratchit's son, 'Tiny Ted', gazes into a toy-shop window, as his father's voice rings in his ears: 'Christmas presents? Pah! Barley sugar! You'll have your Christmas present, my boy – a new surgical boot!'

Another mean Cratchit appears in Andrew Angus Dalrymple's 1985 book, *God Bless Us Every One!* Now senior partner in the firm of 'Cratchit

Cartoon by Peter Brookes from *The Times*, 1990

and Scrooge', Bob has provided a home for the elderly Scrooge, but finds the old man something of an embarrassment. When Cratchit learns that he might soon become Sir Robert, he decides that it is time for his former employer to live elsewhere. This unhappy state of affairs is eventually remedied and – as a reward for helping to cure Queen Victoria's gout – Ebenezer Scrooge also receive a knighthood!

In 'The Ghost of Christmas Endless', a piece published by Russell Baker in the *New York Times* in 1973, Tiny Tim is the successful one, having become a wealthy bookmaker: as for the rest: Mrs Cratchit runs a Turkey Take-away shop, Scrooge's nephew leaves his wife and goes to Samoa to paint, while Scrooge lives in a trailer park in New Jersey.

'Old Scrooge on the Day After', which appeared in the *New York Critic* some years earlier, in 1905, shows Ebenezer suffering a relapse; come Boxing Day he is once more maintaining: 'A rich man has no business wasting his estate on miscellaneous charity at Christmas ... It's plain to me that somebody has been giving the people too much meat to eat and it has made them cocky.'

Scrooge expressed similar views in a rare modern-day interview, conducted by the *Daily Telegraph's* Christopher Fildes on Christmas Eve, 1993. The skinflint is overheard telling Bob Cratchit that he would give Tiny Tim a job as a messenger – not out of compassion, but in order to maintain the company's quota of disabled employees. 'No,' Scrooge interrupts himself, remembering the niceties of political correctness,

'I mustn't say that nowadays, must I? Leglessly challenged.'

Another version in which Dickens' story is turned upon its head was told, by Thomas Meehan, in 'A Christmas Carol, Revised and Updated for 1969'. In this account, published in the magazine *Mademoiselle*, Scrooge is a New York businessman noted for his generosity and philanthropy. However, he acquires more appropriately Scrooge-like attributes following visits from three spirits – named Holly, Belle and Carol – who teach him 'the modern meaning of Christmas' and eventually help him to become 'as mean, miserly and generally unpleasant as any old skinflint could possibly be'. Scrooge, having observed the Cratchits laughing at his gullibility (rather than raising a glass to toast his health), turns over a new leaf and gives his clerk a thoroughly deserved 37 per cent cut in salary!

The *Sunday Telegraph*'s wine writer, Robert Joseph, found Scrooge, in December 1993, in considerably more genial mood as he hosted Mr Dickens' annual Christmas party: serving champagne to Miss Haversham, late-bottled port to Mr Pickwick and a humble country wine to Uriah Heap, while sampling a bottle of Australian chardonnay brought back by Abel Magwitch from his time in penal servitude.

Bernard Levin, writing in *The Times*, pondered on what might have happened if Scrooge's nephew, Fred, had taken seriously the old man's comment: 'I wonder you don't go into Parliament.' Had he done so, he asks, what kind of a career might have followed? Levin imagines him as a Radical MP, attempting to introduce various pieces of seasonal legislation, such as 'The Relief of the Poor in Excessively Cold Weather (Distribution of Hot Chocolate) Bill' and 'The Smile for the Festive Season (Cordiality to Strangers) Bill'; but these enlightened notions sadly win no support, and, 'a sadder and a wiser man', he applies for the Chiltern Hundreds and leaves Westminster. Fred spends his declining years trying to persuade Scrooge to revert to his original anti-Christmas attitude. 'He died,' Levin concludes, 'in an accident at home when a Christmas tree fell on him.'

For John Mortimer, the burning question was: what happened to Tiny Tim in later years? His speculations appeared in a short story, 'The Return of Ebenezer Scrooge', published in the *Sunday Telegraph* in December 1992, and subsequently broadcast on BBC radio as 'Not So Tiny Tim'. The setting is a town in North Africa; the time is Christmas Day, 1894: Sir Timothy Cratchit is entertaining guests – including Oscar Wilde and Lord Alfred Douglas. Gone are the days of 'God bless us every one!' Sir Timothy no longer holds with Christmas: 'That is why,' he explains, 'I have chosen to live in a country without holly, or snow, or carol singers ... Above all, in a country without turkey...'

Sir Timothy's jaundiced view of Christmas sprang from bad memories of a Festive Season past, when 'some foolish fellow' had given the Cratchit family 'a huge beast of a bird, about the size of a Brontosaurus', and they had lived on cold turkey for weeks! Despite this early set-back in life, he had achieved success: as a young employee of 'Scrooge and Marley', he borrowed his employer's Turkey Fund, 'invested it for a month in Oriental railways and made a 200 per cent profit before the company crashed'. Like the late Mr Marley he was, clearly, a good man of business; but (also like Mr M.) he didn't know that mankind should have been his business.

Then comes the ghostly visitation, but only two spirits this time: the Ghost of Christmas Future and the ghost of the man who had been a second father to him, Ebenezer Scrooge. Yanked out of bed and hauled across a century of time, Sir Timothy sees terrible visions of Christmases to Come: visions of rape, massacre, torture and starvation; visions of international warfare and civil disorder. The world's problems, it seems, have not been much relieved by Scrooge's provision of Christmas turkeys. As the spirit explains: 'There simply aren't enough turkeys to go round.' So what can the contrite Sir Timothy do?

> The Spirit had moved very close to him...
> 'All I can tell you to do is to look about you. See everything, however much it distresses you or even turns your stomach. So men and women like you may change a little. It's all we can hope for...'

Those familiar with the characters of Dickens' may not readily identify the name of Constable Porlock, yet – according to a short story published in the *Daily Mail* in 1993, from the pen of the award-winning children's writer, Leon Garfield – this individual was right there, in foggy London, when the events described in

A Christmas Carol actually occurred. Constable Porlock – possible a relation of that person who interrupted Coleridge's dream of 'Xanadu' – calls in at the Queen's Arms (opposite Scrooge's house) for a noggin of rum and brandy. Suddenly, he sees the ghost of Jacob Marley who announces that he is *en route* to haunt his former partner. The Constable further witnesses the other visitations to Scrooge, each of which he carefully records in his notebook:

> Christmas Morning. One o'clock. Fog lifting a little. Observed Mr Scrooge's residence. Light showing in first-floor front. Observed Mr Scrooge, in the company of small, white-clad personage whose head appeared to be lit up like a candle, emerging from the said window and proceeding in an easterly direction, some twenty feet above the chimney-pots.

These strange events spur Constable Porlock to reflect upon his own past, present and future Christmases with Mrs Porlock: once a slender, pretty young thing he had kissed under the mistletoe; now a stout woman and a terrible cook ('with a mania for gravy as thick and sour as the fog'); and soon to be a widow with no tears to shed for her dead husband. At the precise moment that E. Scrooge Esq. wakes up to the fact that he hasn't missed Christmas, the Constable's own daydream comes to an end. Outside the pub, he intercepts a young lad who is running an errand for an hysterical Mr Scrooge:

'Boy!' called out Constable Porlock... 'Do you know the flower shop next to the poulterer's?'

'I'll say I do,' said the boy.

'Do they still have their hot-house flowers?'

'I'll say they do!'

'Then tell 'em to send a dozen red roses to Mrs Porlock of 27 Pentonville Road, and tell 'em to put in a card saying, "A Merry Christmas, darling, and don't forget the mistletoe"!'

Another police investigation is conducted by Inspector Mudrick of Scotland Yard, in Marion Markham's detective story, 'What Really Happened to Scrooge?', published in *Blackwood's Magazine* in 1973. During an inquiry into how and why Scrooge has become a reformed character, suspicion falls on many – including Tiny Tim, whom Mudrick suspects of concealing his real intentions behind a 'pleasant smile and cheerful manner'.

Eventually, Scrooge's housekeeper – a former medium named Mrs Potter – is placed under arrest for using psychic powers to raise spirits with which to scare Scrooge into becoming a philanthropist. Although Mrs Potter clearly hoped to make money out of the altered Scrooge, he chooses not to press charges. He decides, in fact, to maintain his goody-goody image on the principle that he is likely to receive so many invitations to dine out, that he will be able to drastically economize on the cost of living!

In addition to sequels and parodies, there have been any number of stories that, if not direct copies, are certainly very much in the style of *A Christmas Carol*; one such, published in 1850, was *Christmas Shadows* by W.H. Shepstone about a stony-hearted clothing manufacturer named Cranch, whose employees – cutters and seamstresses – suffer from his callous attitude towards pay and working conditions. Visited by Starvation and Conscience, Cranch is shown his own death and the resulting anguish suffered by his daughters who are forced to work as seamstresses until one dies and the other commits suicide; whereupon Cranch wakes up, sees the light and triples his workers' pay.

Published around the same time, was *Faces in the Fire*, done up in an identical format to the Christmas Books: crimson cloth with a gilt design showing a grate with a crowd of strange faces emerging from the smoke and flames. Subtitled 'A Story for the Season', it combined elements from *A Christmas Carol*, *The Haunted Man* and *The Chimes*. It tells of a despairing young man who falls into a melancholic reverie before his fire: 'Everywhere, everywhere, the Faces in the Fire were haunting him, and whispering dreadful words of black Temptation to his Heart. And Shapes of fear and horror, black ugliness and grim tormenting dread, filled all the air...'

Then, 150 pages later, the Presence of the Fire steps from the grate and brings the young man hope (or, rather, Hope) by explaining that 'in everything exists some Good, though it be but an atom':

'Forgive the wrong, and I will doubt no longer,' groaned the wretched man. And the light about Its head grew so bright that he dared not look upon it.

'My subjects must have Faith in Good. Ponder my words: — reflect: do good: be charitable: just: cheerful: pious: and I will believe you doubt no longer!'

If such passages seem to owe some of their inspiration to Dickens' story, then other episodes – particularly those descriptive of Christmas in the City – are little more than downright robbery. Remember Dickens' account of shops on Christmas Eve, and in particular, of the Grocers? Obviously the author of *Faces in the Fire* also remembered them. A brief comparison will illustrate:

A Christmas Carol: There were bunches of grapes ... The figs were moist and pulpy ... The French plums blushed in modest tartness from their highly-decorated boxes ... The blended scents of tea and coffee ... so grateful to the nose ... The sticks of cinnamon so long and straight ...

Faces in the Fire: There were grocers' shops, with windows filled with rich ripe plums and tempting grapes; luscious foreign fruits in natty little boxes set round in paper lace ... glistening tea with the bloom upon it, and coffee with fragrant scent; long sticks of cinnamon ...

Such effrontery is, as Dickens might have said, enough to make the reader 'feel faint and subsequently bilious'!

Faces in the Fire was written by George F. Pardon, hiding behind the pseudonym 'Redgap'. Someone less self-effacing was the popular American writer, Horatio Alger, who contributed a piece entitled 'Job Warner's Christmas' to the December 1863 issue of *Harper's New Monthly Magazine*. Although it is only the palest of ghosts of *A Christmas Carol*, its inspiration is unmistakable. One Christmas Eve, Job Warner, a bank-clerk, asks his boss for a rise in salary, but is refused. On his way home, he comes across a girl in the street who is an orphan. Forgoing family Christmas presents, he spends some money on the child and takes her to his home. Job's employer witnessing this charitable deed, decides to raise his clerk's salary and makes provision for the orphan.

G.K. Chesterton, a keen admirer of Dickens and his Christmas ghost story, ventured a parody of his own in 1909, entitled 'The Modern Scrooge'. This story concerned Mr Vernon-Smith, a gentleman with a mission for civilizing London's poor. Being Christmas Eve, Mr Vernon-Smith gives a reading of *A Christmas Carol* to the charwomen of Tooting, telling them that, in their day and age, 'a mad wicked old miser like Scrooge would be quite impossible'. Returning home, he refuses to give money to a beggar and, the next minute, is knocked out by a well-aimed snowball. Vernon-Smith dreams that he is standing on high ground, looking down on children playing in the snow. He longs to join them, but is afraid to jump. Eventually, he finds the courage to do so, and makes the leap in faith. At which point he wakes up and finds himself being arrested as a drunk. However, says Chesterton, 'he did not mind, since the crime of drunkenness is infinitely less than that of spiritual pride'.

A few months after the publication of *A Christmas Carol*, a religious magazine, the *Christian Remembrancer*, criticized Dickens' use of the phrase: 'It is good to be children sometimes, and never better than at Christmas, when its mighty Founder was a child himself!' This, they maintained was a piece of blasphemous irreverence; nevertheless, Christians have not been slow in turning the story into a tract. One such leaflet turned the story into a cartoon-strip showing Scrooge's reclamation achieved, not through the intervention of supernatural beings,

but through the evangelical witness of Bob Cratchit. The clerk tells his employer that God is going to judge him for his sinfulness and hands him a tract: 'Read this, sir. It will show you how to miss God's wrath!' Thanks to this publication – and the prayers of Tiny Tim – Scrooge sees the error of his ways and becomes a Christian, handing out presents to the Cratchit children.

Another, less edifying, comic-strip parody appeared in 1989, in the adult comic, *Viz*. 'Ebenezer Colon's Christmas Carol' recounts the tasteless tale of hard-hearted toy-shop owner, Mr Colon, and his hard-up assistant, Bob Cricket. Colon is visited by a solitary ghost who shows him, among other things, the grave of Cricket's crippled son, Tiny Tom.

When Colon wakes up on Christmas morning, he is a changed man. He rushes out into

'Humbug?' by J.T.C., a 1980s 'Send The Light' religious tract

Christmas Present and 'Sadstone' (Gladstone). An 1893
Punch cartoon by Sir John Tenniel

the snow to find the child: 'Come along with me, young fellow!' he says, 'I'll see to it there's a grand Christmas dinner at Bob's house this year!'

Ebenezer Colon is true to his word; except that, instead of the ubiquitous turkey, he arrives with Tiny Tom on a platter, stuffed, cooked and with an apple in his mouth. 'Well,' Colon explains, as they sit down to dine, 'he wasn't going to last more than a couple of months anyway. I saw it in this dream...'

Scrooge and Company have also been repeatedly high-jacked by political satirists. As early as December 1885, they were at work in *Punch* with 'A Christmas Carol: Being a few scattered staves, from a familiar Composition...' In this parody, Scroogestone (Liberal Prime Minister, William Ewart Gladstone) is faced with problems from his past and present political career when he receives a visit from the ghost of Bendizzy (former Conservative premiere, Benjamin Disraeli).

Gladstone made another Scroogish appearance in *Punch* – this time disguised as 'Sadstone' – in 1893, shortly before leaving office. The cartoonist, John Tenniel, depicted him confronting a doomful Spirit of Christmas Present, carrying a sword inscribed 'STRIFE' and torch marked 'ANARCHY'. The Spirit's familiar largesse now includes a 'PARTY PIE', a bowl of 'PARTY SPIRIT' and assorted items bearing such labels as 'CAPITAL' (on a cake); 'EASTERN QUESTION' (on a turkey) and 'IRISH QUESTION' (on a sucking pig).

Other political targets of the Christmas Carollers have included: in 1901, the soon-to-be Tory premier, Arthur Balfour, haunted by the Ghost of 'Old Morality'; and, in 1993, a terrified John Major facing Margaret Thatcher (drawn with the deliciously poisoned pen of Gerald Scarfe) as a handbag-carrying Ghost of Christmas Past.

At the opposite end of the political spectrum, Britain's communist newspaper, the *Daily Worker*, carried a polemical parody in 1932, declaring: 'Scrooge still lives! ... His real name is

Mr Profit, Mr G. Profit (G. for Grab).' But they have news for this prosperous gentleman: the people are massing to smash his world and rebuild it for themselves:

Already they are doing it, Scrooge. Your days are numbered... They are gathering in their thousands, and their millions. Demanding work and wages. Fighting hunger. Demanding the release of their comrades. Hunger has not crushed, nor will prisons daunt them. They are gathering, Scrooge...

Workers' power also features in a later parody, written for *The Nation* in 1984, by Richard Lingeman. Scrooge runs a blacking factory and his clerk, Cratchit, is 'a lazy, worthless agitator type' who is trying to get his fellow workers to form a union. When he succeeds in this and calls a strike, Scrooge decides it will be easier to run his blacking factory somewhere else — and moves it to India!

Another story, dangerously challenging the conservative work ethic, appears in 'Famous Stories as Told by Famous People', a series presented in America's satirical *Mad* magazine. Former President Ronald Reagan is cast as the storyteller for *A Christmas Carol* and his Ebenezer Scrooge is 'a hard working businessman', contending with a clerk unwilling 'to roll up his sleeves and do an honest day's work or go to night school and pull himself up by his bootstraps'.

Then Scrooge has 'a terrible nightmare', in which he is visited by the usual quota of spirits who — 'using Marxist-Lenin propaganda techniques' — make Scrooge feel guilty about being successful while Cratchit is a failure. The reformed Scrooge unwisely squanders his fortune on buying Christmas presents and dinners, as well as paying Tiny Tim's medical bills — all of which add to the inflationary spiral. 'Well, we can only pray,' concludes the storyteller, 'that next Christmas, Mr Scrooge will be visited by three Conservative ghosts who will show him the error of his ways.'

It is a testament to our familiarity with Dickens' story that these many rewritings and updatings are so readily understood. For example, it is Scrooge's original encounter with Marley that we are remembering as we laugh at this modern parody, written in 1922, in which Scrooge — manufacturer of doornails — dismisses his secretary on Christmas Eve. Suddenly, the phone rings:

Hello... Who? ... Jacob Marley, my late partner? Don't try to be funny — he's been dead seven years... WHAT? His GHOST? ... No, I don't believe it. Get Conan Doyle to write a magazine article about it and I might listen, but I'm not in the habit of believing anything until I deposit it in the bank...

That version, by George Kaufman and Marc Connelly, was published in the *Bookman* magazine — rather unusually — in the form of a play. Not that there was anything new about the idea of dramatizing *A Christmas Carol*: indeed, people have been turning the book into plays, musicals, operas

An engraving from the *Illustrated London News* showing a scene from Edward Stirling's 1844 dramatization of *A Christmas Carol* staged at the Adelphi Theatre

and ballets ever since it was first published.

Within just two months of the book's publication, musical scores – such as 'The Christmas Carol Quadrille' – were being composed and no less than eight dramatized versions were simultaneously presented on the London stage. At the Royal Surrey Theatre there was C.Z. Barnett's play *A Christmas Carol; or the Miser's Warning!*; while at the Theatre Royal Adelphi you could see Edward Stirling's *A Christmas Carol, or Past, Present, and Future*; and at the Sadler's Wells Theatre they were presenting a version by Charles Webb, who made the most of his rivals' titles by calling his dramatization *A Christmas Carol; or, Scrooge, the Miser's Dream; or, The Past, Present, and Future*. Other productions were performed at the Britannia, Strand, Victoria, Queen's and City of London Theatres – all, to the author's chagrin, without payment of so much as a penny!

Edward Stirling's play was described as 'the only dramatic version sanctioned by C. Dickens, Esqre.' and the author was present at some of the rehearsals. As Stirling recalled in his memoirs: 'Thinking to make Tiny Tim (a pretty child) more effective, I ordered a set of irons and bandages for his supposed weak leg. When Dickens saw this tried on the child, he took me aside: "No, Stirling, no; this won't do: Remember how painful it would be to many of the audience having crippled children." '

Dickens also attended a performance of this production, commenting that it was 'better than usual' and that the actor playing Bob Cratchit seemed to enjoy his part. Nevertheless, Dickens found the whole experience a 'heart-breaking' one. 'Oh Heaven!' he wrote, 'if any forecast of this was ever in my mind!' Scrooge was portrayed by the actor O. Smith – whose real name was Richard Smith, but who had adopted the 'O' after a triumphant run in the role of Obi in *Three-fingered Jack*. Of Smith's performance, Dickens remarked that it was 'drearily better than I expected,' adding that he found it, 'a great comfort to have that kind of meat underdone'. Would that the same might be said of some subsequent Scrooges!

Stirling's dramatization was regularly revived and, in 1859, the actor J.L. Toole had a bizarre experience whilst playing Bob Cratchit, which he later recounted to Dickens. Each night, the theatre management provided a real goose and a real pudding for the Christmas dinner scene and Toole would carve these and distribute them to his 'family', who were being played by the children of the theatre's scene-shifters. The young Cratchits, who probably had little enough to eat, made short work of this dinner, but the little girl portraying Tiny Tim seemingly had the most astonishing appetite and nightly consumed huge quantities of food. At each performance, Toole heaped her plate with goose and she went to Tim's seat by the fire and gobbled it down. Only when half a goose had been thus despatched, did Toole discover that the food was being passed through the fireplace to the child's sister who was then taking it home to share with the rest of her family. Dickens, touched by this story, told Toole: 'You should have given her the whole goose.'

Three years before Dickens wrote *A Christmas Carol*, a popular play being performed was Egerton Wilks' truly romantic *Drama of The Miser*, and C.Z. Barnett's play *A Christmas Carol; or the Miser's Warning!* clearly cashed-in on such theatrical melodramas about misers' and cautionary dreams. Dickens' story underwent various changes in Barnett's dramatization and many of his narrative jokes found their way, inexplicably, into the mouth of Bob Cratchit who, at one point, tells Scrooge: 'I've been trying to warm myself by the candle for the last half hour, but not being a man of strong imagination, failed.'

The same production has mild-mannered Bob – who, in the story, never says a bad word of his employer – rather surprisingly referring to Scrooge as 'Old covetous!' This version, published 1852, also introduced a new character – 'Dark Sam' – who steals Bob's wages, and was still being staged as late as 1920 when, at Nottingham Repertory Theatre, this role was played by a very young George Sanders.

Numerous other dramatizations have followed, in Britain and America, with such titles as *The Miser*, *The Three Spirits*, *Scrooge*, *Old Scrooge* and *The Regeneration of Old Scrooge*. Like the many stage, radio, film and television adaptations which have continued to appear over the years, these versions have added to the Carol mythology. For example, the 1877 stage version, *Old Scrooge*, concludes with him being reunited with Belle, who — by the happiest of coincidences — turns out to be the widowed mother of Fred's wife!

Every time the story is turned into a piece of theatre, dramatists seem to be torn between cutting Dickens' text and putting in extravagant nonsense of their own. In one play, Bob Cratchit is obliged to put his ink back into the bottle, before leaving the office, so that it doesn't freeze overnight; in another, after enjoying the Fezziwigs' lavish hospitality, the young Scrooge pointedly observes: 'I only hope I can be half as kind and thoughtful when I have my own business.'

Sometimes, only the names have been changed to protect the dramatist's integrity; so, in one play, Belle becomes Ellen; and, in another, Mrs Dilber becomes Mrs Mildew. A long tradition of giving names to characters unnamed by Dickens began with C.Z. Barnett's decision to give Scrooge's nephew the name Fred Freeheart; while, in other dramatizations, his wife might be called Agnes or Jane. Similarly, the charity collectors have received such appropriate names

as Mr Cheerly and Mr Heartby; and Scrooge's contemporaries on the Exchange have included such gentlemen as Mr Plumstone, Mr Woolhead and Mr Blunderbone, an unlikely trio who appeared in one of the most fanciful dramatizations. Written in 1949, by Shaun Sutton, the play begins with a prologue in which a modern-day grandmother tells the story of *A Christmas Carol* to three youngsters. All kinds of elaborations have been made beginning with Scrooge finding an error of one halfpenny in Cratchit's book-keeping. Bob protests: 'Mr Marley was good enough to say that my books were the finest he had ever—' But Scrooge interrupts with 'Marley is dead! Dead as a doornail!'

Fezziwig, whom Dickens drew larger than life, is now grown beyond belief to a veritable monster of generosity: arriving home later than expected, he gives his wife a brooch as a peace-offering, to which she protests that he has given her SEVEN Christmas presents already! But it is the two Portly Gentlemen collecting for charity, who almost succeed in eclipsing the central role of Scrooge. When they first appear, they have come from visiting a number of Scrooge's fellow businessmen — companies with such names as 'Pootleberry and Squib' and 'Anderson, Henderson, Sanderson, Richardson and Son' — who have all told them that Scrooge has had 'a particularly good year'. Notwithstanding such cajolery, Scrooge still declines to contribute to their funds.

When, however, he later relents and gives them a sizeable — but, he stresses, anonymous —

donation, the two gentlemen go into a musical routine in which they list the contributions received from their various donors – all of whom turn out to be famous Dickensian characters: Mr Pickwick, David Copperfield, Mrs Gamp, Martin Chuzzlewit, and even Fagin and the Artful Dodger.

This play, which contains a good many lines in cockney dialect – mysterious words such as 'Orlright!' and phrases like: 'Blast yer bottles, they ain't broke!' – concludes with Tiny Tim climbing onto Scrooge's bony knee to demand that the old man sing him a carol; but this Tim does NOT say (and it's a brave production that so dares) 'God Bless Us, Every One!'

This same dramatization also features an interesting guest-list for Fezziwig's ball, including Miss Fanny Fezziwig (replacing Belle as young Scrooge's sweetheart); Miss Emma Fezziwig, in love with Scrooge's fellow apprentice, Dick Wilkins; and Jacob Marley, beau to a young lady named Dora. But some even more fascinating guests attended the Fezziwig's party in Thea Musgrave's 1979 opera. First to arrive are the three Miss Fezziwigs: Liza, Mollie and Belle; then comes Mr Dorrit, 'very weedy and shy' and a character described as 'an unattractive but wealthy suitor for the hand of Belle'. Wasting no time, this gentleman 'surreptitiously helps himself to the sweetmeats that are laid out'. But before he can help himself to Miss Belle, the young Ebenezer whirls her off into the dance. And who might this gentleman be? According to Thea Musgrave his name is Mr Gabriel Grubb – none other than Scrooge's forebear, the goblin-haunted

sexton whose terrible adventures were recounted to Mr Pickwick!

Thea Musgrave, the distinguished British composer of *Mary, Queen of Scots* and other works, was commissioned to write *A Christmas Carol* for Virginia Opera in America. Her powerful work contains many imaginative insights into the character of Scrooge, as when his younger self sings to Belle, who has seen his affections towards her undergo a change:

See the poverty round us drowning men in debts and hopelessness! They all live in squalor, crippled with disease and misfortune. They bear children and watch them suffer from cold and hunger. Then, oh then, the affections cool in the icy hand of anxiety. How long would our love last then?

It is an interesting proposition that Scrooge's attitude towards poverty and suffering stems not from ignorance (which would have been impossible for anyone living in those times), but from an acute awareness – and a deep fear – of the potential hardships of life.

Later, he is confronted by a vision of the Cratchit family, where he hears his cruel philosophy of life ruthlessly parodied by Mrs Cratchit: 'People are poor because they are stupid and lazy and drown themselves in drink. They deserve to be poor! Let them be punished for their poverty!' Scrooge protests:

Here I stand accused – but why, but why? How can I be blamed for all the evil in the world? It's not my fault they live in poverty and their child is ill. The world is cruel and without mercy.

And then, revealing his own deep-seated sorrow, Scrooge asks:

Who comforted me when I was little? When my sister died there was no one who loved me. Harsh words and rough hands greeted me. Never a word of tenderness!

Unfurling his cloak, the Ghost of Christmas Present reveals Ignorance and Want joined, rather surprisingly, by the Cratchit children. 'Several years have passed,' the composer explains in her stage-directions, 'Bob Cratchit no longer has any work and the whole family has to beg.' These children of poverty scream and claw at Scrooge, crawling all over him, pleading for food and money. Scrooge pushes them away, but still they cling to him until he finally hurls them to the ground – and, in doing so, kills Tiny Tim.

Thea Musgrave was not the first composer to give *A Christmas Carol* over to the singers: an early operetta was staged in 1955 and various operatic versions followed in the 1960s and 1970s, including, in 1978, an opera broadcast by Welsh television. With music by Norman Kay and a libretto by John Morgan, it is notable for having Sir Geriant Evans in the role of Scrooge and for its unusual economies. There have been dramatizations where the two gentlemen collecting for charity have been reduced to one, but there cannot be many versions of the story where they have failed to appear at all! However, in John Morgan's libretto (which had to compress the whole story – plus singing – into less than a hour) Bob Cratchit simply tells Scrooge that the two gentlemen called while he was out!

Another delicious absurdity occurs during Scrooge's perambulations through the streets of London with Christmas Present. To avoid stopping off at the home of Scrooge's nephew, the writers have Fred wander amongst the crowd, engaging children and passers-by in playing his celebrated game of 'Yes and No'. Despite the fact that it is snowing hard, they stand around giving wrong guesses until one of the Cratchit brood suddenly announces (and not a moment too soon, for the threat of frostbite must be serious): 'It's horrid old Scrooge!'

A Christmas Carol has also inspired a piano suite, composed by Alex Rowley (1921); a folk dance ballet, *On Christmas Night*, by Ralph Vaughan Williams and Adolph Bolm (1935); a work by Benjamin Britten entitled 'Men of Goodwill: Variations on *A Christmas Carol*' (1947); an avant-garde version for chamber orchestra by Jon Deak in 1986 and, a year earlier, a ballet suite by John Hine which was recorded in a two piano arrangement and has elegantly titled sequences, such as 'Candle in the Wind' for Bob Cratchit; 'Heartlight' for the Ghost of Christmas Present; 'The Circle Unbroken', depicting the Cratchit family's Christmas and 'The Circle Rejoined', conveying Scrooge's final redemption.

Many ballet versions of *A Christmas Carol* have been performed, one of the most spectacular being the Northern Ballet Theatre's 1992 production, subsequently filmed for television. With choreography by Christopher Gable, and music by Carl Davis (utilizing themes from Christmas songs and carols) this production fills the stage with the hustle and bustle of Dickens' Christmas revellers and confronts Jeremy Kerridge's Scrooge with probably the finest trio of spectres Jacob Marley ever summoned up. Christmas Past dances into Scrooge's bedroom dressed in shining tights, a lacy shift and with a garland of spring flowers over her flowing hair; Christmas Present appears bare-chested wearing red tights and a swirling green cloak, while Christmas Future looms out of the mists of time (and dry-ice!): a towering figure, all skull and bones, swathed in tattered grave-clothes and with a huge pair of vulture wings.

A reviewer for *Dancing Times* found these costumes 'unappealing', adding: 'I cannot judge how faithful to Dickens is this realization, but the excellent programme notes indicate that the collaborators have studied the text most carefully.' Unlike the reviewer, who begins her appraisal by confessing: 'I have never read *A Christmas Carol* nor seen any theatrical version; I did not even know the story, although I had heard of Scrooge...'

This is surprising, since there are few dramatic forms in which *A Christmas Carol* has not been presented: it has been performed in mime (by Marcel Marceau), as a pantomime, a marionette play and several dozen musicals – one of which, the 1979 Broadway show, *Comin' Uptown*, had an all-black cast led by Gregory

Hines as a slum landlord in Harlem with a talent for nifty footwork.

As well as the professionals, amateur companies the world over have long enjoyed putting Scrooge & Co. on stage. Many productions in the past would have used J.C. Buckstone's adaptation of *A Christmas Carol*, an enduringly successful one-act drama, first performed on the professional stage in 1901. Running for little more than an hour, the play centres on Scrooge and the scenes set in his office, whilst virtually ignoring the method of Scrooge's conversion and the part played in it by Tiny Tim. The three Spirits are made redundant by Jacob Marley who, unaided, conjures up edited highlights from the Past, Present and Future.

Despite being hacked, this production proved a successful vehicle for two popular actors of the day, Bransby Williams and Seymour Hicks; both of whom, eventually took the play – further truncated to a one-man performance – from the theatre to the music-halls. Describing Seymour Hicks' performance in his book *Dickens as Dramatist*, F. Dubrez Fawcett notes that 'instead of the doddering senility so often portrayed in the first scene of the play, Hicks invested the character with startling aggressiveness, waspish and intolerant to the last degree'. All too rarely do great theatrical performances get recorded for posterity, but Seymour Hicks repeated his performance for the 1935 British film, *Scrooge*.

It was not the first film version of *A Christmas Carol*, nor by any means the last – subsequent versions featured a diversity of stars from Alastair Sim to George C. Scott and Mr

Magoo to Michael Caine — but Seymour Hicks' portrayal is a significant milestone in the long and diverse career of Ebenezer Scrooge, movie-star ...

The Northern Ballet Theatre's
A Christmas Carol; Scrooge (Jeremy Kerridge) with the Ghost of Christmas Present (Royce Neagle)

9

Nice Story, Mr Dickens!

Some actors are irresistably drawn to *A Christmas Carol* — in fact, there are those, it seems, who simply cannot leave it alone! Sir Ralph Richardson played Scrooge on a gramophone recording, on television and on radio; another radio Scrooge, Sir Alec Guinness, subsequently showed up on film as Jacob Marley; while fellow theatrical knight, Sir Michael Hordern, reversed this process, beginning with two appearances as Marley's Ghost and, later, moved on from haunter to haunted. Sir Laurence Olivier ambitiously narrated the story *and* played Scrooge, but ended up doing neither very well.

Alastair Sim twice played the role: once in person and once on behalf of an animated cartoon character; Michael Gough played Scrooge on radio and, elsewhere, appeared as one of the two charitably minded gentlemen; while Frederick March, who portrayed Scrooge on television, later narrated a film version, starring Basil Rathbone. Honourable mention must also be made of a young actor, John Charlesworth, who played Tiny Tim on radio and his elder brother, Peter, on film; and Timothy Bateson, who has twice cavorted through the indefatigably jovial role of Fezziwig!

Getting in character: Michael Gough dressed as Scrooge to publicize a BBC radio adaptation   Copyright © BBC

The tradition of actors associating themselves with *A Christmas Carol*, and in particular with the role of Scrooge, goes back many years to Seymour Hicks and Bransby Williams, who both played the part in the theatre, music hall and, later, on film. Indeed, as late as 1946, Williams was still at it in a live two-hour television version which concluded with the octogenarian actor hoisting Tiny Tim onto his shoulders.

The first filmic telling of the tale was a silent picture, made in Britain in 1901 and entitled *Scrooge, or Marley's Ghost*. Five more silent film versions appeared in Britain and America between 1908 and 1914. Two years later, Bluebird Photoplays in the USA released a version, curiously entitled *The Right to Be Happy*; while, in Britain, two distinguished thespians played the part of Scrooge: Henry Esmond, in 1922; and, the following year, Russell Thorndike.

An early sound version, in 1928, allowed Bransby Williams to reprise his stage performance; while 1935 saw the release of Seymour Hicks' film version, *Scrooge*, consciously conveying its literary origins by a leather-bound edition of Dickens' book which opens to reveal a bizarre title-page declaring it to be 'Controlled throughout the World by Twickenham Film Distributors, London WI'.

Based on J.C. Buckstone's stage dramatization, this film, as its title suggests, is centred on Scrooge to the exclusion of many of the subsidiary characters. Seymour Hicks depicts Scrooge as being old, ill-kempt and very probably rather dirty: his hair is uncombed, his clothes threadbare, his lodgings dusty and dingy. Much is made of the office sequences with Scrooge and his clerk, including an invented exchange about the fire in Cratchit's office which Dickens had described as being so small 'it looked like one-coal'. Here, Bob (Donald Calthrop) recklessly calls it 'his fire'. 'YOUR fire?' snaps Scrooge, 'It is evident to me that my interest is not your interest, my welfare is not your welfare!'

Seymour Hicks' film creates a vivid impression of Victorian London in winter and, like most of the subsequent movie versions, visually captures much of Dickens' fulsome description of Christmas preparations. In all his many film appearances, Scrooge has never walked through a street where the shops are not profusely hung with holly, mistletoe and turkeys; nor does he ever pass shoppers who do not labour under Christmas parcels and presents or baskets overflowing with fruit, sweets and nuts! One notable radio version – cut to the bone and delivered at break-neck speed to cram as much of what is left of Dickens' story into half-an-hour – still manages to include a sequence with link-men lighting people through the fog and invents cries for street-vendors selling 'Fine, fat turkeys!' and 'Scarlet holly, all berries!'

Buckstone's play had omitted the three Christmas Spirits, but they were reinstated for the film version, although only Christmas Present – a tubby, beardless fellow – had any physical presence: Christmas Past appears merely as a blaze of light, while Christmas Future is nothing

Seymour Hicks as Scrooge (1935)

more than a shadow. As for Marley's Ghost, he doesn't appear at all — at least not to the naked eye. 'Look well, Ebenezer Scrooge,' says a disembodied voice, 'because only you can see me.' Fortunately, later film-makers didn't latch on to this technique!

Although subsequent Marleys have consistently put in an appearance, they have not always looked particularly ghostly. Despite the fact that Dickens describes the spectre as passing straight through the door to Scrooge's room, only one see-through movie Marley (Leo G. Carroll) enters in this way. Other, more corporeal Marleys (some of whom even cast shadows) have required the door to unbolt, unlock and open itself in order for them to gain access.

Even a translucent Michael Hordern, who is clearly capable of walking through just about anything, curiously — or, perhaps just politely — waits until the door is opened for him! Bizarrely, Alec Guinness makes an ethereal entry (again through an already open door) and then becomes suddenly solid! However, to compensate for such unspooky behaviour, he is — like several other Marleys — daubed with ghostly white make-up, dusted down with powder and dressed in a monochrome costume suggesting the colour of a bad lobster. Perhaps, after all, the producers of the 1935 film were simply saving themselves a good deal of trouble!

Despite being a feature-length film, Seymour Hicks' Scrooge is a drastically cut-down version of Dickens' story: gone are Ebenezer's schooldays and that centrepiece of Christmas Past, Fezziwig's Ball. Nor is there any place for the children, Ignorance and Want, two frequent casualties of dramatizations.

Other candidates for the chop, over the years, have been Belle, the love of Scrooge's youthful life; and even Scrooge's nephew. As for Old Joe and the trio of ghouls who meet at his shop, this gruesome foursome are rarely shown together. Mrs Dilber might visit Old Joe on her own; or, there again, she might meet the undertaker and sometimes (but not always) the laundress in Scrooge's bedroom — in which case, Old Joe doesn't get a look in. This last

arrangement ought to give Scrooge — who, in the book, is fairly slow on the up-take — a pretty clear idea of who has died; but when, in one radio adaptation, he observes the laundress and the undertaker (minus Mrs Dilber this time) coming out of his own front door, he still doesn't realize what is going on!

Some productions have got more than their money's worth out of the Mrs Dilbers they have employed: two of them — Athene Seyler and Kathleen Harrison — bring Scrooge a tray of tea on the morning after the night before, and provide an audience for his extended monologue about the Spirits and what they did and what he is going to do now that he has another chance... 'I don't know anything!' chortles one Scrooge, 'I never did know anything! But now I KNOW I don't know anything!' And then he stands on his head which, since he is wearing a nightshirt, gives Mrs Dilber a worse fright than any ghosts could have produced!

A rare instance of, some might say, miserly economy, is a television version where the party at the house of Scrooge's nephew finds Fred presiding over a select gathering of four. This particular sequence in the story has been endlessly altered and adapted. In only one movie, for example, is Topper (renamed Tom) permitted to play blind-man's buff; normally, since time is pressing, he is simply allowed a few flirtatious remarks, although some adapters have gone to the bother of having Topper (or sometimes Tupper) banned from taking part (on the grounds that he always catches the plump sister), or excusing his non-participation, because he 'never plays games'!

Not that Topper would necessarily know how to play all the games that have been enjoyed by Fred's party-goers. There are occasional attempts at the game of 'Yes and No' described by Dickens, but there are also a variety of alternative entertainments, such as 'The Minister's Cat', in which participants have to complete the phrase 'The Minister's cat is a **** cat' with an adjective beginning with each letter of the alphabet in turn. Another game is 'Similes', in which Fred gives the beginning of a simile which the participants have to complete. Scrooge's niece, given the phrase 'As tight as –', ignores the obvious answer of 'A drum', and instead offers: 'Your Uncle Scrooge's purse strings!'

The high jinks at Fred's party are so much a part of the collective Carol-memory, that a radio version, from which it was excised, briefly introduced party games to Fezziwig's Christmas celebration replacing 'Sir Roger de Coverley' with Musical Chairs and a rendition of 'Pop Goes the Weasel!' One film solved all worries about what entertainments to provide at Fezziwig's Ball by scrapping it altogether, although to be fair, Mr Fezziwig does invite young Scrooge to dinner on Christmas day, and (since he will 'probably eat too much') gives him the following day off as well!

Rarely included in productions is that passage in the book in which the Ghost of Christmas Present takes Scrooge to see how people, near and far, celebrate the season. There might be the occasional brief stop at a mine or a lighthouse or even aboard a ship, but few versions, presumably for budgetary reasons, have attempted to recreate the effect of cumulative happiness, depicted in Dickens' text.

Certainly none of those scenes are shown in the 1938 MGM film of *A Christmas Carol*, starring Reginald Owen, which was the first of many attempts at building a complex story-line on what even the author recognized as a fairly slight plot. In September 1852, writing a Preface to the first Cheap Edition of the Christmas Books, Dickens confessed:

> The narrow space in which it was necessary to confine these Christmas stories when they were originally published rendered their construction a matter of some difficulty, and almost necessitated what is peculiar in their machinery. I never attempted great elaboration of detail in the working out of character within such limits, believing that it could not succeed.

Certainly MGM's film attempts just such an 'elaboration of detail in the working out of character', even if the relationships and motivations it sets up owe little to Dickens. Its significant device is in establishing a rapport between the story's two 'Forces for Good': Scrooge's nephew and the Cratchit family. This begins, in the opening moments of the film, when Fred encounters Tiny Tim watching other children having fun sliding on the ice. On discovering that Tim can't join in because he is crippled, Fred gives him a piggy-back ride down the slide; only, a moment later, to be knocked off his feet by Tim's brother, Peter Cratchit! Such chance meetings and novel coincidences proliferate throughout the film.

Reginald Owen as Scrooge and Lionel Braham as
Christmas Present in the 1939 film

glassware. According to Dickens all they possessed were 'two tumblers and a custard-cup without a handle' (not much for a family of eight) and yet the film prop-buyers have provided them with a wide range of receptacles from mugs to fine crystal.

The MGM film demonstrates the level to which people 'know' Dickens' book without necessarily recalling specific details; so it is conceivable that whilst audiences probably remember the presence in the story of Scrooge's hale and hearty nephew, they might not be too surprised, on seeing this version, to find that he is not married, but only engaged. This subtle alteration ostensibly strengthens the plot, by giving the reformed Scrooge the power to assist his nephew towards married happiness. It does, however, play havoc with Fred's normally simple invitation to his Uncle to join them for Christmas dinner, obliging him, in this instance, to explain that he is dining with his fiancee's people, but is sure that they would also welcome a visit from Scrooge.

The young lady with such obviously liberal parents is called Elizabeth or Bess; other nephews' wives in other productions have been named Betsy, May, Clara and Janet. As with the various stage versions, the reason for such apparent inconsistency is that Scrooge's niece is one of several characters whom Dickens — that great provider of unforgettable monikers — never named. Indeed, her husband, Fred, has no surname: an oversight which once prompted the critic, Bernard Levin, to speculate on what that name might have been. Levin suggested

This Cratchit family are — compared with some of their counterparts — a fairly well-fed, healthy-looking bunch; reasonably clothed and living in comfortable surroundings. Nicholas Clark has a theory that you can judge a production of *A Christmas Carol* by the Cratchits'

Warmington, Beamish or Wellbeloved; names not dissimilar to the only one he has ever been given in a film: Fred Holywell.

The two gentlemen collecting for charity have also been named: as Mr Twill and Mr Rumidge or as Mr Poole and Mr Hacking; while Scrooge's fellow business men have sported such names as Brady, Billings, Snedrig, Groper and Rosebed. Other name-givings include Scrooge's sister (once called 'Fran' instead of 'Fan') referring to young Ebenezer by such diminutives as 'Ben', 'Eb' or 'Ebby'; and, inexplicably, the re-naming of Scrooge's sweetheart, Belle, as Isabel, Abella or even Alice.

One film includes a sequence in which the married Belle is romping with her children – all seventeen of them! Scrooge might well have remarked, as he does elsewhere: 'Lord what a brood!' The MGM film with Reginald Owen eliminates Belle altogether, her role in the story being covered by a handy generalization from the Ghost of Christmas Past:

My time grows short, I have yet to show you the black years of your life, your gradual enslavement to greed, your ruthlessness, your ingratitude, your wretched thirst for gold...

At which point, Owen's Scrooge can stand no more, and so extinguishes the Spirit by pulling her diaphanous dress (for this ghost is a she) over her head! Looking not unlike a chorus girl from an MGM musical, Ann Rutherford as Christmas Past has a mass of golden curls and wears an air-hostess style cap surmounted by a glittery cut-out star.

Other female Spirits of the Past have included Angela Pleasance, with threads of tinsel in her hair, and Edith Evans dressed in a red gown with a fur muff and a hat that would not have looked out of place in the Ascot sequence of *My Fair Lady*!

Some of the cuts made by MGM were obviously intended to make room for new material such as an early sequence in which Bob, on the way home from the office, has a snowball fight with some street children. One of his snowballs knocks off Mr Scrooge's hat, which rolls under the wheels of a passing cab and is squashed. Scrooge dismisses Cratchit on the spot and, when Bob hesitantly says that 'his papers' say he is entitled to a week's notice, Scrooge replies: 'Your week's salary will compensate me for the price of a new hat,' then, after a quick peep inside the hat, he adds: 'No, as this hat cost me 16/6, and your salary is 15/6, you owe me a shilling!' Although an unnecessary embellishment, Bob's dismissal on Christmas Eve nevertheless intensifies the emotional pressure on Scrooge, and considerable dramatic tension is gained from having the spectre of unemployment hanging over the famous Cratchit celebrations.

There is scarcely a production which does not contain new material: sometimes obviously alien to the original, sometimes attempting to look and sound as if it had come from the Master's pen. One radio production, for example, begins with this piece of bogus – but plausible – Dickens:

Christmas Eve: jollity; plenty; the merry shouting of the urchins; the delicious smells arising from the mounds of mince-pies in the pastry-cooks, the tournedos of turkeys, the garrisons of geese in the poulterers, the barons of beef in the butchers; the rich, ruddy glare from the grocers, the bon-bons, gingerbread, the whole glorious pageant of Christmas. Christmas Eve, piercing, searching, piping and cold and foggy withal . . .

Some additions are little more than detail added to explain apparent discrepancies in Dickens' text. In the original story, Marley gives Scrooge very precise arrival times for the ghosts: 'Expect the first to-morrow, when the bell tolls One . . . Expect the second on the next night at the same hour. The third upon the next night when the last stroke of twelve has ceased to vibrate.' When, however, Scrooge eventually wakes up a new man, he finds that it is Christmas morning and declares: 'The Spirits have done it all in one night. They can do anything they like . . .' Some dramatists, perceiving this as an attempt at explaining away an error in continuity, either have the Spirits make hourly appearances on the same night or announce only the time on which the first spirit is expected to arrive; while, in another version, Scrooge is told: 'Expect the first tonight, when the bell tolls one. Expect the second on the stroke of two. The third, more mercurial, shall appear in his own good time.'

All manner of new scenes have been devised in order to get the Cratchit household — and especially Tiny Tim — on screen earlier than Dickens introduces them in the story. Neat ways of doing this have been to show Tim gazing longingly in the window of a toy shop; or waiting in the snow outside his father's office — where Scrooge mistakes him for a beggar! There have been several attempts at 'building up' the role of Tiny Tim, a risky business, since some of the young actors are hard pressed to cope with anything more complicated than the few lines given them by Dickens. One Tiny Tim manages to fluff his best line by saying: 'God bless us ALL, every one!' In another, presumably intentional variation, Tiny Tim specifically includes the stingy Mr Scrooge in his blessing: 'I say God bless him too, Mother — and EVERYONE!'

In marked contrast to the way in which he reacts to the name of Scrooge in the story, the cinema's more saintly Tiny Tims almost always have a kind word for the old Humbug. One particularly unctuous child tells his sister, Martha: 'We mustn't think poorly of him.' To which Martha wittily, and not unreasonably, replies: 'Why not? It's his thinking that keeps us poor!' Another Tim correctly guesses who has donated the surprise turkey; a suggestion that causes a flabbergasted Bob Cratchit to ask: 'Whatever would make Mr Scrooge take leave of his senses suddenly?' To which Tiny Tim piously replies: 'Christmas!' A suitable antidote to all such goody-goodies is the Tiny Tim who returns home not from church, but from carol-singing — at which enterprise he has earned tenpence-halfpenny. 'Another fantastic coup by young Timothy Cratchit, the financial wizard!' enthuses his father, 'At only seven years of age, the youngest millionaire in the vast Cratchit empire!'

What is most surprising about dramatizations of *A Christmas Carol*, is the number of productions that have managed to inflate entire scenes out of the smallest references in the original text. Dickens observes, in passing: 'The Lord Mayor, in the stronghold of the mighty Mansion House, gave orders to his fifty cooks and butlers to keep Christmas as a Lord Mayor's household should.' Seymour Hicks' film turns this sentence into a major set-piece: cutting between the elaborate preparations in the kitchen at the Mansion House — cooks basting joints, tasting wines, turning out jellies and icing cakes — with Scrooge's 'melancholy dinner in his usual melancholy tavern'. At the banquet itself, the Lord Mayor's guests — several hundred extras dressed in a great deal of hired finery — are invited to raise their glasses to 'The Queen', but instead raise their voices and sing the National Anthem!

Alistair Sim as Scrooge (1935)

Another fanciful addition, this time in the MGM film, picks up on Dickens' joke that the noise made by Marley's Ghost was so hideous 'that the Ward would have been justified in indicting it for a nuisance'. Reginald Owen's Scrooge throws open the window and summons a trio of comic night watchmen to arrest the intruder in his rooms. On finding no one there, the leading Watchman remarks that Scrooge's 'hintruder seems to have hextruded'; and, on being told that it was a spirit, observes: 'A great night for spirits, sir, of one sort or another!'

'Even to those who are not Dickensian purists,' wrote F. Dubrez Fawcett in *Dickens the Dramatist*, 'the grafting of new material, and of unauthorized dialogue, on a Dickens story is anathema.' If true, then Renown Pictures' 1951 film, *Scrooge*, starring Alastair Sim, ought to be held in fairly general contempt, since it contains more new and invented scenes than any other movie version. Opening on the steps of the Exchange, it immediately introduces a new character, Samuel Wilkins, debtor to Scrooge. Begging for time to pay, Wilkins reminds Scrooge that it is, after all, Christmas. 'Christmas has nothing to do with it,' snarls Scrooge, 'You'd still owe me £20 which you're not in a position to repay if it was the middle of a heat-wave on August Bank Holiday!' An interesting (and possibly prophetic) remark, since, in Scrooge's day, August Bank Holidays were yet to be invented!

Another new character, with the suitably Dickensian name of Jorkin, is included: partly to act as a catalyst in various scenes, partly to provide a role for the then popular film and radio actor, Jack Warner. Mr Jorkin is a ruthless businessman, given to denouncing any altruistic views he encounters with such phrases as 'Sage and Onion! Gammon and Spinach!' On his first appearance, Jorkin is attempting to buy out Fezziwig's failing business and tells the young Scrooge that he is easily worth twice the salary that he getting from Fezziwig. When Ebenezer replies that 'Money isn't everything,' Jorkin laughingly replies: 'Well if it ain't, I don't know what is!'

Scrooge accepts Mr Jorkin's offer and goes to work for the Amalgamated Mercantile Society, where one of his fellow clerks is Jacob Marley. Eventually Jorkin takes over Fezziwig's company and the young Scrooge and Marley gain promotion. It seems as though there is truth in Jorkin's motto – 'Control the cash-box and you control the world!' – especially when Jorkin finds himself in dire straits for having embezzled over £3,000 from the company. Scrooge and Marley offer to rescue Amalgamated Mercantile on the understanding that they be allowed to buy up to 51 per cent of its shares.

It is scenes such as these that mark out this film as the first of its kind to attempt an explanation of Scrooge's personality. In 1968, the President of Screen Gems, announcing plans for a new film of *A Christmas Carol*, wrote: 'Dickens is a terrible writer. In the original, Scrooge was mean and stingy, but you never knew why. We're giving him a mother and a father, an unhappy childhood, a whole background which will motivate him.' That particular movie was never

made; but Alastair Sim's films had already done much the same thing.

On first being introduced to his fellow clerk, the young Marley observes: 'The world is on the verge of new and great changes, Mr Scrooge, some of them, of necessity, will be violent.' To which Scrooge replies: 'I think the world is becoming a very hard and cruel place... One must steel oneself to survive it, not be crushed under with the weak and the infirm.'

Scrooge's heart goes on hardening and when, many years later, Marley lies at death's door and sends for his partner, Scrooge refuses to leave the office before closing time. Bob Cratchit (Mervyn Johns) comments that the place will seem odd without Mr Marley. 'Why should it be any more odd than it was with him?' Scrooge replies, 'We've all got to die, Cratchit!' A deathbed scene follows (the only film to include such a sequence) in which the dying Jacob Marley (Michael Hordern) having, apparently, seen the error of his own wicked ways, implores Scrooge to 'save himself' – a request which falls, of course, on deaf ears.

There is much in *Scrooge* that is pure delight – especially Sim's exuberant performance as the miser reformed – all laughter and genial buffoonery. Nevertheless the movie critic of the *New York Times* found the film 'heavy on the Freudian sauce', and it is true that it attempts a psychological reading of Scrooge's character. Whilst most films have been happy simply to describe him as 'Mr Humbug', 'Mr Grim', 'The stingiest man in town' or 'The meanest man in the whole wide world', Noel Langley, screenwriter for the Alastair Sim film, presents valid reasons for Scrooge's meanness of spirit.

On visiting the Past, Scrooge sees his sister, Fan, come to fetch his younger self home from school. She looks, he says, as his mother must have looked just before she died. Then, on being told that his father has sent for him, young Ebenezer (George Cole) replies: 'He doesn't know me or even what I look like.' His mother, it is revealed, died giving him birth. Fan tells her brother that he is 'never to be lonely again – never, as long as I live!' To which, Ebenezer replies: 'Then you must live forever, Fan...' But Fan does not live forever, she marries and – like their mother – dies in childbirth. On her deathbed, she begs Ebenezer to take care of her boy, his nephew; but Scrooge, thinking her dead, and wildly angry with his brother-in-law and the new-born child, has already stormed out of the room; so begins Scrooge's animosity towards his sole surviving relative.

The same explanation for Scrooge's behaviour is employed in the 1984 American television production, *A Christmas Carol* (released in Britain as a feature film), with George C. Scott as Scrooge. This is the only version in which Scrooge's father makes an appearance, arriving at the school with Fan. Young Ebenezer is to begin his apprenticeship with Fezziwig in three days' time. 'Three days, father,' says a disappointed Fan, 'I'd hoped to have my brother home for longer.' 'Three days,' Scrooge Snr coldly remarks, 'is quite long enough – for both us.' Turning to the Ghost of Christmas Past, Scrooge observes that his father was 'a very stern man'. He may also

have been responsible for Scrooge's attitude towards money, since although he is not named in the film, he is listed in the credits as 'Silas Scrooge', which suggests, perhaps, an emotional link with another miser in literature, Silas Marner.

This Scrooge grows up to be a hard-headed businessman, driving a tough bargain on the Exchange over the cost of corn. Having raised his price by 5 per cent from the previous day, he tells the other businessmen that if they delay a further day it will cost them another 5 per cent. 'Damn it, Scrooge,' says one of his fellows, 'It's not fair!' Which prompts Scrooge to the sardonic reply: 'No gentlemen, but it's business!'

This image of Scrooge is unlike that of the greedy, grasping money-lender that he is so often shown as being. Elsewhere, Scrooge is frequently depicted foreclosing on mortgagees and denying debtors time to pay. In one of Lionel Barrymore's many American radio performances in the role, Scrooge sends Cratchit to a debtor named Ephraim Fothergill, to collect the sum of seventeen shillings and sixpence, which has been owing since Michaelmas: 'Tell him,' barks Scrooge, 'I'll have a constable over there if he doesn't pay up at once!' Bob protests that Fothergill's wife is ill, but his employer is unrepentant: 'What do I care about his wife? I just want my seventeen-and-six!'

George C. Scott's Scrooge is a very different character. Hearing Bob and his wife (David Warner and Susannah York) arguing about whether or not to toast Scrooge as 'the founder of the feast', he remarks: 'He's made a point, Bob

George C. Scott as Scrooge (1984)

an unpleasant, vindictive man who first agrees to Cratchit having Christmas day off, and then changes his mind: 'No! You'd better come in around four, there are some accounts I want to go over!' To Seymour Hicks he is an unloved, unlovable man; to Alec Guinness a doddering old fool; to Ralph Richardson and Lionel Barrymore, a cantankerous curmudgeon; to Michael Hordern and Reginald Owen a blinkered individual, incapable of seeing his faults; while to Alastair Sim he was simply a frightened, haunted man.

Sim gave a less anxious performance as Scrooge for the voice-track of the 1971 Oscar-winning animated film version by Richard Williams, who later directed the animation in *Who Framed Roger Rabbit?* Stunningly reproducing the look of the cross-hatched Victorian engraving, the film contains many splendid touches such as a Marley's Ghost, whose jaw really does drop when he undoes the wrapper from around his head and who is, thereafter, able to speak without opening and closing his mouth; and a Ghost of Christmas Past who shape-changes exactly as Dickens described.

A far less prestigious animated version was an hour-long feature released by Burbank films in 1985, which has some particularly crass additions, including the moment when Scrooge starts jigging about at the thought of Fezziwig's party, which prompts the Ghost of Christmas Past to ask: 'What's the matter with you – got a beetle in your pants?' Later, to the Ghost of Christmas Present, Scrooge complains that he doesn't like turkey or pheasant. 'What do you

Cratchit has; without me there would be no feast, no goose at all, my head for business has furnished him employment.' This is a Scrooge for today; less a skinflint than a sharp, successful and apparently unsentimental entrepreneur. Scott's Scrooge is no unshaven, ill-kempt old miser, but a man smartly dressed and well-groomed; when he travels with the Spirits he wears an elegant dressing gown over his shirt and trousers – no ridiculous nightshirt and night-cap for him!

All of which is in striking contrast to earlier Scrooges. To Basil Rathbone, Scrooge is like?' enquires the Ghost and receives the answer: 'Cold toast and a cup of tea!' But the undoubted highlight is the moment when one of the men collecting for charity reports the news of Scrooge's death by saying that he has 'dropped off his perch'!

This version apart, Dickens' story has been performed – rather more successfully – by a variety of well-known cartoon stars. First, in 1962, was *Mr Magoo's Christmas Carol*. The myopic, accident-prone Quincy Magoo is playing the role of Ebenezer Scrooge in a Broadway musical. The film is notable for several delightful Jules Styne/ Bob Merrill numbers; for the astonishing fact that the Ghost of Christmas Present arrives before the Ghost of Christmas Past and for one of the least attractive Tiny Tims of all time, who is constantly lusting after such American-sounding delicacies as 'Woofle-Jelly Cake' and 'Razzleberry Dressing'!

Voiced by the inimitable Jim Backus, Mr Magoo's performance is peppered with jokes based on the character's acute short-sightedness; so, on confronting the Marley door-knocker, he mutters: 'Very strange, very strange! Could I need spectacles?' And when the Ghost of Christmas Present observes: 'You have never seen the like of me before!' Magoo truthfully replies: 'I'm not sure I see the like of you now!'

In Bugs Bunny's *Looney Christmas Tales* (1979), the famous carrot-chomping rabbit plays Scrooge's nephew, while the mustachioed bandit, Yosemite Sam – minus his Stetson and six-shooters – plays an unlikely Scrooge. 'Ooo! I hates Christmas,' he growls, 'and I hates mistletoe and I hates kissing and I say, "Bah, humbug!" to the whole thing!' Porky Pig is a timorous Bob Cratchit while Tweety-Pie plays Tiny Tim – explaining that the only reason he is small is because he lives on bird-seed! When Scrooge evicts the Cratchit family on Christmas Eve, Bugs issues his famous challenge: 'You realize this means WAR!'; and, dressing up in a sheet and chains, sets about 'haunting' his uncle into a better kind of person. When he eventually succeeds, Bugs winks at the camera and laughs: 'Ain't I a little Dickens, though?'

It was not until 1983 that Hollywood's most-celebrated cartoon stars tackled Dickens' novel in the film *Mickey's Christmas Carol*. The genesis of this movie was a story about another mouse, written and illustrated by the Walt Disney studio and published in *McCalls Magazine*, in December 1957. Cedric, a mouse clock-mender, works for a human Scrooge who refuses to give him a holiday on Christmas Day. Rather than miss Christmas with his family, Cedric leaves his job; that night, Scrooge's grandfather clock shows the old man a time to come when his name will represent all that is mean and miserly. The usual reformations and happy endings follow, but it was to be another seventeen years before the Disney studio turned again to the Dickens' classic.

The necessary creative spark was provided by artist Carl Barks, who was responsible for the weekly comic-book *Walt Disney's Comics and Stories*. In 1947, Barks – who was working on a story called 'Christmas on Bear Mountain' – created a new character: a rich uncle for Donald

Scrooge McDuck and Mickey Mouse in *Mickey's Christmas Carol*, 1983 © Disney

Duck, called – Scrooge McDuck. 'His name,' said Barks, 'tattles the fact that he was adapted quite thievishly from Charles Dickens' great character.' Carl Barks drew Scrooge McDuck with side-whiskers (or feathers) and a pair of glasses perched on the end of his beak. Dressed in spats and a dressing-gown (subsequently traded for a coat of broadcloth) Scrooge McDuck sits hunched over his walking stick:

'Here I sit waiting for Christmas to pass! Bah! A curse on it! Everybody loving everybody else... Me – I'm DIFFERENT! Everybody HATES me and I hate EVERYBODY!'

Originally, Carl Barks had no further plans for McDuck; however, he reintroduced the character in a 1948 story, 'The Old Castle's Secret', in which Donald and his nephews help Scrooge search of his family fortune – hidden for nine hundred years in the huge old McDuck Castle on Scotland's Dismal Downs. Scrooge proved popular with comic-book readers and soon had his own magazine – with his name printed on the cover as 'Uncle $crooge'.

In 1974, capitalizing on the success of Scrooge McDuck, the Disney company produced an original gramophone recording of a version of Dickens' story. Described as being 'Presented by the Popular Repertory Company The Walt Disney Players', the recording featured several amusing songs, including a prophetic number for Marley's Ghost entitled, 'Being Tight is Not All Right'!

The cast was headed by Scrooge McDuck, voiced, in a Scottish accent, by Alan Young (of television's 'Mr Ed'); while Bob Cratchit was played by Mickey Mouse, Mrs Cratchit by Minnie Mouse, Scrooge's nephew by Donald Duck and Marley's Ghost by Goofy. The Ghost of Christmas Past was played by Merlin (from *The Sword in the Stone*), Christmas Present by Willie the Giant (from *Mickey and the Beanstalk*) while the Ghost of the Future was portrayed by the cackling Witch from *Snow White and the Seven Dwarfs*.

Another nine years passed and Scrooge McDuck became one of the best known Disney characters – original comic-books and limited-edition lithographs by his creator Carl Barks were being valued in thousands of dollars – yet he had made only one movie appearance, in a 1967 educational film entitled *Scrooge McDuck and Money*. When, however, in the early 1980s, the Disney studio was looking for a vehicle to re-launch the careers of some of its old cartoon stars, it hit on the idea of cashing in on Scrooge's fame (and fortune!) by filming the story they had already released as a record.

Some recasting took place: the role of Christmas Future passed to Mickey's old nemesis, Peg Leg Pete; while Merlin was replaced, in the role of Christmas Past, by Pinocchio's diminutive conscience, Jiminy Cricket – Disney's equivalent of the *Cricket on the Hearth*!

Despite cultural inaccuracies (Scrooge gives the charity-men a donation of fifty sovereigns in a bag with a $ sign on it) and the omission of the songs composed for the original recording, the film succeeds and contains amusing visual gags – such as the shadow of the goofy Ghost of Jacob Marley tip-toeing upstairs behind Scrooge – and witty lines: 'In his will,' Scrooge says of his dead partner, 'he left enough money to pay for his tombstone – and I had him buried at sea!'

Paying Bob Cratchit a wage of two-shillings and a halfpenny, including the price of doing his weekly washing, makes Scrooge McDuck a premiere example of a type of Scrooge which might be categorized as the Super-Meany. An undoubted fellow spirit appears in the 1986 animated film *The Stingiest Man in Town* (based on the 1950s television musical with Basil Rathbone). Narrated by a chirpy little insect called 'B.A.H. Humbug Esq.', it stars the voice and caricatured likeness of Walter Matthau as Scrooge.

One of the lyrics describes him as 'the tightest man since time began,' and, on calling his former partner to mind, this Scrooge remarks: 'You're lucky you're dead as a doornail and don't have to be bothered with Christmas anymore. And I'm lucky, too – I don't have to share the profits with you anymore!' So unscrupulous is he that, when Bob asks for his day's holiday, Scrooge breaks down and weeps, telling him that paying money for no work will beggar him and bring him to the workhouse. Bob naturally forgoes his salary!

Asked for his opinion of Santa Claus, this epitome of meanness grunts: 'I abominate old St Nick, his reckless spending makes me sick; I think St Nick's a lunatic!' Another humbug who dislikes Father Christmas – largely because that's what the street urchins nickname him – is Albert Finney, star of the 1970 Leslie Bricusse musical film, *Scrooge* (later reworked as a stage musical for Anthony Newley). Bricusse re-draws Scrooge as the quintessence of misanthropy; a dark, tragic character (more Quilp than Scrooge) expressing his bleak creed in a song which describes people as, frauds, parasites, hypocrites and scavengers, who feed on their fellow men and corrupt honest individuals like Ebenezer Scrooge!

Where Dickens' Scrooge is merely indifferent towards his fellow human beings, this Scrooge has a deep loathing for all mankind; an attitude which makes his ultimate reformation harder to accomplish and almost impossible to believe. Nevertheless, there he is at the end, happily dressed-up in a Father Christmas outfit, distributing vast quantities of everything to the poor and needy and ripping up his long list of debtors.

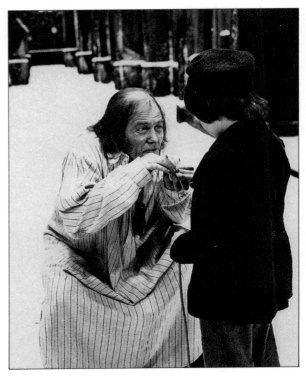

Albert Finney as Scrooge (1970)

The film, *Scrooge*, contains many fanciful embellishments to Dickens' text: such as Kenneth More's Ghost of Christmas Present giving Scrooge a goblet filled with the Milk of Human Kindness; and some curious departures from the original: as when Scrooge's nephew (Michael Medwin) uncharacteristically describes his uncle as 'the most despicable old miser; beyond dispute the most obnoxious and parsimonious of all living creatures!' By far the most ingenious diversion, however, is the sequence in Christmas

Future when one of Scrooge's many debtors, Tom Jenkins (Anton Rogers) leads an army of impecunious Londoners in singing a song of gratitude to Mr Scrooge. What the observing Scrooge does not realize is that the cause for this celebration is, in fact, his funeral!

Funerals – usually Marley's – are a common feature of several film and television productions: Michael Hordern's version opens with Marley lying in his coffin, just before the lid is nailed down; Alastair Sim is shown signing the register of his burial; and George C. Scott's film opens with a plumed hearse passing through the streets of London. For Scrooge himself - particularly in Albert Finney's portrayal – the chief concern is what happens to him *after* his funeral.

Dickens says of the deceased Scrooge: 'Old Scratch has got his own at last.' And it is clearly a notion with movie-potential. Bugs Bunny, for example, tells Yosemite Sam's Scrooge that he is taking him to see the man in the red suit. 'You mean Santy Claus?' asks Yosemite Sam. 'No,' replies Bugs, 'the OTHER man in the red suit!' A song in *The Stingiest Man in Town* describes Scrooge as being the 'Devil's stooge', and suggests that when he reaches Hell, even Satan will be moved to ask: 'How can anybody be that stingy?' While Scrooge McDuck, on being told that he is 'The richest man in the cemetery', finds himself falling into an open grave filled with flames and smoke.

But Albert Finney is the only Scrooge to have been actually taken down to Hell. And when he gets there, he finds his old partner (Alec Guinness) waiting for him. 'I am dead, aren't I?'

he asks Jacob Marley, who gives a smile and replies: 'As a coffin-nail!' Then, ushering Scrooge through a subterranean world of red-hot stalactites and stalagmites, he conducts him to his office, explaining:

Your activities in life were so pleasing to Lucifer, that he has appointed you to be his personal clerk – a singular honour. You will be to him, so to speak, what Bob Cratchit was to you!

Scrooge's new office, whilst in every other respect a replica of the one he had on earth, is freezing cold and filled with ice and snow. 'Lucifer,' Marley explains, 'turned the heat off – he thought it might make you drowsy. You'll be the only person in hell who's chilly!'

Being chilly is not something many Scrooges have bothered about. George C. Scott tells Cratchit that coal is costly and that if he is not warm enough then he should put on more clothes, since garments were created by the human race for protection against the cold! And when, in *The Muppet Christmas Carol* (1992), Michael Caine is approached by Bob Cratchit (Kermit the Frog) and the book-keeping staff (a troupe of rats) to complain that it is so cold their pens are turning to 'ink-cicles', his bellowed threats of unemployment are enough to make them produce grass skirts and start singing: 'This is my island in the sun'!

For the first time since he began his long career with the late Jim Henson, Kermit the Frog plays a part other than himself. But, as he explained in a television interview: 'Bob Cratchit is a kind of mild-mannered guy surrounded by lots of mayhem and craziness, and that's not unlike the job I do with the Muppets.' Indeed, the film is decidedly a Muppet Show version of *A Christmas Carol* with Michael Caine as the human guest-star, playing an ultra-mean Scrooge who actually relishes Christmas – because it is 'Harvest time for the money-lenders!' When, on Christmas Eve, Scrooge tells Cratchit to send out the following day's eviction notices, Bob protests that people will receive them on Christmas Day. 'Then,' says Scrooge ironically, 'you can gift-wrap them!'

The film's supporting roles are taken by well-known Muppet players: the temperamental, but ever-glamorous, Miss Piggy having the feisty role of Mrs Cratchit, who condemns her husband's employer as: 'Odious, stingy, wicked, unfeeling – and badly dressed!' Tiny Tim is portrayed by Kermit's nephew, Robin, while the Cratchits' other children – another boy frog and two girl pigs – are played (or so Kermit told an interviewer) by pig and frog actors in order to avoid unnecessary speculation about the results of such a union - would they be figs or progs? – as well as to deflect gossip about his personal relationship with Miss Piggy!

The Muppet show's resident (unfunny) comic, Fozzy Bear, plays young Ebenezer's first employer – renamed 'Fozzywig'. While his movie forebears have been variously described as merchants, shippers and warehousemen or as dealers in a diversity of products from tea to cloth, Fozzy Bear is probably the only Fezziwig

Michael Caine as Scrooge, Kermit the Frog as Bob Cratchit in *The Muppet Christmas Carol* (1992) © Disney

to own a rubber chicken factory!

Marley's ghost has a double incarnation as The Marley Brothers! Playing Robert and Jacob Marley – complete with rattling chains with singing padlocks and cash-boxes – are Waldorf and·Statler, the elderly hecklers from 'The Muppet Show'. Now plaguing performers from beyond the grave, they greet Scrooge's 'More-of-gravy-than-of-grave' joke with derisive cries of 'What a terrible pun!'

Over the years, *A Christmas Carol* has had many narrators: Orson Welles; Vincent Price; Freddie Jones; Paul Scofield (telling the tale of Ralph Richardson's Scrooge) and Ralph Richardson himself, narrating another version in which he also played Scrooge. The story of George C. Scott's Scrooge is narrated by his movie nephew, Roger Rees; while one of the businessmen in the Alastair Sim film, Peter Bull, got the job of topping and tailing the film because, it is rumoured, Sim wasn't keen on Tiny Tim (Glyn Dearman) getting the last word!

Never, however, until *The Muppet Christmas Carol*, has the story had a narrator quite like that blue, furry geek with bulgy eyes and a bent beak — The Great Gonzo! Not content with simply telling the story, Gonzo dons a waistcoat and a top hat and plays Charles Dickens. Gonzo's comments on the action and his predictions about what is going to happen to the characters prompts Rizzo the Rat to ask how he knows so much. 'Storytellers,' explains Gonzo-Dickens, 'are omniscient; I know everything!' Rizzo sniffs: 'Hoity-toity, Mr God-like, smarty-pants!' But by the end of the film, he is full of compliments for the author: 'Nice story, Mr Dickens!' To which Gonzo replies: 'Oh, thanks! If you like this, you should read the book!'

And, back in 1850, the real Mr Dickens was about to launch a new career for himself, doing just that . . .

10

Hear Dickens, and Die!

In 1850, Dickens returned to his idea of producing a 'weekly journal designed for the instruction and entertainment of all classes of readers', a pot-pourri of amusements and articles on social issues. Unable now to call it *The Cricket*, he needed a new name: suggestions included *The Microscope*, *The Rolling Years* and *The Comrade*, but as he had talked of its being edited by 'The Household Voice, The Household Face', he finally named it *Household Words*. Dickens was well into what is often regarded as his finest novel, *David Copperfield*, and although there was no question of his writing another Christmas Book, he still managed to write about Christmas in *Household Words*.

Dickens wrote about Christmas trees which were 'brilliantly lighted by a multitude of little tapers; and everywhere sparkled and glittered with bright objects'; he wrote of ghost stories filled with haunted sounds of 'a spinning wheel, or a hammer, or a footstep, or a cry, or a sigh, or a horses tramp, or the rattling of a chain'; fairy tales: 'I felt if I could have married Little Red Riding-Hood, I should have known perfect bliss'; and he wrote of the theatre: 'music plays, amidst a buzz of voices ... and the great green curtain rolls itself up majestically, and The Play begins!'

And again and again Dickens was to restate his now well-known philosophies of Christmas: look back and remember the past, the good and the ill, the happy and the sad, learn what lessons you may and then live for the present and the future. In a piece entitled 'What Christmas is as We Grow Older', he wrote:

On this day we shut out Nothing! ... Lost friend, lost child, lost parent, sister, brother, husband, wife, we will not so discard you! You shall hold your cherished places in our Christmas hearts and by our Christmas fires; and in the season of immortal hope, and on the birthday of immortal mercy, we will shut out nothing!

Those sentiments, written in 1851, reflect some of sadness he had experienced that year. The Dickens children now numbered nine – Alfred d'Orsay had been born in 1845; Sydney Smith Haldimand in 1847; Henry Fielding, two years later; and Dora Annie, in 1850. Following Dora's birth, Kate Dickens suffered a breakdown and while she was away recovering, two deaths occurred: one was Dickens' father, the other, the infant Dora.

Dickens moved the family to a new home in Tavistock Square and in 1852, Kate once again gave birth – this time to their last child, Edward Bulwer Lytton. Dickens, meanwhile, began work on his terrible masterpiece *Bleak House*, which was completed in 1853. However, too many years of mercilessly driving himself suddenly took their toll and Dickens seemed to be on the brink of a breakdown. He retreated to Europe on a holiday and recovered, although a fearful restlessness continued to hound him; like Redlaw in his last Christmas book, 'he looked like a haunted man'.

A new novel, *Hard Times for these Times*, began serialization in 1854. Touched with the same grimness that readers had found in *Bleak House*, the new book reflected Dickens' critical view of the industrialization of England. *Hard Times* was followed by *Little Dorrit*, the final part of which was published in 1857. A year earlier, Dickens purchased Gad's Hill Place – that house he had so much admired as a child.

The same year, Dickens' fondness for amateur dramatics was revived with extraordinary ramifications for him and his family. He staged – and acted in – a melodrama by his friend Wilkie Collins, entitled *The Frozen Deep*. Queen Victoria attended an early performance of the play; so did Thackeray, who was moved to remark that if Dickens had chosen to become a professional actor, he could have earned £2,000 a year.

Dickens was invited to take the play to Manchester, and Dickens invited an actress friend, Mrs Ternan, and two of her daughters to undertake the female roles. The younger girl, Ellen, was just eighteen; and, although Dickens was forty-five, he was soon in love with her: 'I told her on the last night that I was sure she had one of the most genuine and feeling hearts in the world...'

This was not the first time that Dickens had been infatuated with a younger woman, but Dickens' love for Ellen Ternan started a chain of ugly events. Kate, seeing a bracelet which Charles was planning to give to Ellen, suspected adultery and the couple were soon in the throes of a separation. Dickens denegrated Kate with a vehemence that had obviously been many years in the making: 'Neither can she get on with herself, or be anything but unhappy'; and, in 1858, foolishly chose to put the facts of his private life before his public.

He passionately defended Ellen's innocence: 'Upon my soul and honour there is not on this earth a more virtuous and spotless creature than that young lady'; but his readers, and the popular press, appear to have thought the novelist protested too much, and expressed disappointment at finding that the household god had feet of clay.

It seems likely that it was was some years more before Ellen became Dickens' mistress. In the meantime, Kate (accompanied by their eldest son, Charles) was established in a house in Gloucester Crescent on £600 a year. Dickens, who was maintaining two other households in London and Kent was, once again, in desperate need of money; it was the penny-pinching Ebenezer Scrooge (along with Pickwick, Bill Sikes and others) who came to his aid. Two weeks before finally splitting from his wife, Dickens began what was to become an alternative career as a performer of his own works — an event that was to breathe new life into Ebenezer Scrooge, Tiny Tim and the cast of *A Christmas Carol*.

Dickens had given his first public reading five years earlier, in 1853, to raise funds on behalf of a recently opened Working Men's Institute in Birmingham. The venue was the Town Hall, the date was 27 December and Dickens read *A Christmas Carol*. He had read the story to an

An engraving in the *Illustrated London News* showing Dickens giving a public reading in March 1870

audience once before, in 1845 in the drawing room of the British Consul in Genoa, but however receptive those listeners might have been, it is doubtful if they were quite as enthusiastic as the audience in Birmingham.

'The success,' Dickens wrote, 'was most wonderful and prodigious — perfectly overwhelming and astounding altogether.' Two nights later, he read *The Cricket on the Hearth* and, the following evening, he gave another reading of the Carol — this time, at reduced prices, for the working men themselves.

The Times reported that the audience for Dickens' reading numbered some '2,000 people, whose lives are one long round of toil'; yet they gave the novelist their undivided attention. 'They lost nothing,' wrote Dickens, 'misinterpreted nothing, followed everything closely, laughed and cried.'

Over the next few years he gave more readings for charity and whenever the ticket prices were reduced or the performance was free, the reading was always from *A Christmas Carol*. Of his first London charity reading, one reviewer wrote:

We have rarely witnessed or shared an evening of such genuine enjoyment, and never before remember to have seen a crowded assembly of three thousand people hanging for upwards of two hours on the lips of a single reader ... At the close there was an outburst, not so much of applause as of downright hurrahing.

It was during 1857, while giving one of these readings, in aid of the Great Ormond Street Children's Hospital, that he remembered the adage which says charity begins at home, and hit upon an idea: 'A great deal of money might possibly be made (if it were not infra dig) by having Readings of one's own books. It would be an odd thing. I think it would take immensely.'

What began as a handful of planned readings of *A Christmas Carol* in London had soon increased to seventeen, and a tour of the provinces took the total to a hundred. In addition to some much-needed cash, it is possible that Dickens saw this new venture as a way of helping to reinstate his reputation with his readers. He expanded his repertoire to include the trial of Mr Pickwick; some comic interludes with Mrs Gamp (from *Martin Chuzzlewit*); and 'Little Dombey', a touching account of the demise of another of his 'little' child characters, this time Paul Dombey (the 'and Son' of the novel).

He had carefully abridged the texts: *A Christmas Carol* at his first reading ran for three hours, but was later edited to two hours, and then to eighty or ninety minutes. What he chose to cut, curiously, were passages (such as the one featuring the children, Ignorance and Want) that showed the righteous indignation that had first fired him to write the book. Gone too, were most of the story's downbeats: Scrooge's sad encounter with his childhood self is managed in a few lines, as is the painful conversation between Belle and the youthful Ebenezer. 'Paradoxically,' observes the Dickens scholar, Kathleen Tillotson, 'the performances which brought him in person so close to the public represented a far less personal version than the original text.'

Dickens' prompt-copies were full of detailed notes on how each piece was to be read. For example, the tone of delivery for important sections were clearly marked – 'Tone down to Pathos' or 'Up to cheerfulness' – with occasional one-word reminders such as 'Weird' to denote the laughter of the three vultures rummaging through the dead Scrooge's possessions. Some passages were underlined, or double-underlined for emphasis, as when the Spirit of Christmas Past reveals: 'A living and moving Picture of Scrooge's former self.' And when Scrooge asks the Last of the Spirits: 'Are these the shadows of things that Will be or are they shadows of things that May be, only?' Dickens underlined the word 'Will' three times, and the word 'May' no less than four times.

In fact, Dickens didn't so much read the passages as enact them. Standing at a specially-designed reading desk, he peopled the otherwise empty stage with dozens of characters. Before performing a piece in public, Dickens would rehearse it as many as two hundred times. And since he had committed the scripts (plus all their vocal and physical mannerisms) to memory he needed no prompting – the books on his reading desk being little more than theatrical props. Once in a while the words would desert him: 'I have got to know the Carol so well,' he said, 'that I can't remember it and occasionally go dodging about in the wildest manner to pick up lost pieces.' But, most of the time, what someone called 'a scarcely credible amount of forethought and preparation' paid off handsomely.

The tour, which began in Plymouth and took him to Edinburgh via Ireland, earned him 3,000 guineas. Equally important for Dickens was the opportunity, given to few writers, to see the extent to which his writings moved an audience to laughter or tears. He played, shamelessly, on those emotions and the public were quick to show how much they adored it. 'There's nothing in the world,' he wrote, 'equal to seeing the house rise at you, one sea of delightful faces, one hurrah of applause.'

'The audience,' noted a reviewer in Dublin, 'stood up and cheered him lustily. It is not that the world knows Mr Dickens to be merely a great man; but we all know him to be a good man.' As another remarked, the reception Dickens received at the end of a performance was 'not mere applause . . . but a passionate outburst of love for the man.'

There was so much for an audience to respond to in all his performances – and particularly those of *A Christmas Carol*. There was the moment when Scrooge pleaded with the Ghost of Christmas Yet To Come: 'Will you not speak to me?' This cry – with 'great emphasis' on the word 'speak' – followed a very long pause during which, we are told, 'Dickens' face looked so anxious that the audience watched him in breathless silence.'

There was the moment when 'Mrs Cratchit entered: flushed, but smiling proudly: with the pudding . . .' at which point audiences erupted with cheers; one observer remarked that 'his description brought down torrents of applause,

so archly was it given'. In contrast there was the moment when Bob Cratchit breaks down over the death of Tiny Tim: after three or four seconds of 'painful silence', Dickens threw back his head and Bob's grief 'burst out, almost in a suppressed scream', as he cried: 'My little, little child! My little child!' Another observer commented that 'here, and only here, Dickens forgets the nature of Bob's voice, and employs all the powers of his own, carried away apparently by the situation'. The effect on the audience was devastating.

Then there was the moment when the nephew's sister-in-law says: 'It's your uncle Scro-o-o-o-oge!' which Dickens pronounced 'long-drawn-out and with tremendous emphasis' in a 'blood-curdling and yet almost loving way'. When Scrooge is finally brought to repentance, Dickens read 'in his richest, fullest, happiest voice'. And when, during one of his charity readings, Dickens delivery of the words: 'Tiny Tim, who did NOT die . . .' the entire audience spontaneously rose to its feet with 'a tremendous burst of cheering', that Dickens described as being like a 'roll of thunder'.

Dickens seldom failed to achieve a powerful effect. Kate Field in her book, *Pen Photographs of Charles Dickens' Readings*, had only one complaint with Dickens interpretation and that was with the 'monotonous' voices which he gave to his ghosts; 'Solemnity and monotony,' she observed, 'are not synonymous terms, yet every theatrical ghost insists that they are, and Dickens is no exception to the rule.'

'I had no conception, before hearing Dickens read,' wrote Thomas Carlyle, 'of what capacities lie in the human face and voice. No theatre-stage could have had more players than seemed to flit about his face.' And Kate Field commented that 'what Dickens does is frequently infinitely better than anything he says, or the way he says it'; thus, in the Fezziwig passage, when he reached the words 'the fiddler struck up "Sir Roger de Coverley",' Dickens' fingers danced along the top of his reading-desk, 'as if it were the floor of Fezziwig's room, and every finger were a leg belonging to one of the Fezziwig family'.

Carlyle described a reading by Dickens as being better than a performance by the great actor, William Macready, since Dickens was 'a whole tragic, comic, heroic theatre visible, performing under one hat'. And even Macready admitted that Dickens read 'as well as an experienced actor'. Reviewers were no less enthusiastic: 'It can honestly be said,' wrote one, 'that Mr Dickens is the greatest reader of the greatest writer of the age.'

Others were less keen on his making a public exhibition of himself with what was being called 'a novelty in literature and in the annals of "entertainment"'. His friend, John Forster – while acknowledging that Dickens had the 'power of projecting himself into shapes and suggestions of his fancy' – considered the readings a distraction from Dickens' 'higher calling' as a serious writer.

Dickens continued with his other work. In 1859, difficulties over *Household Words* had led him to change publishers and start a new journal, entitled *All the Year Round*, which he launched with a new serialized novel, set in the time of the French Revolution, *A Tale of Two Cities*. Similarly, *Great Expectations*, which he began in 1860, was intended to maintain public interest in the magazine.

But Dickens' reading tour had proved a success and was repeated, with new extracts, in 1861 and (following completion of his novel, *Our Mutual Friend*) 1866. Again Dickens played to packed houses. There were various near disasters, as when, in Newcastle, a bar of gas lights crashed onto the stage and almost caused a fire; or, in Birmingham, when Dickens averted another catastrophe by rapidly editing his readings in order to finish before a metal reflector suspended above the stalls – made red-hot by a badly angled gas jet – was able to crash down into the audience.

By this time, Dickens had sold Tavistock House and was living at Gad's Hill, with occasional visits to London and Paris. There were also regular visits to Ellen who lived in Slough, with her mother and sisters, until she moved into a house in Peckham, South London, possibly provided for her by Dickens. They even managed a brief holiday in France together in 1865, although they were subsequently involved in a fearful adventure. They were returning from Paris when the train on which they were travelling to London was derailed. Dickens behaved courageously, rescuing Ellen and other passengers and then tending the injured and dying.

This event affected Dickens, whose health was beginning to fail: he was suffering from neuralgia and gout, and his doctors were anxious about a possible heart condition. His writings and readings had, by now, made him a wealthy man, and he could have afforded to take life a little easier. Nevertheless, in 1867, he decided to embark on yet another five-month reading tour – this time in America.

The American public appeared to have forgiven – or just forgotten – the critical views of

MR. CHARLES DICKENS'S READING.

Doors open at half-past 7.
The Audience are respectfully requested to be in their places by 10 minutes to 8 o'clock.
80 ONE SHILLING.
The Reading will last two hours.

America which Dickens had expressed in *American Notes* and *Martin Chuzzlewit*; and his first reading, in Boston, sold out in eleven hours and earned the author $14,000. The ticket touts also did well, selling $2 tickets for up to $26 each.

Following a reading of *A Christmas Carol*, on Christmas Eve Dickens once more received evidence of the impact made by his little story. Mr Fairbanks, a local industrialist who was in the audience, was so moved that, the very next day, he changed his company's practice of working on Christmas Day and, the following year, began an annual custom of giving a turkey to each factory hand.

From Boston, Dickens travelled to New York and Washington, where President Andrew Jackson brought a party to hear every performance. An American reviewer conveyed the typical feeling of excitement that attended a reading of *A Christmas Carol*:

... At one moment he is savage old Scrooge, at the next, his jolly nephew, and in twinkling of an eye little timid, lisping Bob Cratchit appears. All this is effected by the play of features as well as the varying tones of voice. It is the comical or savage twist of the mouth – the former to the right, the latter to the left – the elongation of the face, the roll or twinkle of the eyes, and above all the wonderful lift of the eyebrows, that produce such surprising and delightful effects....

Although the tour, through grueling winter weather, took its toll on Dickens, it earned him $300,000 (then around £30,000). On returning to England, with his American earnings as an incentive, Dickens decided to undertake another tour of his homeland. This time it was to be a Farewell Tour.

For this venture, Dickens decided to prepare a new reading – the chilling episode from *Oliver Twist*, in which Bill Sikes clubs Nancy to death: Dickens' energized performances had repeatedly put a strain on his health, but the struggle between Sikes and Nancy was to prove too much.

His son, Charles, together with various friends, warned him against performing so emotional a piece, but Dickens had already given a private reading of it and had seen the way in which the terrified audience hung upon his every word and had heaped praise upon him afterwards. There was, therefore, no turning back.

The tour began in October 1868; again the critics fell at Dickens' feet:

Hear Dickens, and die: you will never live to hear anything of its kind so good... His powers of vocal and facial expression are very great... and he applies them heartily and zealously to the due presentment of the creations of his own matchless genius. It has been said that an author is generally either greater or less than his works... In Mr Dickens, as a reader, each is equal to the other. His works could have no more perfect illustrator; and they are worthy of his best efforts as an artist.

However, so devastating was Dickens' portrayal of Nancy's brutal death, that his performances were increasingly followed by complete exhaustion. In April 1869, he collapsed and the rest of the tour was cancelled.

Dickens recovered sufficiently to give one last series of readings in London. Beginning in January, 1870 – against the advice of his doctors – they proved costly to his health long before he reached his Final Farewell on 15 March. On this occasion, he read Pickwick's Trial – although he now had trouble articulating the character's name, which often became 'Pickswick', 'Picnic' or 'Peckwicks'. He also read what has been described as 'the quintessential Dickens reading' – A Christmas Carol...

He began, as he had done more than a hundred times before, speaking the name 'Old Marley' in a low voice and stressing the double-underlined name of Marley's partner in such a way as to, unequivocally present 'Scrooge in the flesh'. At the end, thunderous applause brought Dickens back onto the platform, tears rolling down his cheeks. The passionate excitement he derived from reading his own words, the fevered adulation with which those readings were always received: it was all, now, drawing to an end.

'From these garish lights,' he said, in a voice shaking with emotion, 'I now vanish forevermore, with a heartfelt, grateful, respectful, affectionate farewell.' He left the stage and, when the cheers and applause refused to abate, returned one last time – his face still wet with tears – and, having kissed his hand, turned and made his final exit.

Before Dickens gave his own first public reading of A Christmas Carol, the book had been read by James Staples to an audience at a Domestic Mission in Bristol; and when Dickens finally bowed out, many other readers followed in his footsteps: among them his own son, H.F. Dickens, who was giving readings of the book until his death in 1933.

Actor Emlyn Williams dressed himself up in wig, beard and snazzy waistcoat, and using many of Dickens' famous intonations and gestures attempted to recreate the experience of attending one of the novelist's readings.

Over the years, various readings have been commercially issued, on long-playing record, cassette and compact disc. The first recordings, on cylinder, were simply extracts from the book; and in 1905, Bransby Williams and Albert Whelan both selected the same episode − that concerning the 'new Scrooge' − calling their recordings *The Awakening of Scrooge* and *Scrooge's Christmas Morning*.

Recordings have also been made of *A Christmas Carol* by, among others, Joss Ackland, Tom Conti, Roy Dotrice, Martin Jarvis and Siobhan McKenna − not to mention Eleanor Roosevelt, wife of the former American President. One semi-dramatized version, which more properly belongs in this listing, is Ronald Colman's 1949 recording, which relies heavily on narration which is itself unique, in that it is the only adaptation in which Scrooge tells his own story.

It is, perhaps, hard to imagine that impeccably mannered Englishman, star of such movies as *A Tale of Two Cities* and *Lost Horizon*, ever being capable of playing a grouch like Scrooge, yet there he is! No sooner have a group of young carol-singers started 'God Rest You Merry Gentlemen', then up flies the window and mean old Scrooge shouts out in a harsh voice: 'I want none of your singing here! Get away with you, before I take a stick to you! Get away, all of you!' Then the familiar softly measured tones:

It was I who said those words, may heaven help my soul! It was I who called them out into the night on Christmas Eve, and sent those children scampering away into the fog with fear in their hearts where, but a moment before, had been the love of fellow men and God. I have learned a great deal since then and my story bears telling...

Many listeners, down the years, have found Ronald Colman's reading a satisfyingly reassuring one, especially when − over the swelling strains of 'O Come All Ye Faithful' − he tells us that Tiny Tim did not die: 'He is well and growing stronger day by day. A fine boy. I'll see him tonight at dinner, for it is Christmas once again...'

Each reading has its own distinctive style: Sir John Gielgud is ponderously reverential; Paul Scofield is dry and crisp; Daniel Massey revels in the language but, in almost three hours, scarcely draws breath; Leonard Rossiter, alone among his peers, finds the full richness of Dickens the humourist.

To many, however, the chief attribute of *A Christmas Carol* seems to be the opportunity it provides for the putting on of voices. There are basically two types of Scrooge: one kind speaks in high, querulous tones and unable to say 'Humbug!' other than as 'Hummmmbuuug!'; while the rest tend to growl along in the lowest registers. Rather surprisingly, perhaps, a handful of Scrooges (and one or two Marleys) have been given accents that are even more working-class than those of their down-trodden clerk.

The First of the Three Spirits usually speaks slowly, as if it were as far off as the Past it represents, and in one case lingers so much over such lines as 'My time grows sho-o-o-o-rt', as to suggest that it is actually falling off the top of a very high cliff! The Ghost of

Christmas Present, on the other hand, usually sounds like Father Christmas with a mouth full of mince-pie.

In one, heavily-accented, recording, Fezziwig sounds as if he's had a few too many cups of punch and a cockney Bob Cratchit has a wife from somewhere in the general direction of Devon and Cornwall. In fact, readers have scoured the British Isles for accents: there is a version in which Mrs Dilber, the laundress, is Irish; while Scotland has supplied at least one Jacob Marley and one Ghost of Christmas Present.

Errors, of course, abound: after seeing his former self at Fezziwig's ball, Scrooge expresses the wish: 'I should like to be able to say a word or two to my clerk just now...'; in one version this, inexplicably, becomes: 'I would like to say a word or two to my friend, Dick Wilkins.' Other recordings contain such oddities as 'blind-man's bluff', 'Old Squatch' for 'Old Scratch' (suggesting that the reader wasn't altogether familiar with the Devil in question); and a Mrs Dilber who suddenly turns into a Mrs Dibler — but seems happy to answer to either name!

As with published versions, there have been the usual alterations to the text; sometimes nothing more than a laboured attempt to explain some supposed complexity of language. Thus, 'of all the good days in the year, on Christmas Eve' becomes: 'It was Christmas Eve, the twenty-fourth of December, the evening before Christmas Day...'

In another version, in reply to Scrooge's inquiry about what will happen to Tiny Tim, the Ghost of Christmas Present replies: 'If Tim does

Patrick Stewart reading *A Christmas Carol*, 1988

not get enough to eat, he will die and Bob's heart will break.' And when Bob proposes a toast to Mr Scrooge (an event, according to Dickens, which Tim 'didn't give twopence for') the child enthusiastically responds: 'God bless him!'

Perhaps the most faithful (if least likely) successor to Dickens has been the British actor, Patrick Stewart, who achieved international fame in the role of Captain Jean-Luc Picard in the American television series, 'Star Trek: The Next Generation'. Stewart's one-man production, first staged in 1988, was successfully reprieved on both sides of the Atlantic, gaining many enthusiastic reviews: 'Reciting the litany of Scrooge's scrooginess,' wrote *Newsweek* magazine, 'Stewart relishes the emotional gamut of meanness . . . Humbug seldom sounds so good.'

Tall, bullet-headed and dressed in a sharp suit, Stewart used but a few props – a kitchen table, a chair, a high desk and stool – with which to make the otherwise empty stage into Scrooge's office, the Cratchit's home, Fezziwig's warehouse and, with Stewart curled up on top of the table, Scrooge's bedroom.

'The audience,' said the *New York Times*, 'has entered a magical world dense with character, atmosphere and action.' And, like Dickens himself, Patrick Stewart peopled the stage with the whole teeming cast: men, women, children and ghosts. No moment in the whole *tour de force* showed Stewart's genius better than the party at the Fezziwig's. 'In came a fiddler . . . and tuned like fifty stomach-aches,' wrote Dickens, and Stewart noisily tuned that fiddle till Mr and Mrs F. stood out to dance the 'Sir Roger de Coverley'. Up and down the stage he cavorted, describing the scene, dancing and fiddling seemingly at one and the same time! Dickens would have heartily approved!

The End of It

Although in March 1870, Dickens had left the public stage, he still had other work to do. A new novel, *The Mystery of Edwin Drood*, was in progress, but there was a sense in which the curtain-call he had taken after his last reading of *A Christmas Carol* was really his final bow. Just three months later, on 8 June 1870, he suffered a paralytic stroke and died the following day. 'We have had greater writers in poetry and prose,' noted one obituary, 'but they were not of our day and generation. For us just now this loss is our greatest.'

Dickens had left explicit instructions for a simple, unpretentious funeral with none of the elaborate arrangements beloved by the Victorians, which he considered 'revolting absurdity'. He wanted to be buried outside Rochester Cathedral, with a plain headstone that carried nothing more than his name.

The nation, however, decreed otherwise and, on 14 June, he was laid to rest in Poets' Corner in Westminster Abbey, close to the graves of Johnson and Macaulay and not far from monuments to Shakespeare and Chaucer. For two days, thousands of mourners filed past the open grave, throwing flowers upon the coffin until the whole area was filled to overflowing. The memorial card distributed at the Abbey carried

Dickens in death: a sketch by John Everett Millais showing a wrapper round the corpse's head to keep the jaws closed, as did the ghost of Jacob Marley

words from the farewell speech at his final reading: '... from these garish lights I vanish now forevermore.'

Queen Victoria wrote in her diary: 'He is a very great loss. He had a large loving mind and the strongest sympathy with the poorer classes.' And it is said that, a costermonger's girl in Drury Lane, hearing of his funeral, cried: 'Dickens dead?

Then will Father Christmas die too?'

But neither the memory of Dickens, nor the trappings of the festive season he so much loved, could ever really die; *A Christmas Carol*, more than anything else he had written, ensured that they remained very much alive.

Scrooge in particular, it seems, is ever with us. Whenever a person behaves in a parsimonious or mean-spirited way, someone will inevitably draw the comparison with Scrooge, whose very name has entered the dictionaries as a definition of a miserliness.

Scrooge's likeness — night-cap tassel bobbing and bare, bony legs protruding from the bottom of his night-shirt — has been sculpted in porcelain and cast in brass and pewter. Images of him have adorned plates, mugs, jugs and vases; coasters, horse-brasses, book marks, thimbles and toasting-forks! A Scrooge card game has players winning and losing bank notes inscribed, 'All donations gratefully received', and signed 'Ebenezer Scrooge, Chief Cashier', and Dickens House produced a brass Marley's Ghost door-knocker (with ghostly spectacles turned up upon his ghostly forehead) that lifts to reveal a striking-plate shaped like a lobster!

As we have seen, there has been no shortage of dramatizations of Scrooge's story and when people are not adapting the story for stage, film, television, radio and record, then they are endlessly spoofing and parodying it — from *Carry On Christmas* with Sid James as Scrooge, to a pornographic film, *The Passions of Carol*. Some of the most unlikely re-workings have provided

vehicles for the least likely players. Alan Ladd, for example, starred in a 1951 American radio play entitled *Lefty Gallagher's Christmas Carol*; and, almost thirty years later, in 1979, Henry Winkler ('The Fonz' from 'Happy Days') was aged-up to play a ruthless furniture-dealing Scrooge in a television special, 'An American Christmas Carol', set in the dark years of the Depression.

Another variation on the story featured The Jetsons, Hanna and Barbera's cartoon space-age family. *A Jetson Christmas Carol* (1985), begins with George Jetson flying off to work at Spacely Sprockets Inc., wondering whether his boss will let him leave early so that he and the family can 'gather round the laser-tree for an old fashioned Christmas'. But when Cosmo Spacely (motto: 'Be it ever so dirty, there's nothing like money!') receives a large order for sprockets, he makes George work late to fill the requisition. Jetson wishes that some 'weird Christmas ghosts' would visit his Scrooge-like employer, then adds: 'But he'd probably scare them off!'

That night, Cosmo Spacely is haunted by his former partner, Marsley, and three robotic spectres. In a vision of the past, Spacely sees his money-grabbing childhood-self exploiting young Jetson to run a lemonade-stall for him; in the present, the Jetson's dog, Astro, lies at death's door after swallowing a sprocket from a mechanical cat; and in the future, the Jetsons are fabulously wealthy from having sued Spacely — whose company made the sprocket that killed Astro! The reformed (or, at least, forewarned) Spacely rushes off to get a vet for Astro, gives a 'fat raise' to George, expensive gifts to the Jetson family and – as everyone sings 'We Wish You a Merry Christmas' – doubtless thinks he's had a lucky escape!

The much-loved American television 'sit-com' series, 'The Ghost and Mrs Muir' (about a widow who finds her seaside home haunted by the ghost of a sea-captain, with whom she promptly falls in love) featured a seasonal episode in 1969, called 'The Ghost and Christmas Past'. Other popular TV series to allude to *A Christmas Carol* include 'Family Ties', 'Fame', 'WKRP in Cincinnati' and, in 1986, 'Moonlighting'. In one episode of this Cybill Shepherd–Bruce Willis series, Blue Moon Detective Agency's Maddie Hayes (Shepherd) turns decidedly Scrooge-like one Christmas Eve and is taught some painful lessons. The episode was entitled 'It's a Wonderful Job', making a connection with another classic 'Ghost Story of Christmas' – Frank Capra's 1946 film, *It's A Wonderful Life*.

It is also on Christmas Eve that the central character in *It's A Wonderful Life* – hard-working, generous-hearted George Bailey (James Stewart) – is brought (by the incompetence and dishonesty of others) to the brink of ruin and suicide. He is saved, however, by the intervention of an unlikely (and not too efficient) guardian angel named Clarence. George, who believes the world would have been a better place without him, wishes he had never been born and Clarence grants his wish. Acting as the Ghost of Christmas Future, Clarence shows George Bailey (a kind of Bob Cratchit, given hero-status) how very different the lives of

Lionel Barrymore and James Stewart in
It's A Wonderful Life, 1946

his family and friends would have been if he had never lived: his kid brother dying in a drowning accident and the town of Bedford Falls degenerating into a sleazy slum.

Like Scrooge – but for different reasons – George is allowed a second chance, and all ends as happily and sentimentally as *A Christmas Carol*. Unrepentant and unredeemed, however, is the film's true Scrooge-figure, Mr Henry C. Potter – a rapacious, mean-spirited old man whose links to Dickens' miser are unmistakable: he is an old, curmudgeonly man, dressed in late Victorian clothes. But the cementing bond is the casting of

Lionel Barrymore as Potter, an actor inseparably linked with Ebenezer Scrooge, through eighteen years of portraying him on radio.

Orson Welles introduced one such Barrymore broadcast of *A Christmas Carol*, in 1939, by describing the player and the play as: 'The best-loved actor of our time, in the world's best-loved Christmas story.' Certainly, Lionel Barrymore – like Alastair Sim and George C. Scott – had what Richard Parlour has described as the skill of portraying Scrooge as 'truly sinister while, at the same time, always showing the heart of warmth glowing through the shell of ice; the ember of soul imprisoned in the sin'. As for Henry C. Potter, however, Frank Capra considered giving him a reformation at the end of *It's a Wonderful Life*, so that he might enter into the glow of George Bailey's happy home, but he finally decided to leave this particular Scrooge out in the cold.

In one of Lionel Barrymore's happier endings, Bob Cratchit asks: 'Are you quite yourself, sir?' To which Scrooge replies: 'No, thank heaven, I am not quite myself!' And there have been many Scrooges who are most certainly not themselves! One of these is cynical, ambitious television executive, Francis Xavier Cross (Bill Murray), in the 1988 pastiche, *Scrooged*. Frank Cross, who is producing a TV version of *A Christmas Carol* (narrated by John Houseman and starring Buddy Hackett as Scrooge), is visited by his former boss (John Forsyth from 'Dynasty'), now dead and seriously decomposed. Then come the Spirits: Christmas Past, a demented yellow-cab driver (David Johansen), whose meter clocks up the passing years; Christmas Present, a violent female goblin (Carol Kane), got up in a spangled fairy costume; and Christmas Future, sometimes a grimmer than usual death's-head, sometimes a shrouded figure with a television-monitor instead of a face.

In the past, Frank relives his unhappy childhood and his romance with Claire (Karen Allen), the girlfriend he let go because his job was more important to him; while, in the present, he sees how Christmas is celebrated in the home of Grace, his black secretary, and her young son who, following a traumatizing experience, no longer speaks. In the future, a series of chilling experiences end with Frank waking up inside his own coffin as it trundles into the crematorium furnace.

Alive and penitent, Frank returns to the television studio. 'Francis Xavier Cross!' says one of his colleagues. 'That's me,' he replies, 'but the great thing is it's NOT me.' Interrupting the telecast of *A Christmas Carol*, Frank harangues the audience on the true meaning of Christmas:

> It's the one night when we all act a little wiser, we smile a little easier, we cheer a little more... For a couple of hours out of the whole year, we are the people we always hoped we would be... You have to do something, you have to take a chance, you have to get involved... If you believe in this spirit thing, Christmas can happen every day...

It might almost be Scrooge promising 'to honour Christmas in my heart, and try to keep it all the year.' Frank gets his girlfriend back and Calvin finds his voice — just in time to remind Frank that he's forgotten to say 'God bless us, every one!'

Casting comedian Buddy Hackett as Scrooge in the show-within-the-film is a nice joke, since — one way and another — quite a few laughs have been had at Scrooge's expense. American impersonator, Rich Little, cut a multi-voiced comedy record entitled *Scrooge and the Stars* in November 1963, but, shortly after its release, the recording was withdrawn, following the assassination of President John F. Kennedy, whose voice had been impersonated for the Ghost of Christmas Present, prophetically telling Scrooge: 'My life upon this globe is brief; it ends tonight. In fact, it ends as fast as you can say your name.'

Rich Little subsequently gave a solo television reading of the story in which, again, he spoke for all the characters — this time borrowing the voice of W.C. Fields for Scrooge. In 1967, the popular Smothers Brothers spoofed Dickens' story on their television show, with comedian Jack Benny, not (as might be supposed, considering his reputation for meanness) in the role of Scrooge, but as Bob Cratchit!

British comics who have played Scrooge for giggles include Rowan Atkinson who, in 1988, presented 'Blackadder's Christmas Carol'. 'In the reign of good Queen Victoria,' begins the opening narration, 'there stood in Dumpling Lane in old London town, the moustache shop of one Ebenezer Blackadder, the kindest and loveliest man in all England...'

This unlikely character enters with a shout of 'Humbug!' — and immediately offers round a paper bag full of them! He is, at any rate to begin with, the antithesis of Scrooge, giving all his money, food and Christmas presents away to a series of unattractive cadgers. Fortunately, the Spirit of Christmas (Robbie Coltrane) haunts Blackadder with visions of his conniving

Rowan Atkinson and Tony Robinson in the 1988 television spoof 'Blackadder's Christmas Carol'

ancestors from whom he learns the bitter lesson that 'bad guys have all the fun'. Blackadder's milk of human kindness having now 'gone off', he reforms and becomes a miser. When, however, Queen Victoria and Prince Albert arrive at his shop to reward him for his acts of kindness with £50,000 and the title of Baron, he assumes that they are more spongers, and slams the door in their faces!

Many years earlier, in 1959, The Goons had celebrated what they called 'the greedy-guts season' with 'the radio adaptation from the dinner of the same name – *A Christmas Carol* by kind permission!' Peter Sellers in narrator-type tones, begins the story: 'And here, at Christmas, we see the venerable offices of Scrooge and Marley, importers and exporters for the great year of 1887...'

Scrooge (Sellers again, this time with an ancient crumbling voice) is busy in his office: 'Now to enter certain things in the all-weather ledgers... One barrel of Blungers Violent Stone and Ginger Purge; one gill of rare leopard-oil – in newts; one box of feathered shirt-lifters – Oooohhh!'

Bob Cratchit (obsessed with celebrating this 'time of goodwill and custard') is Neddy Seagoon (a.k.a. Harry Secombe) while Marley is fleetingly portrayed by Spike Milligan. 'Marley is dead!' says Scrooge, 'Marley is dead!' Then comes a distant, protesting voice: 'No, I'm NOT!' There is a pistol-shot; an expiring: 'Ohhhh!'; and Scrooge replies: 'Yes, you ARE!'

The thing is, you simply can't keep a good humbug down! Scrooge turns up all over the place. In 1977, he (and his creator) looked in on the television spectacular, 'Bing Crosby's Merrie Olde Christmas'. Bing is shown spending Christmas in an old English mansion, where he encounters the ghost of Charles Dickens (Ron Moody) who tells Bing that he based Scrooge on one of his neighbours who had 'a nose like a ski-slope' and who was 'very wealthy but very, very tight.' Dickens then names the alleged source of his inspiration as one 'Leslie Townes Hope' – the full name of Bing's old movie-partner, Bob Hope! This zany exchange is followed by a bizarre musical fantasy in which Ron Moody again appears – this time as a night-shirted Scrooge, cavorting through snowy streets with Twiggy, on crutch, as Tiny Tim!

As an amateur conjurer of some note, Dickens would probably have enjoyed Scrooge's appearance in the Christmas 1993 'Paul Daniels' Magic Show'. The popular television magician portrayed Scrooge being warned by a portrait of Jacob Marley (Ali Bongo) that he is to be haunted by three spirits – which then emerge from the interior of a seemingly vacant wardrobe. Paul Daniels' Scrooge also sings 'Who wants to be a millionaire?' whilst producing vast quantities of cash from previously empty cupboards, wastepaper baskets, drawers and even the chamber-pot under his bed!

These money-making activities are a reminder that, like his former partner, Scrooge is 'always a good man of business' and regularly advertises finance and brokerage services. During the early 1980s, Hewlett-Packard Co., an American manufacturer of electronic calculators, ran an advertisement showing nephew Fred producing one to take some of the drudgery out of Scrooge and Cratchit's lives. Scrooge has featured in a variety of advertising media from appearances on American radio in the annual Campbell Playhouse production of *A Christmas Carol* to advertisements for Scrabble; from cigarette cards to a television commercial for Hamlet cigars, a packet of which he keeps in one of his cash-boxes, although – being Scrooge – he naturally cuts the cigar in half before lighting up!

Scrooge has also made a somewhat quirky commercial for a well-known brand of lager. Televised in 1974, it opens with Scrooge hunched over his desk; but, for once, he is not counting his money. 'This Christmas,' says a narrator, 'things are not as they should be.' Outside, church bells ring and carollers sing. The narrator continues: 'The normally grasping fingers of Scrooge are nimbly tying presents... There is obviously a lack of refreshment to Scrooge's traditional meanness...'

Suddenly aware of moaning cries and clanking of chains, Scrooge looks up. 'Disturbed by this, the ghost of Jacob Marley has brought home a whole can of Heineken, a little of which he gives to his partner...' Scrooge drinks and the lager starts to take effect. 'We see Heineken rapidly refreshing Scrooge's meanness... enabling him to enjoy his Christmas in the old familiar way.' Scrooge sweeps the offensive presents from his desk! 'Only Heineken is able to do this, because it refreshes the parts other beers cannot reach.'

The 150th anniversary of the first publication of *A Christmas Carol*, in December 1993, found Scrooge indulging in a positive orgy of commercialism with special tableaux of his experiences decorating the windows of the London store, Selfridges. Shoppers left with their Christmas presents in carrier bags suitably inscribed with the words 'Christmas Present' and a jolly picture of Scrooge's second spirit-visitor, drawn by the popular children's illustrator, Quentin Blake.

The same artist was responsible for a set of five commemorative Christmas stamps illustrating snowy street scenes with Scrooge, Bob Cratchit and Tiny Tim, Scrooge's nephew and niece, Mr and Mrs Fezziwig and the Poulterer carrying the Prize Turkey. Available in a multiplicity of forms including first-day covers (franked with Holly and Christmas-Pudding-shaped cancellations), Quentin Blake's charming

One of Quentin Blake's 1993 Christmas postage-stamp designs

Scrooge at 150: cartoon by Nick Stead from
The Dickensian (Winter 1993)

designs opt only for scenes of goodwill and joviality. There's not a ghost in sight and even Scrooge, though pinched and hunched, is upstaged by a boy carrying an enormous garland of holly. In marked contrast, two earlier stamp issues – from Dominica and from the Turks and Caicos Islands – preferred specific incidents from Scrooge's story, including Christmas Past and Present and Marley's haunting (chains and all) as depicted, respectively, by J. Leech and W. Disney.

Other celebratory events in December 1993 included radio and television programmes, the

publication of a new facsimile of the original manuscript and a special edition of the Dickens Fellowship's journal, *The Dickensian*, given over to articles on various aspects, including a discussion of humour in the story and an examination of the various genres to which the story might be said to belong: is it a ghost story, or a dream-vision, or a parable? In 'Tiny Tim: The Child with a Crippling Fatal Illness', Charles W. Callahan, Jr, considers what might be wrong with the Cratchits' child. Whilst acknowledging that a writer in the *Australian Pediatric Journal* had suggested 'coxalgia', or tuberculosis of the hip, Callahan concludes that Tiny Tim was really suffering from tuberculosis spondylitis. The author then goes on to speculate on how Scrooge might have helped prevent the child's death – possibly by sending him to the Royal Sea Bathing Infirmary in Margate and providing him with a piece of apparatus called the Davis Spinal Assistant.

It must be said, however, that another article, this time in *The American Journal of Diseases of Children*, in December 1992, revealed that pediatric neurologist, Dr Donald Lewis was convinced that since Tiny Tim used only one crutch, his illness probably affected one side of his body more than the other. This led Dr Lewis' to diagnose a kidney disease, not recognized until the twentieth century, called distal renal tubular acidosis.

Dickens' admirers are constantly attempting to identify the origins of various people, places and things in his works and, to date, enthusiasts claim to have located Scrooge's counting-house (in St Michael's Alley, not far from the Exchange); his 'usual melancholy tavern' (Garraway's Coffee House); the nearby church, whose bell Scrooge can hear in bed (St Andrew's Undershaft); and the churchyard where Scrooge is buried (All Hallows Staining, Star Alley).

It has also been suggested that behind the character of Ebenezer Scrooge himself, there may hover the shade of a real misanthrope. Dickens, it is thought, was probably familiar with the eccentric life of an eighteenth century miser, John Elwes, whose bizarre behaviour had been the subject of several popular books and pamphlets. Sometime member of Parliament for Berkshire, John Elwes (1714–89), bore a certain physical resemblance to Dickens' description of Ebenezer Scrooge: 'Both,' wrote Alison Barnes in *The Times*, 'were shrewd, wealthy businessmen with hollow cheeks and pointed noses. Both were too mean to light a fire to keep warm and both were blessed with adorable younger sisters and jovial nephews.' Elwes refused to use candles, wore moth-eaten clothes that dated back to his Elizabethan ancestors and ate meat that was so maggot-ridden it 'walked about his plate'. Unlike Scrooge, however, Elwes was noted for his considerable charm – a quality which won the him the respect of William Pitt, Horace Walpole and His Majesty, George III.

Entire books (in addition to the present volume) have been published about Dickens' little story; notably Paul Davis' scholarly *The Lives and Times of Ebenezer Scrooge* (1990) which examines *A Christmas Carol* as a cultural text (and includes a near-exhaustive listing of its many interpretations); and an earlier book, Michael Patrick Hearn's excellent *The Annotated Christmas Carol* (1976), which contains a mass of fascinating information and ideas: for example, does the name 'Cratchit' perhaps suggest 'the scratching of the clerk's pen'? And is the origin of Tiny Tim's blessing to be found in the following verse from a long-forgotten Christmas carol?:

The meanest of them all
Was but a maiden's son,
Born in an oxen stall.
He said God bless you every one
Your bodies Christ save and see.

Whatever the sources of Dickens' inspiration, how has the story itself stood the passage of time? If some are to be believed, not very well. 'Scrooge has become canned, packaged and neutered,' thundered Peter Millar in the *Sunday Times*, 150 years after the book's publication. 'The pointed morality tale has become just part of the wallpaper; Scrooge's essence has been reduced to a diluted Spirit of Christmas Past rather than an inspiration for Christmas Present.'

Curiously, however, as long ago as 1891 (just fifty years after Dickens wrote the book), William Dean Howells protested that it and Dickens' other Christmas Books had been reduced to 'child's-play, in which the wholesome allegiance to life was lost'. Maybe some views never change! Certainly that is equally true of positive attitudes towards the book.

Reviewing the first edition, the *Sunday Times*' critic wrote, on 7 January, 1844: 'Nowhere do we

Illustration by Ethel F. Everett (1924)

Dickens' old friend, John Forster wrote of *A Christmas Carol* and all his other stories of Christmastide: 'They carried to countless firesides, with new enjoyment of the season, better apprehension of its claims and obligations; they mingled grave and glad thoughts, much to the advantage of both. They comforted the generous, rebuked the sordid, cured folly by kindly ridicule and comic humour.'

Those are the qualities which writers, dramatists, artists and illustrators, animators and film-makers, actors, singers, dancers, comics and entertainers have sought to capture. The results may be beautiful or ugly, inspired or irreverent; funny or facetious, trivial or thought-provoking; but they are seldom if ever dull. For behind every interpretation (and misinterpretation!) stands the ghost of Charles Dickens and the lesson he would teach...

As one of those numerous interpreters, Ronald Colman, put it — many years ago now, in 1949 — using words that aren't by Dickens, and yet which so easily could be:

No greater glory is given us than the love of fellow man, for in that love is love of God. May we keep Christmas always. May its fires burn forever in our hearts.

And so as Tiny Tim observed, 'God Bless Us, Every One!'

remember to have seen a more cheerful or more instructive picture of Christmas, or a truer interpretation of the useful purposes to which its festivities may be applied.'

A century and a half later, Dickens' biographer, Peter Ackroyd, has expressed the view that 'in the writing of *A Christmas Carol*, Dickens created a human myth which may survive as long as the spiritual celebration.' Or, as

Intent Upon His Reading: A Bibliography

Ackroyd, Peter, *Dickens*, Sinclair-Stevenson (London), 1990

Andrews, Malcolm (Ed.), *The Dickensian*, No. 431, Vol. 89, Part 3, The Dickens Fellowship (London), Winter 1993 (*A Christmas Carol* 150th Anniversary issue; articles by James and Patience Barnes; Charles W. Callahan, Jr; Philip Collins; David Dickens; Edwin Eigner; J. Hillis Miller; Michael Slater; Kathleen Tillotson)

Chesterton, G.K., *Charles Dickens*, Methuen (London), 1906

Chesterton, G.K., (Introduction) *Charles Dickens – Christmas Stories*, Everyman's Library; Dent (London) Dutton (New York), 1910

Chesterton, G.K., (Introduction) *Charles Dickens – A Christmas Carol*, A facsimile of the original edition with a Preface by B.W. Matz, Cecil Palmer (London), 1922

Collins, Philip (Ed.), *Charles Dickens – Sikes and Nancy and Other Public Readings*, Oxford University Press (Oxford & New York), 1983

Davis, Paul, *The Lives and Times of Ebenezer Scrooge*, Yale University Press (New Haven & London), 1990

Dent, H.C., *The Life and Characters of Charles Dickens*, Odhams Press (London)

Dickens, Cedric, (foreword), *Charles Dickens – A Christmas Carol*, Specially edited for reading aloud before an audience, 150th Anniversary Edition, with a Preface by Michael Dickens Whinney, The Dickens House (London), 1993

Dickens, Henry, *Memories of My Father*, Victor Gollancz (London) 1928

Dickens, Mamie, *My Father as I Recall Him*, The Roxburghe Press (London), 1896

Dickens, Monica, (Introduction) *Charles Dickens – A Christmas Carol*, A facsimile of the manuscript in the Pierpont Morgan Library, with a Preface by Frederick B. Adams, Jr, The Folio Press (London), 1970

Fawcett, F. Dubrez, *Dickens the Dramatist*, On Stage, Screen and Radio, W.H. Allen (London), 1952

Field, Kate, *Pen Photographs of Dickens's Readings*, J. Osgood (Boston), 1871

Fielding, K.J. (Ed.), *The Speeches of Charles Dickens*, The Clarendon Press (Oxford), 1960

Forster, John, *The Life of Charles Dickens*, Chapman and Hall (London), 1872–74

Haining, Peter (Ed.), *Charles Dickens' Christmas Ghost Stories*, Robert Hale (London), 1992

Hearn, Patrick Michael, (Ed.) *The Annotated Christmas Carol*, Avon Books (New York), 1976

House, Humphrey, *The Dickens World*, Oxford University Press (Oxford), 1941

Johnson, Edgar, *Charles Dickens: His Tragedy and Triumph*, Penguin Books (London), 1986

Miall, Antony and Peter, *The Victorian Christmas Book*, J.M. Dent (London), 1978

Mortimer, John, (introduction), *Charles Dickens – A Christmas Carol*, A facsimile edition of the autograph manuscript in the Pierpont Morgan Library, with a Foreword by Charles E. Pierce, Jr, and an essay, 'John Leech's Illustrations', by David Tatham, Yale University Press (New Haven & London), 1993

Muir, Frank, *Christmas Customs and Traditions*, Sphere Books (London), 1975

Perkins, Donald, *Charles Dickens – A New Perspective*, Floris Books (London), 1982

Slater, Michael (Ed.), *Charles Dickens – The Christmas Books*, Volumes 1 and 2, Penguin Books (London), 1971

Storey, Madeline and Graham, (Eds) *The Pilgrim Edition of the Letters of Charles Dickens*, The Clarendon Press (Oxford), 1965–74

Thomas, Deborah A., (Ed.), *Charles Dickens – Selected Short Fiction*, Penguin Books (London), 1976